Financial Control in HEALTH CARE

A Managerial Perspective

Financial Control in HEALTH CARE

A Managerial Perspective

David W. Young
School of Public Health
Harvard University

DOW JONES-IRWIN
Homewood, Illinois 60430

This publication is designed to provide accurate and
authoritative information in regard to the subject matter
covered. It is sold with the understanding that the
publisher is not engaged in rendering legal, accounting, or
other professional service. If legal advice or other expert
assistance is required, the services of a competent
professional person should be sought.

*From a Declaration of Principles jointly adopted by a Committee
of the American Bar Association and a Committee of Publishers.*

ISBN 0-87094-445-2

Library of Congress Catalog Card No. 83–71735

Printed in the United States of America

1 2 3 4 5 6 7 8 9 0 K 1 0 9 8 7 6 5 4

To my former students

for all our good times . . .
some serious, some not

Preface

As is the case with almost all works of this sort, this book represents the combined contributions of a great many individuals and
organizations. Most of all, it would not have been possible
without the (sometimes unwitting) assistance of my students during the past eight years at the Harvard School of Public Health:
those in the two-year M.S. program in Health Policy and Management, the one-year M.P.H. program, and many executive education programs. Indeed, in many instances it was I who was the
student, and I can only hope that they feel they received something approaching reciprocity.

Gratitude also must go to my colleagues, both at the School of
Public Health and elsewhere, who read the manuscript and provided valuable comments and criticisms. In particular, Nancy
Kane of the School of Public Health, Robert Anthony of the Harvard Business School, and Donald Simons of the Boston University School of Management all read one or more chapters—generally more—and offered delicate advice in places where outrage
frequently would have been more appropriate. Richard Saltman
of the School of Public Health collaborated with me in the preparation of several papers, portions of which have been incorporated into some of the chapters.

I am also most grateful for the support and encouragement I
received from Howard Hiatt, the Dean of the School of Public
Health, Elkan Blout, our Dean for Academic Affairs, and Freder-
ick Mosteller, the Chairman of the Department of Health Policy
and Management at the School. They saw to it that I had, among
other things, an intellectually stimulating environment in which

viii

to develop many of the ideas and concepts which appear in the book.

Various health care organizations also have assisted in one way or another with portions of the book. The Visiting Nurse Association of Greater St. Louis provided financial support for research leading to an article, "Nonprofits Need Surplus Too," which has been incorporated into Chapter 3. Some of the ideas in Chapter 6 emerged from a paper that was prepared with funding from the Hospital Corporation of America. The appendix to Chapter 7 contains a slightly modified version of a budget and reporting system which I developed for the Ministry of Public Health in Kuwait, with funding from the government of Kuwait. And finally, some of the ideas in Chapter 8 emerged from consulting activities some years ago with the Edwin Gould Foundation for Children.

The Pew Memorial Trust, through a sizable grant to our department, provided me with research assistance, secretarial support, and word-processing support, without which the book could not have been completed. I am most appreciative of what I hope they will consider to be their wisdom and foresight in making the grant. The staff of the school's Development Office supplemented this financial assistance by generously sharing their word-processing knowledge and equipment, thereby lightening the task considerably.

Finally—truly last but not least—I would like to thank Beth O'Brien and Debbie Katz. Beth spent a summer as a research assistant pulling together a wide variety of complicated details, freeing me to continue with what at times seemed to be interminable writing. Debbie had no idea, I'm certain, of the monster she was creating when she suggested we put the book on a word processor. I'm sure it occurred to her more than once, though, as chapters entered double-digit drafts. Somehow she maintained her equanimity—and I hope her eyesight—through it all.

I would like to be able to say that any errors or shortcomings in the book are the responsibility of either students who did not correct me, colleagues who failed to spot problem areas, or editors who missed inconsistencies, but I cannot. They are all mine.

David W. Young

Contents

Introduction

The manager of a health care or human service organization of almost any size is faced with a wide array of problems and choices. Among the most significant are those that bear directly on the processes of accounting, finance, and management control. The purpose of this book is to address managerial concerns in these three areas. The book focuses exclusively on health and human service organizations, and has two interrelated goals: first, to assist both practicing managers and students of management in analyzing accounting, financing, and control problems, and in deciding among alternative courses of action; second, to the extent feasible, to put these problems in their broader organizational context.

The focus on organizational context is essential to a full understanding of the more specific issues and techniques. One cannot talk in a meaningful way about matters of accounting, control, or finance in any specific organization without some fundamental understanding of that organization's strategy and structure. An organization that is growing rapidly and receiving a large portion of its revenue from third-party reimbursement sources, for example, will have different financing needs than an organization that is growing slowly or not at all and serves a large percentage of private-pay patients. Furthermore, an organization that is decentralized and has given a great deal of autonomy to its functional units generally will need, if it is to be successful, a different control structure and process than an organization that is highly centralized.

DISTINGUISHING FEATURES

The integrative focus described above, combined with a focus on important concepts and techniques in accounting, finance, and control, is one of the principal distinguishing features of the book. While not all chapters devote the same amount of attention to this integrative and conceptual focus, most chapters pay at least some attention to it, and some give it a considerable amount of time.

A second distinguishing feature of the book is its focus on managers and the kinds of decisions managers must make, either in terms of everyday operations or in the development and implementation of management control systems to assist them in daily operational activities. As such, there is an absence of detailed explanations of basic techniques in accounting, control, and finance. Many textbooks are available that explain both basic and advanced techniques quite well, for both profit-oriented and nonprofit organizations, and this book does not attempt to cover that ground again. On occasion, a chapter is textbook-like and explains some fundamental principles, but in all instances I attempt to avoid *detailed* explanations of this material. A good example is the chapter on financial accounting. The chapter begins with a description of the basic principles of financial statements and their value in communicating important information about the status of an organization. No explanation is provided, however, of the accounting *process* that underlies the statements. Entire textbooks are devoted to financial accounting principles and processes, with many more textbooks available covering both intermediate and advanced financial accounting. Readers are directed to this information—and to comparable information in other chapters—by means of a bibliography at the end of each chapter.

A third distinguishing characteristic of the book is its focus on a wide range of organizations in the health and human service field, not just hospitals. Some examples have a small-institution orientation, some are about larger organizations, but regardless of their institutional focus, the examples illustrate principles that are applicable to organizations of all sizes. Additionally, the textual material that refers to the examples in each chapter should be useful to individuals in health and human service organizations of all sizes.

Finally, and perhaps most important, the book introduces the reader not only to a description of the applicability of some basic accounting, finance, and control concepts to health care but to some unique ways of looking at these concepts in the context of health and human service organizations. In large part, the book puts into writing the explanations and relevant principles that have been developed during eight years of both executive and graduate-level teaching. These explanations and principles have proven useful in describing what frequently is seen as a very difficult body of material to senior and middle-level managers in health and human service organizations of all sizes, to physician chiefs of service in large teaching hospitals, and to graduate students having little organizational experience or those having as many as 24 years of full-time professional activities.

Because these concepts have been tested and refined over several years, they should prove of importance and utility to managers of almost all health and human service organizations, as well as to students studying the management of such organizations. The cost accounting process, for example, is described as a series of decisions, some of which are made for managers by third-party payors, but some of which are left open to judgment. Differential cost analysis is described in light of the complexity introduced by cost-based reimbursement. The role of surplus is described, not as a *reward* but as a critical element in maintaining an institution's financial viability. The topic of "profit centers" is described in a management control context as an important consideration in a decentralized management structure for nonprofit as well as profit-oriented organizations. And so on.

UNDERLYING PREMISES

Several fundamental premises underlie the material in this book: (1) managers are decision makers; (2) rarely is there a "right" decision under any set of circumstances; (3) while there is never enough information for decision-making purposes, whatever information is available *can be* structured to facilitate decision making; and (4) other things equal, better structured information will lead to better decisions. Based on this set of premises, the book attempts to build a language system that can assist managers in structuring information for purposes of decision making. As with any language, the system has both structure and process. The intent of each chapter is both to describe to the reader some important structural elements or concepts and to discuss the way in which those concepts interrelate.

The above focus gives the book a special character. In particular, it should *not* be viewed as a "cookbook" with recipes for solving organizational problems, but rather as the description of a conceptual structure with which to address the wide variety of organizational problems and concomitant decision-making efforts in which managers engage. In short, the book describes ways of

4

thinking about organizational problems, rather than sets of solutions to those problems.

This latter objective is reinforced by means of a "managerial checklist" at the end of each chapter. Unlike some checklists, however, these do not purport to tell a manager what to do. Instead, they consist of issues and concepts for managers to think about in the context of their own organizations. In some sense, they serve to summarize chapters; but their intent is to have more of an action orientation. Each checklist suggests a series of questions for managers to ask themselves about their own organizations, and thus provides readers with a directed approach toward applying the concepts to their own settings. In some instances, a checklist question can be answered with a simple request to the accounting department. In others, answering the question may require one or more meetings and some in-depth staff analysis. In still others, the question may be simply food for thought—one more item to put into the set of concerns and issues that managers ponder on a day-to-day basis.

STRUCTURE OF THE BOOK

In accordance with the structure of many books of this sort, the first topic introduced is financial accounting, including a discussion of some fundamental financial accounting concepts and their relationships to health and human service institutions. Although Chapter 1 is in no way intended to be an all-inclusive discussion of financial accounting, it does contain a discussion of several important financial accounting concepts, including fund accounting, and an explanation of their relevance to managers in health and human service organizations.

Chapter 2 builds on the information in Chapter 1, going into greater depth on some of the important techniques of financial analysis. In particular, this chapter looks at ratio analysis and the use of the statement of changes in financial position. The chapter also illustrates some ways in which one can analyze a set of financial statements.

Chapter 3 moves into the area of financial management, discussing capital investment decision making, the concept of leverage, and the role of surplus in a nonprofit organization.

Chapter 4 shifts from the externally oriented approach of the first three chapters into the realm of management accounting, addressing the topic of full cost accounting. The chapter first describes the relationship between resource utilization and cost measurement. It then looks at the various decisions that are made in a full cost accounting context, including the important but frequently ignored question of process versus job order cost-accounting systems, and the relevance of this distinction for health care institutions. The chapter uses as an example a home health agency with a relatively simple cost-accounting system, which becomes progressively more complex as additional decisions are incorporated into the analysis. The chapter concludes with a discussion of the relationship between full cost accounting and third-party reimbursement. An appendix to the chapter gives the interested reader additional details on third-party reimbursement systems.

Chapter 5 continues with the topic of management accounting. Here the focus of the analysis is on alternative-choice decisions, the nature of cost behavior, and the question of how costs will change under different scenarios. Some important principles related to differential cost analysis are discussed, as are the concepts of contribution, sunk costs, and break-even analysis. This chapter concludes with a discussion of differential analysis under cost-based reimbursement.

Chapter 6 is devoted to the topic of management control systems, stressing the importance of their relationship to an organization's strategy and structure, and the necessity of obtaining a *fit* between the control system and various organizational elements. The chapter begins by looking at the relationship between full cost accounting and management control, focusing on the important concept of cost-influencing variables, and the necessity of attaining a match between controllability and responsibility. In particular, the chapter identifies the key role played by the attending physician in influencing costs, and emphasizes the need to incorporate physicians into the management control system. The design of a management control system is assessed in terms of both structure and process; and the important topic of budgeting is discussed in detail, highlighting places where misfits can take place between an organization's budgetary system and its broader organizational and strategic activities.

Chapter 7 looks in depth at an important but frequently underdeveloped feature of management control systems: the control reports. The concepts of flexible budgeting and variance analysis are introduced and described in detail, along with a discussion of some important concepts related to the development of managerially useful control reports. The chapter concludes with a description of the criteria for a good management control system. An appendix provides the interested reader with a sample reporting system using a flexible budget.

Chapter 8 addresses the topic of management information systems and their role in health and human service institutions. In particular, this chapter is designed to help the manager answer the questions: "Why an MIS?" And, if an MIS, "Which one?" The chapter's focus, however, is almost entirely on the behavioral and managerial issues associated with MIS efforts, not on matters of technology.

Finally, Chapter 9 attempts to obtain some closure by relating the various activities discussed in the preceding chapters not only to each other but to an overarching framework of the organization's strategy and structure. This integration is achieved through the concept of administrative systems, and organizations are described in terms of the various administrative systems of concern to management.

1

Financial Accounting

Although all organizations typically prepare a variety of information for internal and external purposes, the one set of information prepared in a reasonably consistent manner for all organizations is that contained in the financial statements. Despite this attempt at consistency, however, managers have some latitude in determining the kinds of information to be included on their organization's financial statements, as well as in the ability to influence how these statements will be presented to readers. Consequently, managers of both large and small health and human service organizations have a need to understand the fundamentals of financial accounting. This understanding is essential to both a sophisticated reading of statements prepared by other organizations and to an ability to manage the process by which statements are prepared for one's own organization.

This last point is particularly important, but frequently misunderstood. Clearly, most managers will not become involved in the details of the accounting process. Nevertheless, they must be aware of both the kinds of decisions being made by their accountants and of the various accounting options open to their organizations. This is essential if appropriate and consistent directions are to be given to the accounting staff.

The purpose of this chapter is to discuss financial statements in a general way, describing some fundamental concepts that are of importance to managers. The chapter begins with an overview of the three most common statements: the balance sheet, the income statement, and the statement of changes in financial position. The discussion then moves to some of the key managerial decisions that influence the financial statements. Finally, the topic of fund accounting is explored.

THE FINANCIAL STATEMENTS: AN OVERVIEW

The three financial statements of concern to for-profit and non-profit organizations alike are the income statement, the balance sheet, and the statement of changes in financial position (SCFP). It is important to recognize that, since the statements all emerge from the same accounting *system,* there is a high degree of interrelationship among them. This interrelationship is based on the fundamental notion that financial accounting is a process of measuring levels and flows. Specifically, the balance sheet describes the *level* or status of each account *on a particular date;* the income statement describes the *flow* of revenues and expenses (not necessarily cash) into and out of the organization *during a particular time period;* and the SCFP describes, in an organized way, the *flows* that took place in the balance sheet accounts also *during a time period.*

Interrelationships among the Statements: A Simple Example

The interrelationships among the three statements can best be seen by using a simplified reporting cycle. Let us assume that the Spy Pond Hospital begins its fiscal year with the balance sheet shown in Table 1-1. Note that total assets are equal to the total of liabilities and fund balance. Essentially, the left side of the balance sheet indicates what the organization owns or has claim to (i.e.,

TABLE 1-1

SPY POND HOSPITAL
Balance Sheet
As of December 31, 19A
($000)

Assets		Liabilities and Fund Balance	
Cash	$1,000	Accounts payable	$ 500
Accounts receivable (net)	800	Short-term loan payable	900
Prepaid expenses	200	Mortgage payable	5,000
Land, buildings, and		Total liabilities	6,400
equipment	7,000	Fund balance	2,600
		Total liabilities and	
Total assets	$9,000	fund balance	$9,000

its assets), while the right side describes the sources of financing for those assets. As we can see, a portion of the hospital's assets has been financed by parties *outside* the organization (i.e., liabilities) and a portion has been financed by the organization itself with its internally derived funds (i.e., fund balance). Beyond this, however, there generally is no one-to-one correspondence between a given asset and a given liability or the fund balance.

Now, let us assume that during the course of the year 19B the hospital earned revenue of $3,000,000 by selling or otherwise being reimbursed for its services, and incurred $2,500,000 in expenses in delivering its services. The income statement might then look like the one shown in Table 1–2. If all revenue had been received in cash, and all expenses paid in cash, the balance sheet as of December 31, 19B, would look like the one in Table 1–3.

Note that the balance sheet has been prepared as of the last day of the period covered by the income statement. The entire amount of the excess of revenue over expenses shows up in both the cash account on the left side of the balance sheet, and in the fund bal-

TABLE 1–2

SPY POND HOSPITAL
Income Statement
For the Year 19B
($000)

Patient revenue		$3,000
Expenses:		
Salaries and wages	$1,500	
Supplies	500	
Other	500	
Total expenses		2,500
Excess of revenue over expenses		$ 500

TABLE 1–3

SPY POND HOSPITAL
Balance Sheet
As of December 31, 19B
($000)

Assets		Liabilities and Fund Balance	
Cash	$1,500	Accounts payable	$ 500
Accounts receivable (net)	800	Short-term loan payable	900
Prepaid expenses	200	Mortgage payable	5,000
Land, buildings, and		Total liabilities	6,400
equipment	7,000	Fund balance	3,100
		Total liabilities and	
Total assets	$9,500	fund balance	$9,500

ance account on the right side. Thus, it would be possible to determine an organization's excess of revenues over expenses[1] for any given year simply by comparing the fund balance account on the balance sheet at the beginning of the year with the fund balance at the end of the year.[2]

Despite the fact that a comparison of two balance sheets would give us the amount of surplus (or deficit), almost all organizations prepare an income statement that presents additional details on the inflows and outflows (revenues and expenses) to the fund balance account. As such, the bottom line of the income statement (i.e., the excess of revenues over expenses) will be identical to the net change in the fund balance account between the balance sheets. Whatever detail one finds on an income statement, therefore, serves only to provide readers of the financial statements with as much information as the organization would like them to have about the reasons behind the change in the fund balance account.

Similarly, the detail that one finds in the various accounts on the balance sheet reflects the extent to which the organization wishes to provide readers of financial statements with information on the detailed characteristics of that organization's assets, liabilities, and fund balances.

As indicated above, Table 1–3 assumed that all revenues and expenses were in cash; therefore, the cash account increased by the same amount as the fund balance account, which is $500,000. Obviously, the chances of all revenue and expenses being incurred in cash are highly unlikely; and, even if this were to occur, a variety of cash-influencing transactions would most likely take place that would not be shown on the income statement. Such transactions include the collection of outstanding accounts receivable, the payment of accounts payable, principal payments on the mortgage, and so on. Thus, it is almost certain that our balance sheet as of December 31, 19B, will have different totals in all of the accounts. Importantly, however, the total of each side will still be $9,500,000 ($500,000 more than 19A), since the sum of *all* assets and the sum of *all* liabilities and fund balances can only be increased (or decreased) by a *net inflow* (or *outflow*) of resources into (or out of) the organization. Revenues represent resource inflows; expenses represent resource outflows.

---

[1]Sometimes called a surplus (or deficit).

[2]This is actually for "normal operations" only, since fund balance also can be changed by other means, such as contributions of one sort or another. Nevertheless, the normal operations activity is sufficient for our purposes here. Furthermore, for reasons discussed below, we ordinarily could not determine the organization's surplus by comparing the change in the cash account.

This latter point is an extremely important but frequently confusing one. Two examples can help to illustrate it. First, the collection of an account receivable is *not* an inflow of resources, since it simply represents the *exchange* of one asset (accounts receivable) for another (cash). Second, the payment of an account payable is not an outflow of resources, since it represents the exchange of a reduction in an asset (cash) for a reduction in a liability (accounts payable). Thus, none of the transactions, other than those shown on the income statement, represent resource inflows or outflows.

Bearing this important concept in mind, let us assume that the Balance Sheet as of December 31, 19B, looked like the one shown in Table 1–4. By comparing Tables 1–4 and 1–1 we can see that the balances in all accounts are now different. Only the Fund Balance increased by the excess of revenue over expenses. The other accounts increased or decreased by varying amounts.

The SCFP allows us to organize the changes which took place in these other accounts so they can be more easily understood by readers of the financial statements. To illustrate the explanatory power of the SCFP, however, we must first develop our existing financial statements more fully and make them somewhat more realistic.

TABLE 1–4

SPY POND HOSPITAL
Balance Sheet
As of December 31, 19B
($000)

Assets		Liabilities and Fund Balance	
Cash	$900	Accounts payable	$1,400
Accounts receivable (net)	1,300	Short-term loan payable	800
Prepaid expenses	100	Mortgage payable	4,200
Land, buildings, and		Total liabilities	6,400
equipment	7,200	Fund balance	3,100
		Total liabilities and	
Total assets	$9,500	fund balance	$9,500

A More Realistic Example

Table 1–5 contains the same information as Table 1–1, but has classified assets into "current" and "fixed," and has classified liabilities into "current" and "long-term." The distinction is that current assets are what theoretically can be converted into cash within a year, and current liabilities are those due and payable in cash within a year. Fixed assets and long-term liabilities do not possess this one-year-convertibility characteristic. Even though an

TABLE 1–5

SPY POND HOSPITAL
Balance Sheet
As of December 31, 19A
($000)

Assets			Liabilities and Fund Balance	
Cash...............	$1,000		Accounts payable..............	$ 500
Accounts receivable			Short-term loan payable........	900
(net)	800		Mortgage payable, current.......	800
Prepaid expenses	200		Total current liabilities	2,200
Total current			Mortgage payable, long-term ...	4,200
assets........	2,000		Total liabilities............	6,400
Land, buildings, and			Fund balance..................	2,600
equipment, at				
cost $10,000				
Less accumulated				
depreciation...... 3,000	7,000		Total liabilities and fund	
Total assets	$9,000		balance	$9,000

organization could supposedly sell its land, buildings, or equipment during a year and, thereby, convert all or some of that asset into cash, this transaction is not a normal aspect of ongoing operations; thus, the asset is considered noncurrent. Similarly, the mortgage could be paid off entirely within a year, but normally would not be; rather, only the portion actually due (i.e., the current portion) would be paid during the course of a year.

The revised balance sheet also specifies initial cost totals of all fixed assets. It then indicates the amount of accumulated depreciation on the Land, Buildings, and Equipment account (i.e., the amount of those assets that already have been "expensed" or "depreciated") on prior income statements. The result is a "net" figure, which is the same as that shown in Table 1–1.

The income statement contained in Table 1–6, has the same "excess of revenue over expenses" figure as Table 1–2, but it specifies two expenses not shown previously: depreciation and interest; the "other" expense has been reduced to compensate for the shift.

Finally, the balance sheet shown in Table 1–7 is similar to that in Table 1–4, but with the expanded format. Note, in particular, that the accumulated depreciation figure has been increased by the amount of depreciation shown in the income statement, which, of course, is what reduces the "net" or book value of the Land, Buildings, and Equipment account. Also, however, note that the "at cost" portion of the Land, Buildings, and Equipment account has been increased by $500,000—reflecting a purchase of some new fixed assets.

We are now ready to look at the SCFP, which explains the

TABLE 1–6 _____

SPY POND HOSPITAL
Income Statement
For the Year 19B
($000)

Patient revenue		$3,000
Expenses:		
Salaries and wages	$1,500	
Supplies....................................	500	
Depreciation	300	
Interest....................................	50	
Other	150	
Total expenses		2,500
Excess of revenue over expenses...............		$ 500

TABLE 1–7 _____

SPY POND HOSPITAL
Balance Sheet
As of December 31, 19B
($000)

Assets			*Liabilities and Fund Balance*	
Cash................		$900	Accounts payable..............	$1,400
Accounts receivable			Short-term loan payable........	800
(net)		$1,300	Mortgage payable, current......	800
Prepaid expenses		100	Total current liabilities	3,000
Total current			Mortgage payable, long-term ...	3,400
assets........		2,300	Total liabilities............	6,400
Land, buildings, and			Fund balance.................	3,100
equipment, at				
cost	$10,500			
Less accumulated				
depreciation......	3,300	7,200	Total liabilities and fund	
Total assets		$9,500	balance	$9,500

changes taking place between the balance sheets shown in Tables 1–5 and 1–7. We know that the excess of revenue over expenses, shown in Table 1–6, provides a partial explanation, and this is listed first on the SCFP. The remainder of the SCFP is devoted to explaining the flow of funds, depicted by changes in the other accounts, which ultimately resulted in a decrease in cash from $1,000,000 to $900,000.

The SCFP is contained in Table 1–8. It shows that, although cash *would have* increased by $500,000 from the excess of revenue over expenses—if all revenues had been received in cash, all expenses paid in cash, and there were no other cash transactions—it actually fell by $100,000 (i.e., a $600,000 shift). The shift resulted from a net positive cash flow of $1,300,000 from operations (de-

TABLE 1–8 _____

SPY POND HOSPITAL
Statement of Changes in Financial Position—Cash Basis
For the Year 19B
($000)

Sources of cash:
  From operations:
    Excise of revenue over expenses............................... $500

Sources of cash:		
From operations:		
Excess of revenue over expenses.............................	$500	
Add (deduct) adjustments to convert to cash basis:		
Depreciation expense	300	
Accounts receivable increase...........................	(500)	
Prepaid expenses decrease	100	
Accounts payable increase.............................	900	
Net cash generated from operations		$1,300
Uses of cash:		
Payment on short-term loan	100	
Payment on current portion of mortgage......................	800	
Acquisition of land, buildings, and equipment.................	500	
Total cash used during period..........................		1,400
Net increase (decrease) in cash during period		$ (100)

preciation, accounts receivable, prepaid expenses, and accounts payable), and $1,400,000 in outflows as a result of the payments on the short-term loan and mortgage, and the acquisiton of additional Land, Buildings, and Equipment assets.[3]

The Importance of Cash Projections

In essence, then, the SCFP shows the effect on the cash account[4] of the changes that have taken place in all the other balance sheet accounts during a time period. Since the changes in other accounts, essentially, are the result of management decisions, and, since cash is such an important aspect of an organization's viability, the importance of *projecting* the changes in an organization's cash account should be clear. Simply preparing a pro forma (projected) income statement (on an accrual basis) is not enough to determine if the organization will have sufficient cash on hand to meet its ongoing obligations. Indeed, if Spy Pond Hospital had assumed that its $500,000 excess of revenue over expenses would

_____

[3]The process for actually preparing a SCFP is somewhat complicated. For purposes here, it is sufficient to recognize that an increase in a current asset, such as accounts receivable, is a *use* of cash and, hence, is shown as a negative amount (i.e., in parentheses). Similarly, a reduction in a current asset is a *source* of cash. Current liabilities operate exactly the opposite: an increase is a *source* of cash, while a decrease is a *use* of cash, resulting in parentheses.

[4]Or the organization's working capital if the SCFP is prepared on a "working capital basis."

all be realized in cash, it easily could have faced some serious un-anticipated cash flow difficulties.

Effectively, then, one of the most important aspects of manage-ment in any organization—health and human services, or other-wise—is that of accurately projecting cash. Generally, projections are made for each month of the organization's fiscal year, and up-dated as appropriate (i.e., as significant assumptions change, which, in turn, affect the cash flow projections). Since many of an organization's strategic and programmatic activities will influence these assumptions, it is essential that management becomes in-volved in the cash projection process. The purchase of new assets, increase in inventory, expansion of programs, changes in accounts receivable collection policies, and the like, all will influence these projections. Frequently, top and middle management are the only sources of information about these assumptions.

Types of Accounts

As the preceding discussion has indicated, all accounts can be classified into one of two categories: income statement (revenue and expense), and balance sheet (assets, liabilities, and fund bal-ances). Every account in the accounting system, regardless of how complicated its title, can be placed into one of these catego-ries. Indeed, the only purpose for giving specialized names to the accounts is to provide the reader of financial statements with more detailed information than otherwise would be available about the nature of the activities that transpired in the organiza-tion. Take, for example, the question of revenue. All revenue re-ceived by the organization, regardless of its source, could, if we wished, be classified into an account called Revenue. If this were the case, the income statement would then have only one line for revenue, such as we saw in Table 1-6. Alternatively, we could classify revenue into a variety of categories, such as Medicare, Medicaid, Blue Cross, private pay, commercial insurance, and so forth. By providing for this additional detail in the accounts, the income statement could then give readers much more information about the activities of the hospital.

It is important to recognize, however, that, even with addi-tional refinements, all of the above accounts are revenue accounts, and, at any time the organization receives revenue, one of these accounts must be incremented. The same is true for the various expense accounts on the income statement, and for the asset, liability, and fund balance accounts on the balance sheet. The American Hospital Association can provide interested readers with information about acceptable charts of accounts; and the

American Institute of Certified Public Accountants (AICPA) pre-
pares audit guides describing acceptable accounting practices for
various types of nonprofit organizations.[5]

MANAGERIAL DECISIONS

Although the AICPA audit guides stipulate that certain information must be made available to readers of financial statements if
an organization is to be in compliance with audit standards, nevertheless there is some flexibility. Certainly organizations can provide more information than the audit guide requires, and frequently choices exist about alternative ways to present information. Thus, within audit guide limits, a key set of managerial
decisions concerns the nature and extent of information to be presented to readers of the financial statements. This makes it im-
perative that managers become involved in working with their accounting staffs to determine the various options that exist, the
approximate cost of each (in terms of staff requirements and other
information processing expenses), and the value to the organization of presenting the additional information to readers. Although, frequently, decisions of this sort are left to the accounting
staff, this need not, and, in many instances *should* not, be the
case.

Beyond the choice of accounts to be included on the financial
statements, a manager's knowledge of financial accounting can be
useful in a variety of other decisions made in the context of preparing the financial statements. Frequently, for example, it is necessary to (*a*) determine when the organization will recognize that
it has earned revenue, (*b*) make financing decisions related to asset acquisition and cash flows, (*c*) estimate the levels of various
accounts, and (*d*) establish depreciation schedules. These and a
variety of similar decisions can have a significant impact on the
eventual content of the financial statements, and are decisions
which generally should not be delegated to the accounting staff.
A discussion of some of the more important areas for managerial
decision is contained below.

Revenue Recognition

The decision about when revenue should be recognized as earned
has no clear answer, and thus is one frequently requiring manage-

---

[5]There are four AICPA audit guides: hospitals, voluntary health and
welfare organizations, educational institutions, and "other." They may be obtained from the American Institute of Certified Public Accountants, New York.

rial intervention. The following sections, Example and Analysis, illustrate the dilemma.

> *Example:* The manager of a local YWCA began a cooperative effort with a neighboring YMCA to solicit community contributions as part of a capital fund drive. The YMCA was designated as custodian of the funds, which were to be divided equally between the two organizations. At the end of one year, a total of $50,000 had been collected and another $30,000 had been received in the form of pledges. None of the collected money had been transferred from the YMCA to the YWCA. The YWCA recognized no contribution revenue for the year.[6]

> *Analysis:* The revenue recognition principle states that revenue shall be recognized and included on the income statement when there is "reasonable certainty" that it will be received. This implies that, of the $50,000 collected by the YMCA, $25,000 (i.e., the YWCA's 50 percent share) should have been recognized as revenue by the YWCA. By not recognizing this revenue, an unfavorable audit report could result. It is possible that the accounting staff had no knowledge of the agreement made between the two organizations, and thus no way of knowing that any contribution revenue should be recognized. The responsibility of management here is to make this information known to the accounting department so the appropriate amount of revenue can be included.

Beyond this, however, there is a question of how much of the *pledges receivable* should be recognized as revenue. It is reasonable to assume not all of these promises will be kept, with the result that not all of the pledges should be recognized as revenue. Just as the determination of an allowance for bad debts for an organization's accounts receivable (discussed below) is a subjective matter, so is the determination of an allowance for uncollectible pledges. Although historical data frequently can be used as a basis for making these determinations, these data frequently are not appropriate for a new set of circumstances. Again, managerial intervention is called for.

Accrual Accounting and Cash Flows

As indicated in an earlier section of this chapter, the essence of accrual accounting is recognition and recording of events when they occur, rather than when cash is received or dispersed. Thus, revenue generally is recognized before the organization actually receives the cash payment. In the same manner, some expenses

---

[6]See "San Bernardino YWCA," in R. N. Anthony and R. Herzlinger, *Management Control in Nonprofit Organizations* (Homewood, Ill.: Richard D. Irwin, 1980), pp. 147–52.

are recognized and included on the income statement, even though the cash payment for those expenses has not occurred. While the accrual concept leads to greater consistency and comparability among financial statements, it poses some important and frequently confusing concerns for managers. This confusion is particularly troublesome in the interaction among revenue, expenses, and cash, since:

---

1. *Revenue earned is not necessarily cash received.* Generally, for example, a hospital recognizes revenue when the bill is sent out, but the cash payment may not come until several months later.
2. *An expense incurred is not necessarily cash paid out.* Depreciation (discussed in detail below) is a good example of an expense for which there is no associated cash payment.
3. *Cash received is not necessarily revenue earned.* The receipt of payment for the bill sent in item 1 above is a cash inflow, but the revenue was earned when the bill was sent.
4. *Cash paid out is not necessarily an expense incurred.* The purchase of inventory requires a cash outlay, but expenses are incurred only as the goods are actually used up.

The result is that, although accrual accounting provides more accuracy in terms of recording events, and hence greater reliability in comparing financial statements either across organizations or from one year to the next in the same organization, it says relatively little about the ability of an organization to maintain itself in a "liquid" state during any given accounting period. As a result, some organizations find themselves needing to borrow sizable amounts on a short-term basis to finance their cash shortages. Occasionally, more thoughtful planning of cash flows could avoid this need, and frequently better financing terms could be arranged if a cash need could be anticipated well in advance.

Estimates of Account Levels

Although accounting is a relatively precise activity, there are, as indicated above, aspects of the process which are subjective and require the preparation of estimates. In the calculation of the "net" figure of accounts receivable for Spy Pond Hospital, shown in Tables 1–5 and 1–7, for example, an estimate had to be made concerning the amount of accounts receivable on the books that actually would not be collected. Although, for simplicity of presentation, the details were left off these tables, the estimate would actually show up on the income statement as a "bad debt expense," and would be contained on the balance sheet as an "allowance for doubtful accounts." The balance sheet item for accounts receivable shown in Table 1–7 might then look as follows:

```
Accounts receivable  ...........................  $1,500
Less allowance for doubtful accounts  ...........    200    $1,300
```

Again, since there is no right way to make such estimates, management intervention and decision making are important aspects of the accounting process.

Depreciation

The concept of depreciation is one of the most important but frequently misunderstood aspects of accrual accounting. Effectively, depreciation provides recognition of the fact that an asset does not wear out in one year, but rather has a useful life which extends for several years. In many instances, though, the cash payment associated with the acquisition of an asset takes place in the year of purchase.[7] The purpose of depreciation is simply to recognize that the *expense* associated with the asset (such as a piece of equipment) is *not* the cash payment made to purchase it (since that is only an exchange of one asset for another, i.e., cash for equipment, and therefore not an outflow of resources). Rather, the expense represents the *using up* of that asset over its useful life. Depreciation attempts to estimate how much of the asset is used up each year. In some instances, required depreciation schedules are provided in audit guidelines, or by third-party payors; but frequently some managerial decisions are required, particularly in estimating an asset's salvage value, or in determining the cash flow benefits of using accelerated depreciation. Here again, managerial judgment is called for.[8]

Depreciation will appear on an organization's income state-

---

[7]Debt or lease financing obviously changes this somewhat, but not totally. With debt financing the bank (or other lending institution), rather than the organization itself, makes the cash payment in the year of acquisition.

[8]In for-profit organizations, the depreciation expense is not paid for directly by consumers; instead, it is one of many cost items included in the analysis used for setting prices. By contrast, in most health care and in many human service organizations, the depreciation expense is included on a "cost report" and reimbursed directly by third-party payors. Fundamentally, however, this distinction is immaterial, since depreciation also would be included on the "cost report" of a for-profit organization performing an analysis to assist it in setting prices.

ment; but, since the actual cash outflow took place when the asset was purchased, it is a *noncash* expense (i.e., item 2 on the above list). Consequently, it has important cash flow implications, which is why it was *added* in preparing the SCFP in Table 1–8. Effectively, the excess of revenue over expenses had included depreciation as an expense; but, since it is a noncash expense, we must add it back when analyzing the effect of an organization's activities on its cash account.

Funding Depreciation

In many instances, either because of third-party payor requirements or otherwise, health care and other nonprofit organizations will "fund" their depreciation. It is important to understand that, in this instance, there is a cash outflow association with depreciation, which is not seen otherwise. Specifically, an organization that funds depreciation is transferring cash from an unrestricted to a restricted account, and thus has given up the ability to use that cash for operating purposes. To understand this concept more fully, we will now look at the technique of fund accounting.

FUND ACCOUNTING

The practice of fund accounting consists of separating an organization's accounting system into a series of smaller individual accounting systems. The separation is based on the restrictions that are placed on the organization's assets by their contributors, such as private donors, third-party payors, and others. In many states, for example, Blue Cross requires a hospital to maintain a separate *fund* for its land and buildings. Moreover, private donors may place any number of restrictions on their contributions to a nonprofit organization, specifying that their donations be used only for specific services, programs, kinds of equipment, and so forth. And finally, an organization's board of directors may designate certain monies as restricted to certain uses.

To meet these various restrictions, and to provide for clarity in presenting the information to readers of the financial statements, a system called fund accounting has evolved. There are four essential elements of fund accounting which are important to managers of health and human service organizations, as well as to nonprofit organizations in general.

The first and perhaps most important element is that fund accounting is only slightly more complicated or difficult than non-fund accounting. Each fund has a set of financial statements similar to those discussed above: an income statement, a balance sheet, and, if necessary, a statement of changes in financial position. In working with these statements, the accounting department simply must decide what fund is affected by a particular transaction, so the proper entry can be made.

The second element is the one that links the various funds: interfund transfers. For a variety of reasons, such as the funding of depreciation, it frequently is necessary to transfer amounts from one fund to another. The result is an additional financial statement, which shows the net effect of all interfund transfers. This statement contains both the effect of revenues and expenses for each fund, as well as the amount of transfers among the organization's funds that took place during the reporting period.

A third element is that of restrictions on the use of assets in the funds. It is essential for managers to develop reporting mechanisms outside the formal financial accounting system which assure them that the restrictions—whatever they may be—are being observed. Misuse of restricted funds not only may damage the organization's ability to raise funds in the future but can also have legal ramifications.

Juxtaposed with the obligation to assure that contributors' restrictions are observed, managers also must pay attention to the flexibility they need to maintain a financially viable organization. On the one hand, this flexibility requires that they shift amounts into their unrestricted funds, whenever legal and feasible, to provide for ongoing operations. On the other hand, however, many potential funding sources may eliminate or curtail contributions if an organization's unrestricted fund shows what they believe to be an "excessive" fund balance. Clearly, to the extent that options are available on the amount of the balance in each fund, these are choices that should be made by the organization's managers and not by its accountants.

The fourth and final element of importance to managers in a fund accounting system is the presentation of the financial statements. It is important to recognize that the financial statements typically do not show each individual fund, but rather combine the funds into categories for purposes of presentation to outside readers. The result frequently can be a highly simplified overview of an organization's fund structure, one which tells readers very little about the degree to which funds in, say, the restricted category are actually restricted and the nature of the restrictions. Thus, the reading of fund accounting statements should be done with some caution.

SUMMARY OF THE CHAPTER

This chapter has only skimmed the surface of the broad topic of financial accounting. Its intent has not been to provide either a primer or a sophisticated description of the financial accounting process. Indeed, many books are devoted to the general topic of financial accounting, and many more focus exclusively on fund accounting. A few of these books are listed at the end of the chapter for readers who wish to pursue certain topics.

Instead, the intent of this chapter has been to describe financial accounting as it relates to managers of health and human service organizations. In particular, the focus has been, first, on a description of the relationships among the three key financial statements: the balance sheet, the income statement, and the statement of changes in financial position. Second, it has attempted to provide an indication of the importance of managerial intervention into the financial accounting system, and a description of where such intervention is important to the well-being of an organization.

MANAGERIAL CHECKLIST

1. Do our financial statements present information to readers in sufficient detail? How do organizations similar to ours present their financial statements? If they are different, why?

2. What kinds of strategic or programmatic directions are we taking that will influence our cash flows (e.g., the purchase of new buildings, equipment, or inventory; the initiation of a new program for which cash inflows may be delayed, and so on)? Are middle managers involved in the process of making these determinations? should they be?

3. How often does the accounting department prepare cash forecasts? Do they have the information from question 2, above, for use in preparing their forecasts? Do we occasionally have "cash crises," implying that more frequent or more accurate forecasts would be desirable?

4. When does our organization recognize revenue? Is our revenue recognition policy the same as other similar organizations? If not, why not?

5. Which of the accounts in our accounting system require estimates (e.g., depreciation schedules, bad debt rates, uncollectable pledges)? What is the estimating process in each case? How accurate has it been? Can it be changed if necessary?

6. What are our various funds and what are the restrictions? Are we abiding by these restrictions in the use of each fund's assets? **7.** Have we had reductions in contributions because our unrestricted fund had what donors believed to be an "excessive" fund balance? What options are available to allow us to shift assets to other funds?

Bibliography

American Health Care Association. *Uniform Chart of Accounts for Long-Term Care Facilities.* Washington, D.C.: American Health Care Association, 1976.

Anthony, R. N. *Financial Accounting in Non-Business Organizations.* Stamford, Conn.: Financial Accounting Standards Board, 1978.

————. *Essentials of Accounting.* Reading, Mass.: Addison-Wesley Publishing, 1982. A programmed text.

————. "Making Sense of Non-Business Accounting." *Harvard Business Review,* May–June 1980.

Anthony, R. N., and D. W. Young. *Management Control in Nonprofit Organizations.* Homewood, Ill.: Richard D. Irwin, 1984.

Davidson, S., et al. *Accounting: The Language of Business.* Glendridge, N.J.: Thomas Horton and Daughters, 1975.

Estes, R. *Dictionary of Accounting.* Cambridge, Mass.: MIT Press, 1981.

Gross, M. J., Jr., and S. F. Jablonsky. *Principles of Accounting and Financial Reporting for Non-Profit Organizations.* New York: John Wiley & Sons, 1979.

Hanke, E. O. *Accounting for Non-Profit Organizations.* 2d ed. Belmont, Calif.: Wadsworth, 1977.

Hay, L. E. *Accounting for Governmental and Nonprofit Entities.* Homewood, Ill.: Richard D. Irwin, 1980.

Herzlinger, R. *Note on Accounting for Hospitals.* Boston: Harvard Business School, 1977.

Herzlinger, R. E., and H. D. Sherman. "Advantages of Fund Accounting in Non-Profits." *Harvard Business Review,* May–June 1980.

Karling, J. W., and E. C. King. "Accounting for Multi-Unit Systems." *Modern Health Care,* March 1980.

Kraus, W. D. *Accounting Guidelines for Home Health Agencies.* New York: National League for Nursing, 1978.

Lynn, E. S., and J. W. Thompson. *Introduction to Fund Accounting.* Reston, Va.: Reston Publishing, 1974.

Newman, B. R., and L. A. Friedman. "Replacement Cost Accounting: An Alternative to Price Indexes." *Hospital and Health Services Administration,* Fall 1979.

Rhoads, J. L. *Basic Accounting and Budgeting for Nursing Homes.* Washington, D.C.: American Health Care Association, 1978.

Vancil, R. G., and R. L. Weil. *Replacement Cost Accounting: Readings on Concepts, Uses, Methods.* Glenridge, N.J.: Thomas Horton and Daughters, 1976.

Welsch, G. A., and R. N. Anthony. *Fundamentals of Financial Accounting.* Homewood, Ill.: Richard D. Irwin, 1981.

2

Financial Analysis

Another way of looking at the financial statements discussed in Chapter 1 is in terms of the information they convey about the way an organization has financed its growth and other activities. A great deal of information concerning an organization's financial management strategies is conveyed by means of both the balance sheet and the statement of changes in financial position. In particular, as Chapter 1 indicated, the balance sheet contains information about what the organization owns or claims title to (assets) and the means by which those items were financed (liabilities and fund balances). This perspective might be thought of as the "long-run" view of an organization's financial decisions, since it is the result of all of the organization's historical financial activities viewed at a given point in time.

The long-run view can be supplemented by a shorter-run examination of management's specific financing choices and activities over the course of a year. This latter information typically is conveyed via the statement of changes in financial position (SCFP). As was shown in Chapter 1, the SCFP gives specific information on the organization's sources of funds during a given accounting period (usually a year) and the uses to which those funds were put.[1] Thus by using the SCFP, a reader of financial statements can determine the extent to which the organization acquired more fixed assets or current assets during a year, and how those assets were financed (e.g., short-term debt, long-term debt, surplus, contributions). Consequently, the SCFP and the balance sheet together provide a reader of financial statements with some indication of the financial decisions made by an organization's

---

[1] In fact, the statement used to be called Sources and Uses of Funds.

management both over time and during the course of the most recent accounting period.

The purpose of this chapter is to look at questions of financing from several perspectives. The first is the technique of ratio analysis, focusing on the kinds of comparisons that ratios make possible between or among different sets of financial statements. The chapter then turns to the somewhat broader topic of which ratio analysis is a part: financial statement analysis. Here the discussion centers on the characteristics of a "good" set of financial statements. Although there is no one "right" set of financial statements for an organization, certain standards can be employed to determine if and where financial problems exist. Finally, a rather complex set of financial statements is analyzed to illustrate the ways in which the chapter's tools might be employed.

RATIO ANALYSIS

In addition to using the SCFP, an individual interested in analyzing the way in which an organization has carried out its financial management strategies can utilize a variety of financial ratios. Ratio analysis allows one to look at four critical areas of the financial management process: profitability, liquidity, asset management, and long-term solvency.[2] Effectively, a ratio is a mathematical relationship between two or more items on an organization's financial statements. Generally, a ratio is calculated by dividing the sum of one or more elements on the statements by the sum of one or more others. The principal purpose of ratio analysis is to facilitate comparisons, either for a single organization over a period of several years or among several similar organizations for a given time.

Because of lack of a uniformity in financial accounting among health and human service organizations, however, the use of ratio analysis to make comparisons between or among several organizations can be somewhat misleading. Not all organizations, even those of the same type (e.g., hospitals, or visiting nurse associations), prepare their financial statements in the same way or incorporate the same information in accounts of similar names. Thus, when ratios are used to compare organizations, particularly if the ratios included in the comparison utilize very specific accounts on the financial statement, the results should be viewed with some skepticism. This is also true if a given organization is

---

[2]Numerous articles have been written which both explain ratio analysis and apply it to the hospital sector of the health care system. Several of the more comprehensive of these are listed at the end of the chapter.

being compared to some sort of industry "norm." In general, then, while comparisons among organizations *can* be made, or a given organization can be related to some industry norm, the most valid comparisons usually are those that are made over time for a single organization.

Profitability Ratios

Profitability ratios generally measure the ability of an organization to generate sufficient funds from its operations to both sustain itself and provide an acceptable return to its owners. Although nonprofit organizations have no ownership obligations as such, they do have a need to sustain themselves financially to (1) replace assets as they wear out, (2) purchase new assets as programs and services grow, and (3) provide for the working capital needs associated with program and service growth. Profitability ratios provide some partial evidence of how well an organization is satisfying these requirements. One such measure is profit margin.

$$\text{Profit margin} = \frac{\text{Operating surplus}}{\text{Operating revenues}}$$

This ratio effectively measures how much of each dollar in revenue received by the organization ultimately becomes surplus (or "excess of revenue over expenses"). As indicated above, and as will be argued in greater detail in Chapter 3, an excess of revenues over expenses is an essential requirement for an organization which is growing or which must replace assets in the face of an inflationary economy. Thus, the ratio provides a partial indication of an organization's ability to sustain itself via surplus generation.

A second profitability ratio is return on assets.

$$\text{Return on assets} = \frac{\text{Operating surplus}}{\text{Total assets}}$$

Although, as discussed in Chapter 1, depreciation provides for the recovery of the cash expenditures associated with asset acquisition, the depreciation figure is based on the historical cost of the asset, and thus in no way compensates for the effects of inflation. Although there are a variety of other factors to consider with respect to the replacement of assets, the return on asset ratio provides at least a rudimentary indication of whether an organization is earning a sufficiently large surplus to at least maintain itself in a steady state. Accordingly, one would hope to see a return on asset figure which approximates the rate on inflation in an organization's service area. This issue will also be explored in greater detail in Chapter 3.

The final profitability measure is return on investment.

$$\text{Return on investment} = \frac{\text{Operating surplus}}{\text{Fund balance}}$$

This ratio, generally abbreviated as ROI, is perhaps the most commonly used indicator of profitability in for-profit organizations. It allows an investor or potential investor in an organization to compare the earnings on his or her investment in that organization with a variety of alternative uses of the investment funds (e.g., savings certificates, treasury notes, and the like). As will be argued in Chapter 3, the ratio has less value in a not-for-profit context, but it is presented here since third-party insurers occasionally discuss the issue of including a return on investment or return on equity (the two are synonymous) factor in their reimbursement formulas.

Liquidity Ratios

As the name implies, liquidity ratios measure the extent to which an organization has an ability to convert its noncash assets into cash (i.e., "liquidate" assets). Liquidity ratios generally are computed by comparing some portion of an organization's current assets with its current liabilities. By definition, current assets are those assets which will be, or have a reasonable expectation to be, converted into cash within a year. Current liabilities are those obligations which must be discharged within a year. Consequently, the most commonly used liquidity ratio is the current ratio.

$$\text{Current ratio} = \frac{\text{Current assets}}{\text{Current liabilities}}$$

A variety of other liquidity ratios that measure some portion of the current ratio also can be computed. The most frequently used is the quick (or acid-test) ratio.

$$\frac{\text{Quick}}{\text{ratio}} = \frac{\text{Cash} + \frac{\text{Marketable}}{\text{securities}} + \frac{\text{Net accounts}}{\text{receivable}}}{\text{Current liabilities}}$$

The purpose of the quick ratio is to eliminate those current assets which, for one reason or another, may *not* be readily or fully convertible into cash. Notably, the quick ratio excludes inventory and prepaid expenses.

Although included in both the current and quick ratios, accounts receivable frequently can be somewhat speculative. Both ratios attempt to compensate for this uncertainty by using a *net* accounts receivable figure (i.e., with estimates for doubtful accounts and other uncollectibles excluded). Nevertheless, more detail on accounts receivable frequently is considered necessary. A third liquidity ratio, average days receivable, allows us to make an assessment of the collectability of an organization's accounts receivable.

$$\text{Average days receivable} = \frac{\text{Net accounts receivable}}{\text{Sales revenue}/365}$$

The lower portion of this ratio gives us the average revenue earned per day. When this figure is divided into accounts receivable, we have an estimate of the average number of days worth of revenue which are included in the accounts receivable figure, and therefore we have a rough estimate of how many days are required to collect the average account receivable.

Asset Management Ratios

In reality, the average days receivable ratio lies at the intersection between liquidity and asset management, since it has aspects of each included in it. Asset management ratios allow us to determine the effectiveness of an organization's use of its assets, of which accounts receivable is one.

A second commonly used asset management ratio is asset turnover.

$$\text{Asset turnover} = \frac{\text{Operating revenues}}{\text{Total assets}}$$

This ratio allows us to determine how many dollars of revenue the organization earns for each dollar it has invested in assets. If the organization is fairly capital intensive, such as a hospital, a third ratio may shed more light on the quality of its asset management; this is the fixed-asset turnover ratio.

$$\text{Fixed-asset turnover} = \frac{\text{Operating revenue}}{\text{Net fixed assets}}$$

In a rough sense, this ratio permits us to assess the relative productivity of new assets, compared to ones that are highly depreciated. One would expect that, as assets depreciated (and, hence, *net* fixed assets fell), the ability of those assets to earn revenue would fall, also. The magnitude of this fall can be compared in percentage terms by use of this ratio. The comparison might be made to the organization's past performance (when the assets were newer) or to other organizations with relatively new assets.

A final asset management ratio is one which is comparable to accounts receivable turnover: inventory turnover.

$$\text{Inventory turnover} \ = \ \frac{\text{Operating revenue}}{\text{Inventory}}$$

Clearly this ratio, which indicates the amount of revenue earned for every dollar invested in inventory, and is a surrogate for the number of days of revenue contained in inventory, has limited use in some health and human service organizations, since generally they have relatively little inventory, compared to other assets. Nevertheless, if used in a comparative way, it may help certain organizations to determine an area of potential weakness in asset management.

Long-Term Solvency Ratios

Long-term solvency ratios provide an indication of the way the organization has financed itself over the long term (i.e., for the period extending beyond one year). Generally, two issues are of concern here. First, the extent to which the organization has financed itself using debt, rather than internally generated funds (donations, surplus, and so on). Second, the ability of the organization to meet its debt obligations. With the first issue, the most commonly used ratio is the debt/equity ratio.

$$\text{Debt/Equity} \ = \ \frac{\text{Total liabilities}}{\text{Fund balance}}$$

The higher this ratio, the greater the organization's "leverage" (i.e., the extent to which it has utilized outside funds to supplement internal funds). Several other measures of leverage exist. One of the most common is assets to equity.

$$\text{Leverage} \ = \ \frac{\text{Assets}}{\text{Fund balance}}$$

Effectively, this ratio is the same as the debt/equity ratio plus one,[3] a distinction which will become more important in Chapter 3.

Because of the need to make both long and short-term assessments, analysts frequently distinguish between short- and long-

---

[3]This is true by virtue of the fundamental accounting identity: Assets = Liabilities + Equity. If A = L + E, then A/E = L/E + E/E, or A/E = L/E + 1.

term debt (i.e., between current and long-term liabilities). This gives rise to a modified—and more frequently used—version of the debt/equity ratio: the long-term debt/equity ratio.

$$\text{Long-term debt/Equity} = \frac{\text{Noncurrent liabilities}}{\text{Fund balance}}$$

Looked at over time, this ratio can reveal the extent to which an organization is increasingly relying on long-term debt to finance its fixed-asset acquisition, a phenomenon that characterized many hospitals' growth strategies during the 1970s and early 1980s.

One of the concerns managers and policy analysts have about debt is that of an organization's ability to meet both its interest and principal payments, or what is termed *debt service*, in a timely way. An organization's ability to service its debt generally is measured by a ratio called debt service coverage.

$$\frac{\text{Debt}}{\substack{\text{service} \\ \text{coverage}}} = \frac{\text{Surplus} + \text{Depreciation} + \substack{\text{Interest} \\ \text{payments}}}{\text{Principal} + \text{Interest payments}}$$

Since principal payment amounts frequently are not known to individuals outside an organization, a surrogate ratio is sometimes used, termed *times-interest-earned*.

$$\text{Times-interest-earned} = \frac{\text{Surplus} + \text{Interest payments}}{\text{Interest payments}}$$

Obviously, this is not a perfect measure, since it does not include the principal payments on the debt; but, as with other ratios, it provides an approximation, and generally is available from the financial statements. In this case, the ratio looks at the ability of internally generated cash to meet at least one set of fixed-cash payments.[4] Because most organizations have many more fixed-cash obligations than debt service, however, it is most important that this ratio—or that of debt service coverage—be analyzed in the context of other related ratios, most notably those relating to liquidity.

FINANCIAL STATEMENT ANALYSIS

Ratio analysis is an important aspect of financial statement analysis, because it allows us to look at the relationship among various

---

[4]The assumption underlying this ratio is that the cash flow resulting from depreciation will be approximately equal to the principal payments on the debt, a reasonable assumption if the organization has come close to matching the term of its debt (i.e., number of years) with the "life" of the assets being financed with that debt.

parts of a single statement, such as the balance sheet, or to look at the relationship between elements on two different statements, generally the income statement and the balance sheet. The current ratio—which examines the relationship between current assets and current liabilities—is an example of the former; the return on investment ratio—where we compare surplus (from the income statement) with fund balance (from the balance sheet)—is an example of the latter.

To fully analyze a set of financial statements, we need to consider two additional mechanisms: the industry norms and the statement of changes in financial position (SCFP). To put the discussion of these two mechanisms in proper perspective, the ratios described in the previous section have been calculated for the financial statements for a large suburban community hospital. The financial statements are contained in Tables 2-1 through 2-4, and the calculations in Table 2-5.

Industry Norms

To understand more fully the meaning of the calculations in Table 2-5, we need to think in terms of industry norms. A great deal of empirical work has been done over the past 10 years or so in an attempt to develop industry norms for the health care field—particularly for hospitals—and much has been written on the subject. Two of the more definitive studies have been done by Cleverley and Nilsen,[5] and by Choate and Tanaka,[6] who arrived at the industry norms shown in Table 2-6.

Several points should be made about these industry norms. First, the ratios presented here comprise only a few of many ratios which might be calculated and compared. Several of the articles listed at the end of the chapter describe other ratios, and the interested reader should consult them for a more complete treatment of the subject.

Second, the industry norms generally have been derived from published data, and, as indicated earlier in this chapter, managers comparing their own institutions with the norms should be certain that the elements contained in their ratios are the same as

---

[5]W. O. Cleverley and K. Nilsen, "Assessing Financial Position with 29 Key Ratios," *Hospital Financial Management*, January 1980. They analyzed 15 hospitals in New York City, looking at their statements four years before failure and again one year before failure.

[6]M. Choate and K. Tanaka, "Using Financial Ratio Analysis to Compare Hospitals' Performance," *Hospital Progress*, December 1979. They used a 1977 sample of 209 nonprofit hospitals, which were members of the Catholic Hospital Association. The hospitals were from 43 states, some heavily regulated and some not.

TABLE 2–1

THE ANNUAL REPORT OF SALEM HOSPITAL, 1976
Balance Sheet
September 30, 1976 and 1975

Assets	1976	1975
Current assets:		
Cash	$ 283,639	$ 303,116
Certificates of deposit	435,000	—
Receivables—Patient care, less allowance of $718,000 in 1976 and $443,000 in 1975 for uncollectible accounts	4,369,756	4,307,917
Other	484,355	408,722
	4,854,111	4,716,639
Inventories at cost (first-in, first-out)	354,560	319,910
Prepaid expenses	74,527	43,017
Total current assets	6,001,837	5,382,682
Investments	3,831,965	3,558,989
Building fund pledges receivable, pledged as collateral for first mortgage bonds, less allowance of $24,000 in 1976 and 1975 for uncollectible pledges	64,005	98,980
Hospital property and equipment at cost	20,318,734	19,828,490
Less accumulated depreciation	6,493,044	5,796,150
	13,825,690	14,032,340
Deferred charges:		
Third-party contractual settlements	382,372	542,000
Financing costs, net of amortization	52,983	66,856
Other	33,262	42,765
	468,617	651,621

Liabilities and Fund Balances	1976	1975
Current liabilities:		
Trade accounts payable	$ 1,069,092	$ 1,191,947
Accrued expenses	1,135,419	1,336,129
Current installments of long-term debt	309,344	165,900
Reserve for contractual settlements	1,871,215	1,917,273
Current financing advances from third-party payors	242,620	152,100
Deferred tuition income	38,107	49,292
Deferred revenue	387,500	—
Total current liabilities excluding interim financing	5,053,297	4,812,641
Interim financing—Demand note payable to a bank	—	3,944,440
Total current liabilities	5,053,297	8,757,081
Long-term debt:		
Series A, first mortgage bonds payable	2,175,000	2,340,000
7% mortgage loan payable	26,012	26,950
Interim financing note payable	3,811,096	—
	6,012,108	2,366,950
Less current installments	309,344	165,900
	5,702,764	2,201,050

Fund balances:		
Unrestricted funds	9,162,573	8,856,982
Restricted funds:		
Building	900,755	662,152
Special purpose	1,329,553	1,234,441
Endowment	2,043,172	2,012,906
Total restricted funds	4,273,480	3,909,499
Total fund balances	13,436,053	12,766,481
Total liabilities and fund balances	$24,192,114	$23,724,612

Total assets................................ $24,192,114 $23,724,612

Note: All references to "Notes to the Financial Statements" have been deleted.
Source: R. E. Herzlinger, "The Annual Report of the Salem Hospital, 1976," case no. 4-178-063, Case Services, Harvard Business School, Boston.

TABLE 2–2 _____

THE ANNUAL REPORT OF SALEM HOSPITAL, 1976
Statement of Revenues and Expenses
For the Years Ended September 30, 1976 and 1975

	1976	1975
Operating revenue:		
Patient revenue	$27,063,480	$26,339,493
Less:		
Contractual adjustments absorbed on third-party payor accounts (including credits of $144,000 in 1976 and charges of $246,000 in 1975 for prior year adjustments)	1,504,083	3,405,489
Charity, courtesy, and other discounts	211,460	200,061
Provision for doubtful accounts	1,358,524	796,948
	3,074,067	4,402,498
Net patient revenue	23,989,413	21,936,995
Other operating revenue	1,150,760	685,645
	25,140,173	22,622,640
Operating expenses:		
Salaries and wages	13,976,615	12,653,522
Professional fees	1,783,551	1,994,284
Supplies and other expenses	7,536,742	6,541,094
Depreciation	715,217	810,056
Pension costs	393,339	265,848
Write-off of deferred financing costs	—	122,823
Interest expense and financing costs	564,146	636,673
	24,969,610	23,024,300
Income (loss) from operations	170,563	(401,660)
Nonoperating revenues:		
Unrestricted gifts and bequests	58,394	223,274
Unrestricted investment income	128,772	196,844
Other nonoperating revenues	1,400	38,229
Total nonoperating revenues	188,566	458,347
Excess of revenues over expenses	$ 359,129	$ 56,687

Note: All references to "Notes to the Financial Statements" have been deleted.
Source: R. E. Herzlinger, "The Annual Report of the Salem Hospital, 1976," case no. 4-178-063, Case Services, Harvard Business School, Boston.

those included in the calculations shown. The lack of a uniform chart of accounts or uniform reporting for hospitals (as well as for other health care organizations) means there is a good possibility that some of the comparisons will not be valid ones.

Third, there may be regional variations from the norms. For a variety of reasons, such as regulatory requirements, fund accounting distinctions, regional payment patterns by third-party payors, and so on, a hospital in a particular region of the country may, by necessity, have a ratio which diverges from the so-called norm.

Finally, apart from regional variations, a "norm" is not necessarily the "right" level for a ratio. For one thing, as indicated in footnote 5, Cleverley and Nilsen looked at institutions which ultimately went bankrupt; thus, their figures cannot be considered norms. For another, health and human service organizations are now facing a significantly different environment from what they have faced for the past 15 years or so. Philanthropy as a source of financing has been diminishing rapidly, and health care institutions increasingly have been financing fixed assets with debt. Thus, what was a norm at the time the research shown in Table 2–6 was conducted may no longer be appropriate. In short, man-

TABLE 2–3

THE ANNUAL REPORT OF SALEM HOSPITAL, 1976
Statement of Changes in Financial Position
For the Years Ended September 30, 1976 and 1975

	1976	1975
Funds were provided by:		
Income (loss) from operations	$ 170,563	$ (401,660)
Add (deduct) charges not requiring or (credits) not providing funds:		
Depreciation	715,217	810,056
Amortization of deferred financing costs.............	13,873	13,873
Write-off of deferred financing costs................	—	122,823
Reductions of (additions to) deferred third-party contractual settlements	159,628	(349,000)
Funds provided by operations	1,059,281	196,092
Nonoperating revenues	188,566	458,347
Less transfers from special purpose funds to nonoperating revenues for free services and other expenses	(106,939)	(139,895)
Funds provided from operations and nonoperating revenues	1,140,908	514,544
Reclassification of interim financing note payable to long-term debt	3,677,752	—
Net gain on sales of securities in restricted funds.......	27,960	123,227
Restricted gifts and government grants................	195,838	187,477
Restricted investment income	225,760	150,493
Collections of building fund pledges, net..............	34,975	73,886
Decrease in investments (net)	—	318,859
Total funds provided	5,303,193	1,368,486
Funds were used for:		
Hospital construction and equipment purchases, net of retirements	472,152	1,084,643
Decrease in long-term debt.........................	176,038	165,926
Additions to deferred charges	—	69,428
Increase in investments, net........................	272,976	—
Fund-raising expense...............................	22,000	—
Other	37,088	20,743
Total funds used	980,254	1,340,740
Increase in working capital..........................	$4,322,939	$ 27,746

TABLE 2–3 *(continued)* _____

	1976	1975
Changes in working capital:		
Increase (decrease) in current assets—		
Cash	$ (19,477)	$ 65,967
Certificates of deposit.............................	435,000	—
Receivables	137,472	1,142,440
Inventories	34,650	(26,747)
Prepaid expenses.................................	31,510	(17,751)
	619,155	1,163,909
(Increase) decrease in current liabilities—		
Accounts payable.................................	122,855	1,155,834
Accrued expenses	200,710	(315,667)
Current portion of long-term debt..................	(143,444)	(15,050)
Reserve for contractual settlements.................	45,058	(1,917,273)
Current financing advances	(90,520)	(45,900)
Deferred tuition income...........................	11,185	(13,667)
Interim financing.................................	3,944,440	15,560
Deferred revenue.................................	(387,500)	—
	3,703,784	(1,136,163)
Increase in working capital..........................	$4,322,939	$ 27,746

Note: All references to "Notes to the Financial Statements" have been deleted.
Source: R. E. Herzlinger, "The Annual Report of the Salem Hospital, 1976," case no. 4-178-063, Case Services, Harvard Business School, Boston.

agers should view industry norms with a great deal of skepticism.[7]

Statement of Changes in Financial Position

Apart from the ratios, the SCFP (described in Chapter 1) can be a very powerful tool for understanding the kinds of financing decisions which management has made during an accounting period, as well as their ability to manage the organization's assets. The SCFP shown in Chapter 1 has been reproduced as Table 2–7. What it shows is that, despite Spy Pond Hospital having earned a $500,000 surplus, it put much of that surplus into accounts receivable, although it did have a more than corresponding increase in accounts payable. This, coupled with its purchase of $500,000 of fixed assets, and the payment of the mortgage principal were the most significant reasons why a strain was placed on the cash account. In a similar fashion, the SCFP can be used to determine the extent to which an organization is financing itself appropriately (i.e., using short-term debt to finance its seasonal and

_____

[7]See S. A. Finkler, "Ratio Analysis: Use with Caution," *Health Care Management Review,* Spring 1982, for additional discussion of some of these issues.

TABLE 2-4

THE ANNUAL REPORT OF SALEM HOSPITAL, 1976
Statement of Changes in Funds Balances
For the Two Years Ended September 30, 1976

	Unrestricted Funds	Restricted funds			
		Building	Special purpose	Endowment	Combined
Balance September 30, 1974:	$8,357,062	$ 892,728	$1,238,368	$1,911,923	$4,043,019
Excess of revenues over expenses	56,687				
Investment income added to principal		23,097	76,856	50,540	150,493
Net gain on sales of securities		28,426		94,801	123,227
Restricted gifts and government grants		123,129	47,848		170,977
Additions to hospital property and equipment purchased with restricted funds	616,285	(590,841)	(25,444)	—	(616,285)
Additions to building fund pledges receivable		16,500			16,500
Transfers from special purpose funds to nonoperating revenues for free services and other expenses			(139,895)		(139,895)
Transfers from unrestricted funds for payments to the bond sinking fund	(325,000)	325,000			325,000
Transfer from building fund for payments to bondholders	150,000	(150,000)			(150,000)
Restricted endowment fund income transferred to special purpose funds			50,540	(50,540)	
Other transactions	1,948	(5,887)	(13,832)	6,182	(13,537)
Balance September 30, 1975:	8,856,982	662,152	1,234,441	2,012,906	3,909,499
Excess of revenues over expenses	359,129				
Investment income added to principal		31,404	92,826	101,530	225,760
Net gain on sales of securities				27,960	27,960
Restricted gifts and government grants		98,067	48,208		146,275
Additions to hospital property and equipment purchased with restricted funds	83,162	(57,598)	(25,564)		(83,162)
Additions to building fund pledges receivable		51,230			51,230
Transfers from special purpose funds to nonoperating revenues for free services and other expenses			(51,273)	(55,666)	(106,939)
Transfers from unrestricted funds for payments to the bond sinking fund	(300,000)	300,000			300,000
Transfer from building fund for payments to bondholders	165,000	(165,000)			(165,000)
Restricted endowment fund income transferred to special purpose funds			45,864	(45,864)	
Fund raising expenses		(19,500)	(2,500)		(22,000)
Other transactions	(1,700)		(12,449)	2,306	(10,143)
Balance September 30, 1976:	$9,162,573	$ 900,755	$1,329,553	$2,043,172	$4,273,480

Source: R. E. Herzlinger, "The Annual Report of the Salem Hospital, 1976," case no. 4-178-063, Case Services, Harvard Business School, Boston.

TABLE 2-5
Ratios for Salem Hospital

	1976	1975
Profitability:*		
Profit margin	$\frac{359,129}{25,140,173} = .014$	$\frac{56,687}{22,622,640} = .003$
Return on assets	$\frac{359,129}{24,192,114} = .015$	$\frac{56,687}{23,724,612} = .002$
Return on investment	$\frac{359,129}{13,436,053} = .027$	$\frac{56,687}{12,766,481} = .004$
Liquidity:		
Current ratio	$\frac{6,001,837}{5,053,297} = 1.19$	$\frac{5,382,682}{8,757,081} = .61$
Quick ratio	$\frac{5,088,395}{5,053,297} = 1.01$	$\frac{4,611,033}{8,757,081} = .53$
Average days receivable	$\frac{4,369,756}{23,989,413/365} = 66.5$	$\frac{4,307,917}{21,936,995/365} = 71.7$
Asset management:		
Asset turnover	$\frac{25,140,173}{24,192,114} = 1.04$	$\frac{22,622,640}{23,724,612} = .95$
Fixed-asset turnover	$\frac{25,140,173}{18,190,277} = 1.38$	$\frac{22,622,640}{18,341,930} = 1.23$
Inventory turnover	$\frac{25,140,173}{354,560} = 70.9$	$\frac{22,622,640}{319,910} = 70.7$

Long-term solvency:

Debt/equity	$\dfrac{10,756,061}{13,436,053} = .80$	$\dfrac{10,958,131}{12,766,481} = .86$
Leverage	$\dfrac{24,192,114}{13,436,053} = 1.80$	$\dfrac{23,724,612}{12,766,481} = 1.86$
Long-term debt/equity	$\dfrac{5,702,764}{13,436,053} = .42$	$\dfrac{2,201,050}{12,766,481} = .17$
Debt service coverage†	$\dfrac{359,129 + 715,217 + 564,146}{176,038 + 564,146} = 2.21$	$\dfrac{56,687 + 810,056 + 636,673}{165,926 + 636,673} = 1.87$
Times-interest-earned	$\dfrac{359,129 + 564,146}{564,146} = 1.64$	$\dfrac{56,687 + 636,673}{636,673} = 1.09$

*Sometimes calculated for operating accounts only.
†Uses "Decrease in long-term debt" from Table 2–3 for principal payments.

TABLE 2–6 _____

Hospital Industry Norms

| | Cleverley and Nilsen | | |
| | 4 Years
before | 1 Year
before | Choate
and |
Ratio	failure	failure	Tanaka
Profitability:			
Profit margin	−.12	−.11	.037
Return on assets	−.13*	−.11*	.031
Return on investment	.08†	.32†	.06
Liquidity:			
Current ratio	.78	.75	1.81
Quick ratio	.58	.68	1.57
Average days receivable	54.21	42.29	60.70
Asset management:			
Asset turnover	1.74	2.11	.85
Fixed-asset turnover	2.33	3.51	1.32
Inventory turnover	60.85	56.69	59.80
Long-term solvency:			
Debt/equity	NC‡	NC	NC
Leverage	2.38	9.09	2.04
Long-term debt equity	NC	NC	NC
Debt service coverage	−3.82	−4.89	NC
Times-interest-earned	−8.51	−31.36	NC

*(Operating income + Interest) ÷ Total assets.
†Positive, in many instances, since deficit was divided by a negative fund balance.
‡NC = not calculated.

TABLE 2–7 _____

SPY POND HOSPITAL
Statement of Changes in Financial Position—Cash Basis
For the Year 19B
($000)

Source of cash:
  From operations:
    Excess of revenue over expenses . . . . $ 500
      Add (deduct) adjustments to convert to cash basis:
        Depreciation expense. 300
        Accounts receivable increase . . . . (500)
        Prepaid expenses decrease 100
        Accounts payable increase 900
        Net cash generated from operations $1,300

Uses of cash:
  Payment on short-term loan. 100
  Payment on current portion of mortgage 800
  Acquisition of land, buildings, and equipment 500
    Total cash used during period 1,400
Net increase (decrease) in cash during period. . . . . $ (100)

other short-term needs, and long-term debt and equity to finance its fixed assets).

Summary of Financial Statement Analysis

We now are able to draw on the three tools available to us—ratio analysis, industry norms, and the SCFP—to analyze the financial statements shown in Tables 2–1 to 2–4. Turning first to profitability, we can see that Salem Hospital has a relatively low profit margin, at least compared to the Choate and Tanaka (C&T) study, but not so low (i.e., negative) as those hospitals approaching bankruptcy in New York in the Cleverly and Nilsen (C&N) study. Of significance is that the profit margin, return on assets, and return on investment ratios have been improving, although, even with the improvements, the latter two also are well below the C&T averages.

By viewing several ratios as a system, we can gain greater insight into the reasons for the improvement in return on investment:

$\dfrac{\text{Surplus}}{\text{Revenue}}$	$\times$	$\dfrac{\text{Revenue}}{\text{Assets}}$	$\times$	$\dfrac{\text{Surplus}}{\text{Assets}}$	$\times$	$\dfrac{\text{Assets}}{\text{Fund balance}}$	$=$	$\dfrac{\text{Surplus}}{\text{Fund balance}}$
Profit margin	$\times$	Asset turnover	$=$	Return on assets	$\times$	Leverage	$=$	Return on investment
1975								
.003	$\times$	.95	$=$	.002	$\times$	1.86	$=$	.004
1976								
.014	$\times$	1.04	$=$	.015	$\times$	1.80	$=$	.027

We can now see how improvements in both profit margin and asset turnover contributed to a higher return on assets; indeed, had there not been a slight reduction in leverage, the hospital's return on investment would have been increased by even more. Thus, in both the profitability and asset management areas, the hospital is doing a better job in 1976 than in 1975. The fixed-asset turnover and inventory ratios tend to confirm this; in fact, the hospital is above the C&T averages in all three asset-management categories, particularly inventory turnover.

It is in the area of liquidity where the hospital is perhaps the weakest, with both its current and quick ratios quite a bit below the C&T averages, although nowhere near the dangerously low levels of the hospitals in the C&N study. If, however, we note from the SCFP that the hospital reclassified an interim financing note payable (current liability) to long-term debt, we are given even greater cause for concern, since we can see that almost all of the improvement in the hospital's liquidity appears to have come from this reclassification. Here we would want to review the Notes to the Financial Statements to determine the nature of the reclassification and how much liquidity the hospital has in fact gained from it. If the note were due in a period very close to a year, we should then recalculate the liquidity ratios using it as a current liability, which would bring the 1976 figures very close to those for 1975 and below those in the C&N study.

In terms of long-term solvency, we note that the hospital has a lower leverage figure than the hospitals in the C&T study, and thus is not as "exposed" financially as those hospitals. Given its precarious liquidity, this seems fortunate. We can see from the SCFP that approximately $1.5 million in construction has been put in place during the last two years, which implies some potential for an increase in revenues in the next few years. We can also see that the cash inflows from depreciation reimbursement are substantially greater than the cash outflows for principal payments (decrease in long-term debt), implying that the liquidity "crisis" may not be as severe as it first appears; but we would want to know more about the hospital's plans for additional construction and the means for its financing before we could be totally certain about this.

Finally, it is encouraging to note that the financing of the hospital's construction appears to be appropriate. While the specific financing terms are not available, it certainly appears that construction is being financed with long-term debt and equity, rather than short-term debt, and that both measures of debt service coverage are improving.

In summary, we are left with some uncertainty about the hospital's ability to meet its current liabilities; but, given the improvement in debt service coverage, we can be fairly confident that it will be able to meet those obligations (the interim financing issue being the key unanswered question). Lastly, however, although the hospital is improving both its margin and asset turnover, we must raise some serious doubts about its longer-term viability. Although these ratios are positive, they allowed for a return on assets of only 1.5 percent in 1976, hardly enough to compensate for the eroding effects of inflation.

SUMMARY OF THE CHAPTER

This chapter has provided an overview of some important aspects of financial analysis. Essentially, financial analysis consists of assessing the quality of an organization's financial statements— and thus its overall financial performance—through the use of ratio analysis, industry norms, and the statement of changes in financial position. This latter financial statement, although not always used as fully as it might be, provides some valuable insight into the way in which an organization has financed its activities over the course of the most recent accounting period, generally a year. Thus, it assists us in making the transition from financial *analysis* to financial *management,* or the managerial activities necessary to assure that an organization has the funds available to it which it needs to sustain its activities—in both the short and long term. This is the topic of the next chapter.

MANAGERIAL CHECKLIST

1. What is our return on assets? If it is not equal to the inflation rate, what provisions are we making to replace assets as they wear out?
2. What are our debt service obligations? How will they change over the next year? What will be the resulting cash flow implications?
3. Has our liquidity been changing over the past five years? If we are more liquid now than five years ago, should we be putting more cash into interest-bearing accounts? If we are less liquid, do we need to consider some changes in our financing strategies to increase our liquidity?
4. How close are our ratios to the norms shown in Table 2–6? What accounts for any differences? Are they significant? What "trouble signs," if any, exist.
5. If an analysis similar to that performed in the chapter for Salem Hospital were performed for our organization, what would be the conclusions? Do those conclusions have any significance for our organization's financial strategy?

Bibliography

Caruana, R., and E. T. McHugh. "Comparing Ratios Shows Fiscal Trends." *Hospital Financial Management,* January 1980.

Choate, G. M. "Financial Ratio Analysis." *Hospital Progress,* January 1974.

Choate, M., and K. Tanaka. "Using Financial Ratio Analysis to Compare Hospitals' Performance." *Hospital Progress,* December 1979.

Cleverley, W. O., and K. Nilsen. "Assessing Financial Position with 29 Key Ratios." *Hospital Financial Management,* January 1980.

Finkler, S. A. "Ratio Analysis: Use with Caution." *Health Care Management Review,* Spring 1982.

Fitschen, F. "Look to Ratios to Measure Financial Health." *Hospital Financial Management,* November 1976.

Hay, L. E. *Accounting for Governmental and Nonprofit Entities.* Homewood, Ill.: Richard D. Irwin, 1980.

Healthcare Financial Management Association. *Hospital Industry Analysis Report.* Oak Brook, Ill.: Health Care Financial Management Association, 1983.

_____. *User's Guide to the Hospital Industry Analysis Report.* Oak Brook, Ill.: Health Care Financial Management Association, 1983.

Helfert, E. A. *Techniques of Financial Analysis.* Homewood, Ill.: Richard D. Irwin, 1972.

Perry, H. C. "Sizing up Your Hospital's Financial Performance." *Trustee,* June 1981.

3

Financial Management

Chapter 2 looked at how one might analyze a set of financial statements to learn about the decisions taken by management over a time period, ranging from one year to the life of the organization; but it touched only briefly on the substance behind those decisions. The purpose of this chapter is to look at some of the underlying rationale for financial decision making, describing some important concepts and techniques used in a for-profit context, and discussing their transferability to health and human service organizations.

The chapter begins with a discussion of the quantitative techniques used for capital investment decision making. While a variety of nonquantitative considerations must take place in any capital investment decision,[1] an important aspect of the decision-making process is the calculation of the financial feasibility of a proposed investment project, generally the acquisitoin of some kind of fixed asset. Next, the chapter looks both at the effect of cost-based reimbursement on capital investment decisions. The chapter then turns to the topic of financing considerations for capital investments and discusses the concept of leverage, a term de-

---

[1]Nonquantitative factors can range from the need to meet certain regulatory standards to the influence of internal political factors. See, for example Robert N. Anthony and G. A. Welsch, *Fundamentals of Management Accounting* (Homewood, Ill.: Richard D. Irwin, 1980); Joseph L. Bower, *Managing the Resource Allocation Process* (Boston: Division of Research, Graduate School of Business Administration, Harvard University, 1970).

fined in Chapter 2 but given more managerial substance here. Following this, the role of surplus in a nonprofit organization is discussed, particularly in terms of its relationship to leverage. Finally, the chapter attempts to answer the question, "How much surplus is enough?"

CAPITAL INVESTMENT DECISION MAKING

An important aspect of financial management is the decision to purchase fixed assets. Decisions of this sort can have a major impact on an organization's financial statements in both the short and long run. In the short run they may affect cash management, either via a reduction in the cash account to purchase the fixed asset or in terms of an increase in liabilities to finance the asset acquisition. In this latter instance, assuming the debt is of a long-term nature, the short-term impact on the institution is mitigated somewhat, resulting only in annual debt service outlays (principal and interest payments) rather than in the large outlay of cash, which otherwise would be necessary.

The longer-run effect on the organization comes about as a result of the impact which the new fixed asset has on annual revenues and expenses. Although, as discussed in Chapter 1, the depreciation expense associated with the new fixed asset is not a cash outlay, it nevertheless is of some significance for health care entities whose reimbursement is all or partially cost based, since in most states depreciation is a reimbursable expense. Apart from depreciation, however, there are instances in which the acquisition of a fixed asset, generally a piece of equipment or machinery, but occasionally a new facility of some sort, will result in some fairly significant cash flow effects. The cash flow effects can come about either as a result of decreased operating costs or of increased revenues. In almost all instances, these effects will be felt for several years (i.e., over the life of the new asset).

While it is clear that a variety of considerations go into the decision to purchase a new fixed asset, particularly in hospitals where strategic concerns, physician needs, certificate of need requirements, and the like play a major role in such decisions, one important aspect of many capital investment decisions is that of financial feasibility. In essence, financial feasibility consists of comparing the cash inflows (cost savings or additional revenue, or both) with the purchase price of the asset. The three most common techniques utilized to do this are payback period, net present value, and rate of return.

Payback Period

The easiest technique, and one that is used by a variety of organizations, both for-profit and nonprofit, is the payback period. Effectively, this technique consists of simply dividing the investment amount (generally the cost of the new asset minus any revenue being received for disposal of an existing asset that it replaces) by the estimated annual cash inflows resulting from the investment. The result is the number of years of cash inflows necessary to recover the investment amount.

> *Example:* Nido Escondido Hospital is considering the purchase of a $10,000 piece of equipment for its laboratory. The new equipment will replace an existing piece of equipment, which the vendor has offered to repurchase for $2,000. It will also result in labor savings of approximately $4,000 a year.
>
> *Analysis:* The net investment amount is $8,000 ($10,000 − $2,000 trade-in value of the old equipment). With a labor savings of $4,000 a year, the payback period, thus, is two years ($8,000/$4,000).

As the reader can see, the principal advantage of the payback period approach is its simplicity, and it frequently is used to gain a rough approximation of the feasibility of a particular investment opportunity.

Net Present Value

The main disadvantage of the payback method is that it ignores the time value of money. If the payback period is relatively short, such as it was in the above example, this is not a particularly serious limitation; but, with longer payback periods, the value of the technique for assessing the feasibility of different capital investment projects, and particularly the comparison of alternative projects, is quite limited.

The net present value technique avoids these limitations by building into the analysis considerations of the time value of money. It does so, as its name implies, by calculating the present value (i.e., the value today) of future cash inflows. This technique rests on the concept that a dollar received one year from now is worth something less than a dollar received today; that a dollar received two years from now is worth even less today; and so on. Presumably, for example, if I offered to give you a dollar one year from now, you would not, unless you were a good friend or somewhat altruistic, give me a dollar today, since you could invest your dollar today and earn something on it over the course of the next year and have more than a dollar a year from now. If, for example, you could earn 10 percent on your money, you could invest your dollar and have $1.10 in a year. Alternatively, if you had $0.91 and invested it at 10 percent you would have $1.00 a year from today. Thus, if I offered to give you $1.00 a year from today and you were a shrewd investor, looking for a 10 percent return, you would most likely give me only $0.91 today. With a 10 percent interest rate, the $0.91 is the *present value* of a dollar received one year hence.

In the same fashion, we could make a calculation for a dollar received two years from today. Here, however, we must build in the concept of compounding interest.

> *Example:* A business associate says that she needs to borrow some money from you and will be able to repay $100 to you two years from today. You are currently investing your money at 10 percent. How much will you lend her?
>
> *Analysis:* As a shrewd investor you would lend her $82.65, since at an interest rate of 10 percent compounded you could earn the following on your $82.65:
>
> | | | |
> |---|---|---|
> | *Year 1* | $82.65 × .10 | = $8.26 |
> | *Year 2* | ($82.65 + $8.26) × .10 | = $9.09 |
>
> Total at end of Year 2 = $82.65 + $8.26 + $9.09 = $100.00

The above example consists of a promise to pay a given amount two years hence, with no intermediate payments. Another possibility to consider is the situation in which we have even cash flows being received every year for several years in a row.

> *Example:* Suppose your colleague offers to pay you $100 one year from now and a second $100 two years from now. How much would you lend her now, assuming you have the same interest-earning possibility on your money?
>
> *Analysis:* We must now combine the two elements of the analysis described above. Specifically, for the $100.00 received two years from now we would lend her $82.65, and for the $100.00 received one year from now we would lend her $90.90. Thus, the total amount we would lend her would be $173.55.

Our ability to make these determinations is simplified by means of present value tables. Two such tables, Exhibits 3A and 3B, are included at the end of this chapter. The first is entitled "Present Value of $1." This is what we would use to determine present value of a single payment to be received at some specified time in the future. Exhibit 3B, "Present Value of $1 Received Annually for N Years," would be used when we have even cash flows over some given time period. Looking at these tables, we can see that the present value in Exhibit 3B of 1.736 (for a payment of $1 received each year for two years at 10 percent) is the same as the sum of the two amounts shown on Exhibit 3A (.909 for one year hence, and .826 for two years hence). Thus, Exhibit 3B simply sums the various elements in Exhibit 3A in order to facilitate calculations.

The capital investment decision process using the net present value technique takes an important step by incorporating the concept of the time value of money, recognizing that money received in the future does not have as much value as money received today.

As a result of the above considerations, a capital investment analysis using the technique of net present value involves five steps:

---

1. Determine the estimated annual cash flows from the investment. These may be either increased revenues or decreased costs to the organization, but they must result *exclusively* from the investment itself and not from any activities that would have taken place without the investment.

2. Determine the estimated economic life of the investment. This is not, it should be emphasized, the physical life of the new asset, but rather the time period over which the cash flows will be received.

3. Determine the *net* amount of the investment. This would be the actual purchase price of the asset, plus any installation costs, plus any disposal costs on the old asset, and less whatever salvage value will be received for the old asset.

4. Determine the required rate of return. As a general rule, this would be at least the organization's weighted cost of capital,[2] and generally would be increased to reflect whatever level of risk is associated with the investment. That is, the

---

[2]The weighted cost of capital is the percentage rate of interest that results from applying the portion of each financing source to its interest rate. For example, assume that an organization has a debt/equity ratio of 40 percent. It is paying 12 percent on its debt, and feels it should be earning 15 percent on its equity. Its weighted cost of capital is calculated as follows:

40% × 12% = 4.8%
60% × 15% = 9.0%
Weighted cost of capital = 4.8 + 9.0 = 13.8 percent.

If several sources of debt are in use, each at a different interest rate, each would be weighted separately.

riskier the investment, the higher rate of return we would need in order to justify it.

5. Compute the net present value according to the following formula:

$$\text{Net present value} = \left(\text{Cash flow} \times \begin{array}{c} \text{Present} \\ \text{value} \\ \text{factor} \end{array} \right) - \text{Investment}$$

or

$$NPV = (CF \times pvf) - I$$

The present value factor for even cash flows every year can be obtained from Exhibit 3B at chapter's end by finding the factor that lies at the intersection of the year row and percent column selected in steps 2 and 4 above. Present value factors for one-time cash flows can be found in Exhibit 3A.

Example: Nido Escondido Hospital has an opportunity to purchase a piece of equipment that will result in labor savings of approximately $2,000 a year. The equipment has a purchase price of $10,000 and is expected to produce the labor savings for approximately 10 years. The hospital's board has decided that an acceptable project must produce a rate of return of at least 10 percent a year.

Analysis:

1. Annual cash flow = $2,000
2. Economic life = 10 years
3. Net investment amount = $10,000
4. Rate of return = 10 percent
5. NPV = (CF × pvf) − I
       = $2,000 × 6.145) − $10,000
       = $12,290 − $10,000
       = $2,290

The investment, therefore, is financially feasible.

Several important points should be made about an analysis of net present value. First, once we have determined our desired rate of return, a project which yields a net present value of 0 (zero) or greater should be acceptable. It is not important that the project produce a present value significantly greater than 0 since, if this were the case, the implication would be that we should raise our desired rate of return.

Second, although an analysis of this sort appears to have a great deal of precision, we should recognize that its significant elements are, for all intents and purposes, estimates or guesses, and may be quite imprecise. Specifically, projected cash flows beyond a period of two to three years cannot be considered particularly precise, nor can the economic life of an investment. Thus, we should be careful about attributing too much value to the precision that the formula seems to give us.

Third, inflation is a factor. It is quite likely that labor savings from an investment will be greater five years from now than they would be today, because of potential increases in wage rates. If, however, we are to adjust our cash flow factor for the effects of inflation, we also would need to adjust the required rate of return to reflect our need for a return somewhat greater than the rate of inflation. By excluding an inflation effect from both the cash flow calculations and the required rate of return, we neutralize the effect of inflation, however, and thus do not need to undertake the very complex calculations which otherwise might be necessary.

Fourth, as mentioned earlier in the chapter, nonquantitative considerations are essential. These considerations can include (1) quality of care arguments; (2) the need for a full range of services; (3) requirements by such organizations as the Joint Committee on the Accreditation of Hospitals (JCAH), the Occupational Health and Safety Administration (OSHA), and other similar organizations; and (4) political considerations.

In sum, when we perform our calculation of net present value, we should be satisfied if it is fairly close to 0 (zero). If it is much greater than 0, the project has a much higher financial feasibility; but if it is close to 0, or even slightly negative, we should recognize that it is in the ballpark and turn to the nonquantitative considerations to further evaluate the project. Also, if a project is *required* for nonquantitative reasons (e.g., JCAH), its net present value is irrelevant.

Rate of Return

The rate of return method is similar to that of net present value; however, instead of determining a required rate of interest for making the calculations, we set net present value equal to zero and calculate the effective rate of return for the investment. Although this method is somewhat more complicated than the net present value approach, it has the advantage of giving an exact rate of return, rather than simply concluding that a proposed project meets (or fails to meet) an organization's stipulated rate of return. This, in turn, makes it easier to rank proposed projects in terms of their financial feasibility, and, since an organization may not have sufficient capital investment funds to engage in all projects, it can determine its financial priorities somewhat more easily.

The rate of return approach begins with the net present value (NPV) formula:

$$NPV = (CF \times pvf) - I$$

but sets NPV equal to zero, so

$$CF \times pvf = I$$

or

$$pvf = \frac{I}{CF}$$

Once the present value factor has been determined, it can then be located on Exhibit 3B, using the number of years of economic life of the project, so the resulting interest rate, or rate of return, can be determined.

> *Example:* Nido Escondido Hospital wishes to determine the rate of return for the project described in the last example.
>
> *Analysis:*
>
> $$pvf = \frac{I}{CF} = \frac{\$10,000}{2,000} = 5.00$$

Looking at the table in Exhibit 3B in the row for 10 years (the economic life of the investment), we find that the present value factor for an interest rate of 15 percent is 5.019. Thus, our project's rate of return is very close to 15 percent.

Effect of Cost-Based Reimbursement

The presence of cost-based reimbursement in health care functions in much the same way as the tax system does for for-profit organizations.[3] That is, any cost savings which accrue to a hospital must be shared with cost-based third-party payors. As a result, the hospital does not receive the full effect of the savings. Similarly, just as depreciation serves as a "tax shield"[4] in for-profit organizations, it results in reimbursement from cost-based payors in health care organizations. Specifically, a portion of the depreciation on the investment, equivalent to the percentage of the hospital's cost-based payors, would be a cash inflow resulting from the reimbursable expense of depreciation.

---

[3] See H. W. Long and J. B. Silvers, "Hospital Reimbursement Is Federal Taxation of Tax-Exempt Providers," *Health Care Management Review,* Winter 1975.

[4] See Anthony and Welsch, *Fundamentals of Management Accounting,* chap. 9, for a description of the tax shield effect of depreciation.

Example: Of Nido Escondido's patients, 52 percent have their bills paid by cost-based payors. How does this change the cash flow described in the previous example?

Analysis: Of the $2,000 in anticipated cost savings, $1,040 ($2,000 × .52) will be lost due to the reduced payments from cost-based payors. Additionally, however, with annual depreciation of $1,000 (10,000/10), $520 ($1,000 × .52) of reimbursement will be received from the depreciation expense associated with cost-based payors. The net effect of the analysis is:

1. Annual cash flow = $2,000 − (.52 × 2,000)   = $ 960
           + $1,000 × .52   =   520
                                                       $1,480

       or

$$2,000 − [(2,000 − 1,000) \times .52] = \$1,480$$

2. Economic life = 10 years
3. Net investment amount = $10,000
4. Rate of return = 10 percent
5. NPV = (CF × pvf) − I
      = ($1,480 × 6.145) − $10,000
      = $9,095 − $10,000
      = ($905)

The investment is no longer financially feasible.

The financial analysis of a capital investment decision when no external financing is involved (i.e., assuming that the entire investment is made using equity funds) is generally carried out by means of one of the three methods described previously. As indicated, this quantitative analysis is only one aspect of the capital investment decision process, a process which frequently involves a variety of organizational, strategic, and other nonquantitative considerations.

The introduction of external financing considerations, such as the use of debt to purchase the asset, or the possibility of leasing the asset, raises some further complications. These complications can be addressed via a two-step analysis. First, the investment itself should be evaluated according to the net present value method to determine its feasibility. Next, the financing options should be explored. When leasing is used, the lease payment serves to reduce the organization's surplus by the amount of the payment. Leasing also removes reimbursement for depreciation. When debt is involved, the interest payments become additional reimbursable items (depending on the percentage of cost-based payors); but they, as well as the principal payments, serve to reduce the net cash inflows.

Table 3–1 looks in more detail at the impact of three options for financing a $160,000 piece of equipment: (1) full equity financing, (2) full debt financing, and (3) leasing. It is important to note that the equity financing methods would first be used to determine if the investment is feasible; in this case, assuming a 10 percent required rate of return, it has a net present value of $38,500.

Once the investment decision has been made, the various financing options may be examined to determine which gives the highest present value. In the example in Table 3–1, the debt option—with a net present value of $59,000—is the highest and, other things equal, would be most desirable.

LEVERAGE

The introduction of debt financing considerations raises the issue of leverage. The reader will recall that the Ratio Analysis section of Chapter 2 defined leverage as:

$$\frac{\text{Assets}}{\text{Fund balance}}$$

With Salem Hospital in Chapter 2, we saw an example of an organization that had a comparatively low leverage ratio. One question which may have arisen in reviewing this analysis is, "Why doesn't Salem Hospital have more leverage?" Indeed, the value of leverage to an organization, along with its attendant risks, is a subject of great concern to managers of hospitals and other health and human service organizations. The purpose of this section is to describe leverage more fully, and to put it in a context for a discussion of the role of surplus in nonprofit organizations.

If an organization had no debt whatsoever, its assets and fund balance would be equal, and its leverage ratio, therefore, would be equal to one. As an organization begins to rely on debt to finance its assets, however, this ratio will begin to increase. Table 3–2 contains a simple example, beginning with a balance sheet in which assets and fund balance are equal, then moving to a situation in which total debt and the fund balance are equal. As can be seen, the ratio increases to a level of 2.0 under these circumstances.

The importance of leverage is that it allows an organization to finance more assets than would be possible if it relied only on its own fund balance. In a very real sense, the organization is using its equity as a "lever" to obtain funds from outsiders and, thus, expand its asset base. This, in turn, allows it to deliver more services or to produce more goods than otherwise would be possible.

Leverage does not come without some drawbacks, however.

TABLE 3-1

Alternative Financing Methods ($000)

Determination of cash flow	Investment (a)	Cost savings (b)	Depreciation* (c)	Interest or lease payments (d)	Surplus (e) = b − c − d	Cost-based reimbursement loss† (f) = .52e	Principal payments (g)	Net cash flow (h = b − d − f − g)
Equity financing:								
Year 0	160.0							−160.0
Years 1–10		50.0	16.0	—	34.0	17.7	—	+ 32.3
Debt financing‡:								
Year 0	0§							—
Year 1		50.0	16.0	12.8	21.2	11.0	40.0	− 13.8
Year 2		50.0	16.0	9.6	24.4	12.7	40.0	− 12.3
Year 3		50.0	16.0	6.4	27.6	14.4	40.0	− 10.8
Year 4		50.0	16.0	3.2	30.8	16.0	40.0	− 9.2
Years 5–10		50.0	16.0	—	34.0	17.7	—	+ 32.3
Lease financing:								
Year 0	0§							—
Years 1–10		50.0		40.0	10.0	5.2	—	+ 4.8

Computation of present value:

General formula: $\text{NPV} = (\text{CF} \times \text{pvf}) - I$

Equity financing: $\text{NPV}^{||} = (32.3 \times 6.145) - 160 = 198.5 - 160 = 38.5$

Debt financing:$^{||}$

Year 1	− 13.8 × .909 =	−12.5
Year 2	− 12.3 × .826 =	−10.2
Year 3	− 10.8 × .751 =	− 8.1
Year 4	− 9.2 × .683 =	− 6.3
Years 5–10	+ 32.3 × 2.975 =	+96.1
Total		59.0

NPV = 59.0 − 0 = 59.0

Lease financing:$^{||}$ NPV = (4.8 × 6.145) − 0 = 29.5 − 0 = 29.5

*Assumes straight line.

†Assumes 52 percent of patients are cost based.

‡Assumes a note for the full $160,000 with principal payable annually in four equal installments. Interest rate is 8 percent.

§Under debt and lease financing, there is no "investment" as such. The investment in the case of debt is made in the four equal principal payments indicated, each of which is a cash outflow in the year when it takes place. In the lease option, the lessor makes the investment and recovers it through the lease payments.

||Using a 10 percent required rate of return.

TABLE 3–2

Leverage

Situation 1:	No debt		
	assets	*Liabilities*	
	1,000	0	Leverage = 1,000/1,000 = 1.0
		Fund balance	
		1,000	
Situation 2:	Debt of $250		
	assets	*Liabilities*	
	1,000	250	Leverage = 1,000/750 = 1.3
		Fund balance	
		750	
Situation 3:	Debt of $500		
	assets	*Liabilities*	
	1,000	500	Leverage = 1,000/500 = 2.0
		Fund balance	
		500	

Funds borrowed must be repaid, and generally there is an interest charge. Organizations that rely heavily on borrowed funds spend considerable effort predicting their payment requirements for principal and interest (i.e., debt service) to assure themselves that they will have sufficient cash on hand to meet those requirements. Additionally, it should be noted that leverage in the Cleverley and Nilsen hospitals in Table 2–6 rose from 2.38, four years prior to failure, to 9.09 a year before failure. Thus, it seems quite safe to say that excessively high leverage contributed to the failure of these institutions.

In general, hospitals have tended over the past 10 to 15 years to increase their leverage significantly. Not only were many hospitals expanding their asset bases with new plant and equipment, but interest payments were fully reimbursable by third-party payors. Therefore, there was a significant incentive to rely heavily on debt. Moreover, lending sources by and large were favorably disposed to provide debt to hospitals, given the virtual certainty of repayment guaranteed by the existence of third-party payors, and, therefore, the minimal possibility of revenue shortfalls on the part of hospitals. On occasion, difficulties would arise from disallowances by third parties or a mismatch between a hospital's reimbursement for depreciation and its principal repayment requirements; but, in general, most hospitals increased their leverage with few problems.

Recently, however, hospitals have begun to encounter difficulties both in expanding their leverage and occasionally in meeting their debt service obligations. Difficulties in expanding leverage have resulted from the intense tightening of the capital markets, with the consequence of either a lack of availability of debt or extremely high interest rates. Difficulties in meeting debt service obligations also have arisen as third-party payors—particularly in states with prospective reimbursement systems—have become much more stringent in their willingness to reimburse interest payments.

In part, the problem has been exacerbated by inflation, since many hospitals are finding that the depreciation reimbursement they have been allowed to retain (rather than pay back to lenders in the form of principal payments) is insufficient to replace worn-out assets. In effect, these assets were financed with philanthropy; but if additional philanthropy is insufficient to provide for the higher cost of replacing those assets, the hospital has lost ground and must turn to the debt markets for the additional funds. The result is that simply to maintain a constant base of fixed assets is forcing many hospitals to incur higher and higher leverage. In the next section, an argument is presented that a reasonable solution to this problem is for hospitals and other health and human service organizations to earn larger surpluses from operations.

THE ROLE OF SURPLUS[5]

Economists frequently cite profit as a fundamental characteristic of capitalism. According to them it motivates, measures success, and rewards. Indeed, economists see an adequate profit as a legitimate cost of operating an organization. It is excess profits (i.e., those greater than a normal return) that provide an impetus for new organizations to enter a market. In the purely competitive model, when there are excess profits new organizations will enter a market and increase the supply of goods and services until the price falls to a level at which all organizations can earn a normal profit. At that point, the market is considered to be in "equilibrium."

The accountants' and managers' view of profit is somewhat different from the economists'. In the first place, as indicated in Chapter 1, profit (or surplus) is simply the numerical difference between revenues and expenses. Second, in addition to providing a return to the owners of the organization, one of profit's principal purposes is to finance capital acquisitions. In fact, as mentioned above, a basic financial management maxim is that an or-

---

[5]This section has been adapted from D. W. Young, "Nonprofits Need Surplus Too," *Harvard Business Review*, January–February, 1982.

ganization should finance its current assets with current liabilities and short-term debt, and finance its fixed assets with some combination of long-term debt and equity capital. In for-profit organizations, direct contributions by the owners or shareholders of the company, as well as retained earnings, are the sources of equity capital. For a nonprofit organization, equity sources consist of donated funds (endowments, grants, and the like) and retained surpluses.

The financing role of profits in for-profit organizations is directly comparable to the role surplus funds could play, if allowed, in nonprofit organizations. Since no one owns a nonprofit organization, managers have no need to repay profits in the form of dividends. But nonprofit organizations do engage in activities that require financing, and, in many instances, those activities involve acquiring fixed assets. Hospitals that add wings, equipment, or technology have large fixed-asset bases and require large amounts of such financing. But even small organizations, such as visiting nurse associations and community health centers, which must add desks, typewriters, and dictating machines as their programs develop and grow, have financing needs. Moreover, any organization that wishes to remain in a steady state must provide for the replacement of assets, since inflation effectively serves to erode its asset base.

While it is true that organizations could avoid the need for a surplus by relying exclusively on donated funds and long-term debt, this is not an adequate approach. In the first place, many organizations cannot obtain donated funds for this purpose. Nonprofit organizations, particularly those in the human services, frequently serve clientele or administer programs for which donated funds are not available. Their operating revenues come from public sector sources (such as Medicare and Medicaid) or from local funding agencies (such as the United Way). Second, donated funds may not be available until after managers have established and documented the need for a program and have implemented it.

Finally, in many nonprofit organizations the funds that long-term debt might provide have been diminishing as managers have increased their debt to the maximum levels allowed. In fact, as indicated previously, many *for*-profit organizations are finding it difficult to obtain long-term debt in the inflationary, credit-tight economy of the 1980s. The patterns that cause these financing difficulties will most likely persist for some time.

Managers who rely on long-term debt may also be imprudent, however, because of the financing needs that growth creates. Even if an organization—nonprofit or otherwise—engages in no net expansion of its fixed assets, it will, if it is growing, require increasing amounts of working capital. Specifically, because of the time-lag inherent in collecting accounts receivable, an organization that is both growing and extending credit to clients or third parties has an increasing amount of funds tied up in accounts receivable. If managers use debt to finance these receivables, the organization's indebtedness will continue to expand.

While a variety of financing or strategic options, other than debt, exist for the rapidly growing organization, the three that have the greatest impact are (1) slowing growth, (2) shortening the collection period for accounts receivable, and (3) generating equity via either a surplus or contributions. For managers to rely on debt—either long-term or short-term—instead of relying on one of these other options simply will not suffice, since such debt will itself not be repayable until management invokes one of these options.[6]

How Much Surplus Is Enough?

Because these two uses of surplus (i.e., for asset replacement and growth) are so different, managers need to take two different approaches to assess how much is sufficient for each. The first is related to the financing of fixed assets; the second concerns provision of adequate working capital.

Financing Fixed Assets. In many respects, judgments about the appropriate level of surplus in a nonprofit organization parallel those made in for-profit organizations. Specifically, for-profit organizations have a need for retaining some of their earnings, and establish selling prices to provide dividends plus the desired amount of retained earnings to meet capital needs. The company's price, then, becomes one element of the profit formula, a formula that includes both volume and cost. Further, the required profit level generally is related to the organization's desired return on investment (ROI).

As indicated in Chapter 2, ROI is closely related to another figure of concern to managers: return on assets (ROA). Indeed, if an organization does not obtain a sufficiently high return on assets, it will be unable to sustain itself in the future. As assets wear out or become technologically obsolete, management must replace them and, because of inflation, doing so will require more funds than depreciation provides.

---

[6]See David W. Young, "Charge Control Is Not the Answer to Containing Hospital Costs," *Hospital Financial Management,* May 1979, for an illustration of this dilemma and its implications.

The system of ratios, discussed in Chapter 2, shows the relationships among these elements:

$$\frac{\text{Profit}}{\text{Revenue}} \times \frac{\text{Revenue}}{\text{Assets}} = \frac{\text{Profit}}{\text{Assets}} \times \frac{\text{Assets}}{\text{Equity}} = \frac{\text{Profit}}{\text{Equity}}$$

$$\frac{\text{Profit}}{\text{margin}} \times \frac{\text{Asset}}{\text{turnover}} = \text{ROA} \times \text{Leverage} = \text{ROI}$$

The equations highlight some key managerial concerns. In particular, two important questions emerge from a careful analysis of the distinction between ROA and ROI: (1) "Which is the preferable measure?" and (2) "How much is enough?" The first question is not trivial. By using leverage, an organization can transform a low ROA into a high ROI. A high ROI, however, is no guarantee that assets can be replaced as they wear out. Indeed, if an organization is highly leveraged, and if managers wish to replace assets without a decline in ROI, they must maintain their organization's leverage at the initial level; but they often cannot either obtain more debt or refinance existing debt.

Some examples in Table 3–3 show how the ratios interact. In these examples, an organization begins with a margin of 12.5 percent, asset turnover of 1.2, and no debt. Both ROA and ROI, therefore, equal 15 percent. As the table indicates, increasing leverage to a level of 1.33 can, other things equal, raise ROI to 20

TABLE 3–3 _____

Effect of ROI on Asset Replacement

Assumption: An organization has a margin of 12.5 percent, asset turnover of 1.2, and no debt.

$$\frac{\text{Profit}}{\text{Revenue}} \times \frac{\text{Revenue}}{\text{Assets}} = \frac{\text{Profit}}{\text{Assets}} \times \frac{\text{Assets}}{\text{Equity}} = \frac{\text{Profit}}{\text{Equity}}$$

	Profit margin	Asset turnover	ROA	Leverage	ROI
Base case	.125	1.2	.15	1.00	.15
Changes to assumptions:					
1. Increase debt/equity ratio to 33.	.125	1.2	.15	1.33*	.20
2. Keep D/E ratio at .33 but restrict ROI to .15.	.094†	1.2	.11	1.33	.15
3. Keep D/E ratio of .33 but restrict ROI to .02‡	.013	1.2	.015	1.33	.02
4. Reduce D/E ratio to 1 but maintain .02 restriction on ROI.	.017	1.2	.02	1.00	.02

*Calculations are as follows: Assets = Liabilities + Equity. If liabilities = 0, all capital comes from equity, and assets/equity = 1/1 = 1. If D/E ratio = .33, liabilities = 1, equity = 3, assets = 4 (1 + 3), assets/equity = 4/3 = 1.33.
†Either margin or asset productivity or both could change. The assumption is that the margin only will change.
‡This is the figure used by the PRRB; see text footnote 7.

percent. Given this leverage ratio, however, a restriction in ROI to 15 percent (as happens in some regulatory environments) will force the organization to reduce either its profit margin or its asset turnover ratio, or both. In this example, the margin is reduced to 9.4 percent. Note, though, that the chain of events is such that the restriction on ROI reduces not only profit margin but ROA. In this case, ROA falls to a level of 11 percent.

Finally, the table indicates some of the potential implications of limiting the hospitals' ROI to 2 percent (a figure previously used by the Provider Reimbursement Review Board, a division of the Health Care Financing Administration of the Secretary of Health and Human Services[7]). With a 1.33 leverage ratio and asset turnover of 1.2, the margin is cut to 1.3 percent and ROA to 1.5 percent. Under these circumstances, the best ROA the organization could obtain is 2 percent (the same as ROI); but to reach this level requires repayment of all debt, which would bring a leverage figure back to 1.00. At this point, unfortunately, any improvement in managerial efficiency—by, say, cost cutting or improving asset turnover—would increase ROI to unacceptable levels.

One can draw three related conclusions from this analysis. First, any regulation of ROI may also restrict either margin or asset productivity. If an organization's allowed ROI is reduced, for example, and its leverage ratio remains unchanged, its ROA must fall. This means either its margin or its asset turnover must decline.

Second, if a given level of ROA is necessary to replace assets, a certain combination of margin and asset turnover is also required. Thus, by determining a necessary ROA level and a desired asset turnover level, managers can deduce the necessary margin percentage.

Third, information of this sort should be of great interest to regulatory agencies. Specifically, if regulators can agree with managers on (*a*) the required ROA, (*b*) the necessary profit margin *percentage*, and (*c*) the desired asset turnover ratio, they can then calculate allowable costs. In so doing, they can specify an organization's allowed *dollar* margin (i.e., its surplus).[8]

Working Capital. The need for working capital is another outcome of growth that organizations face, independent of fixed-asset expansion. This need arises from a combination of three fac-

---

[7]Provider Reimbursement Review Board, Hearing Decision 79-D95, case no. 78-385G, September 18, 1979.

[8]See Young, "Nonprofits Need Surplus Too," for further details and an example of how managers and regulators might use an ROA model to determine an organization's allowed surplus for purposes of financing asset replacement.

tors: profit margin, changes in current asset needs (especially accounts receivable), and changes in current liabilities (especially
accounts payable). Table 3–4 illustrates why organizations need
additional working capital. The table looks at the effect of growth
on cash that arises only out of the time-lag in collections of ac-

---

TABLE 3–4 _____

Cash Needs Associated with Growth

Assumptions: 1. Growth in revenue and expenses of 2 percent a month.
           2. Accounts receivable collection lag of two months.
           3. Accounts payable paid immediately.
           4. Inventory, prepaid expenses, and other current assets grow at
               same rate as revenue.
           5. Current liabilities (other than payables) grow at same rate as in-
               ventory, prepaid expenses, and other current assets.*

	|	|	Month			
	1	**2**	**3**	**4**	**5**	**6**
Income statement:						
Revenue	100	102	104	106	108	110
Expenses	100	102	104	106	108	110
Surplus	0	0	0	0	0	0
Cash flow:						
Cash in†	96	98	100	102	104	106
Cash out	100	102	104	106	108	110
Change in cash	(4)	(4)	(4)	(4)	(4)	(4)
Cumulative change	(4)	(8)	(12)	(16)	(20)	(24)

  *Assumptions 3 and 4 are very conservative. Unless inventory, etc., equals payables, still more
working capital will be required.
  †From two months ago.

---

counts receivable. Although additional working capital requirements will result from the growth rate in the remaining current
assets, which exceeds the growth rate in current liabilities, accounts receivable generally is the most significant factor in a
growing organization. Indeed, it is immaterial whether the
growth is real or inflationary; in either case, organizations need
working capital.

As with fixed assets, organizations must finance their working
capital needs from either debt or equity sources. As Table 3–4 indicates, if managers use debt they will not be able to repay it unless the growth rate slows or they take other measures (such as
increasing liabilities) to lessen their need for working capital.
Therefore, under these circumstances, managers generally consider debt to be an undesirable alternative, and, once again, a surplus is called for. In the simplified example in Table 3–4, a surplus
equivalent to the "Change in cash" line would be satisfactory.

SUMMARY OF THE CHAPTER

This chapter has built on the previous two to cover several important financial management topics, some quite technical. Although most managers will not engage in the day-to-day analyses of capital investment projects, they frequently become involved in both the project decisions as well as decisions about the approaches their organizations will take to finance those projects. For this reason, the chapter went into some depth not only on capital investment techniques but on financing considerations as well.

Financing considerations inevitably result in the need to pay some attention to the issue of leverage, and the chapter attempted to address both the advantages and some of the risks of leverage. Indeed, it can easily be argued that one of the most important aspects of the managerial process is the management of debt, or leverage. Further, however, managers must be aware of the need to earn a sufficiently large surplus to provide for both asset replacement and the working capital needs associated with growth, since to incur debt for these activities is to flirt with serious financial difficulties.

In the next several chapters we turn to managerial activities that move us from this somewhat externally oriented, or macro, view of the organization to a more internally oriented, or micro, one. This latter perspective frequently is called management accounting, and the discussion begins with the topic of full cost accounting.

MANAGERIAL CHECKLIST

1. What is the nature of the capital investments we have made over the past three to five years? Have any resulted in increased revenue or in cost reductions? If so, what form of financial analysis did we use? If we did not use the payback period, net present value, or rate of return, could our analysis have been improved by doing so?

2. What is our weighted cost of capital? Do we attribute an interest rate to our equity funds? If not, why not? What arguments might be presented for doing so?

3. What are our fixed-asset replacement needs over the next three to five years? What additional fixed assets will we need to acquire which are associated with our anticipated growth? What working capital needs will be associated with that growth?

4. What is our leverage? How does it compare to other similar organizations? What will our fixed-asset replacement and expansion

plans do to our leverage? What are their debt service implications?
5. Do any of our third parties allow us to earn a surplus? If not,
would any be amenable to the argument that we should be allowed to earn one? If so, how much should we be allowed to
earn, and how might we best present our case?

Bibliography

Anthony, R. N., and G. A. Welsch. *Fundamentals of Management Accounting.*
Homewood, Ill.: Richard D. Irwin, 1981.

Bower, J. L. *Managing the Resource Allocation Process.* Boston: Division of Research,
Graduate School of Business Administration, Harvard University, 1970.

Cleverley, W. O. "Profit and Growth: Three Questions." *Hospital Financial Management,* January 1978.

_____. "Capital Management: Accounting Return on Equity in the Non-Profit
Hospital." *Hospital Financial Management,* July 1981.

Colandis, J. "Net Present Value: A Better Way to Evaluate Capital Expenditures."
Hospital Financial Management, December 1977.

Collis, R. H. "Financial Forecasts: Overcoming the Obstacles." *Hospital Financial
Management,* March 1980.

Forsyth, G. C., and D. G. Thomas. "Models for Financially Healthy Hospitals."
Harvard Business Review, July–August 1971.

Furst, R., and R. L. Roenfeldt. "Estimating the Return on Equity Capital." *Hospital Financial Management,* June 1981.

Lightle, M. A. "Changes in the Sources of Capital." *Hospital Financial Management,* February 1981.

Long, H. W. "Valuation as a Criterion in Not-for-Profit Decision Making." *Health
Care Management Review,* Summer 1976.

Long, H. W., and J. B. Silvers. "Hospital Reimbursement Is Federal Taxation of
Tax-Exempt Providers." *Health Care Management Review,* Winter 1975.

Neumann, B. R., and L. A. Friedman. "Should Financial Statements Disclose
Cost of Replacing Hospital Assets." *Health Care Management Review,* Winter
1980.

Neumann, B. R., and J. D. Suver. "ROI: A Diagnostic Tool for a Healthy Bottom
Line." *Hospital Financial Management,* July 1980.

Silvers, J. B. "Capital Management: In the Beginning and Some Conclusions."
Health Care Financial Management, October 1982.

Silvers, J. B., and B. Spitz. "The Nursing Home: Capital Formation and Funding." *Hospital Financial Management,* April 1981.

Silvers, J. B., and C. K. Prahalad. *Financial Management of Health Institutions.*
Flushing, N.Y.: Spectrum Publications, 1974.

Tiscornia, J. F. "Coping with a Capital Shortage." *Trustee,* October 1980.

Vraciu, R. A. "Three Rules for Selecting Capital Financing Options." *Hospital Financial Management,* April 1980.

Weinstock, N. B., and T. P. Weil. "Hospital Capital Formation: Why More Difficulty Ahead?" *Hospital Financial Management,* August 1981.

Young, D. W. "Charge Control Is Not the Answer to Containing Hospital Costs."
Hospital Financial Management, May 1979.

_____. "Nonprofits Need Surplus Too." *Harvard Business Review,* January–Feb-
ruary 1982.

EXHIBIT 3A
Present Value of $1

Years Hence	1%	2%	4%	6%	8%	10%	12%	14%	15%	16%	18%	20%	22%	24%	25%	26%	28%	30%	35%	40%	45%	50%
1	0.990	0.980	0.962	0.943	0.926	0.909	0.893	0.877	0.870	0.862	0.847	0.833	0.820	0.806	0.800	0.794	0.781	0.769	0.741	0.714	0.690	0.667
2	0.980	0.961	0.925	0.890	0.857	0.826	0.797	0.769	0.756	0.743	0.718	0.694	0.672	0.650	0.640	0.630	0.610	0.592	0.549	0.510	0.476	0.444
3	0.971	0.942	0.889	0.840	0.794	0.751	0.712	0.675	0.658	0.641	0.609	0.579	0.551	0.524	0.512	0.500	0.477	0.455	0.406	0.364	0.328	0.296
4	0.961	0.924	0.855	0.792	0.735	0.683	0.636	0.592	0.572	0.552	0.516	0.482	0.451	0.423	0.410	0.397	0.373	0.350	0.301	0.260	0.226	0.198
5	0.951	0.906	0.822	0.747	0.681	0.621	0.567	0.519	0.497	0.476	0.437	0.402	0.370	0.341	0.328	0.315	0.291	0.269	0.223	0.186	0.156	0.132
6	0.942	0.888	0.790	0.705	0.630	0.564	0.507	0.456	0.432	0.410	0.370	0.335	0.303	0.275	0.262	0.250	0.227	0.207	0.165	0.133	0.108	0.088
7	0.933	0.871	0.760	0.665	0.583	0.513	0.452	0.400	0.376	0.354	0.314	0.279	0.249	0.222	0.210	0.198	0.178	0.159	0.122	0.095	0.074	0.059
8	0.923	0.853	0.731	0.627	0.540	0.467	0.404	0.351	0.327	0.305	0.266	0.233	0.204	0.179	0.168	0.157	0.139	0.123	0.091	0.068	0.051	0.039
9	0.914	0.837	0.703	0.592	0.500	0.424	0.361	0.308	0.284	0.263	0.225	0.194	0.167	0.144	0.134	0.125	0.108	0.094	0.067	0.048	0.035	0.026
10	0.905	0.820	0.676	0.558	0.463	0.386	0.322	0.270	0.247	0.227	0.191	0.162	0.137	0.116	0.107	0.099	0.085	0.073	0.050	0.035	0.024	0.017
11	0.896	0.804	0.650	0.527	0.429	0.350	0.287	0.237	0.215	0.195	0.162	0.135	0.112	0.094	0.086	0.079	0.066	0.056	0.037	0.025	0.017	0.012
12	0.887	0.788	0.625	0.497	0.397	0.319	0.257	0.208	0.187	0.168	0.137	0.112	0.092	0.076	0.069	0.062	0.052	0.043	0.027	0.018	0.012	0.008
13	0.879	0.773	0.601	0.469	0.368	0.290	0.229	0.182	0.163	0.145	0.116	0.093	0.075	0.061	0.055	0.050	0.040	0.033	0.020	0.013	0.008	0.005
14	0.870	0.758	0.577	0.442	0.340	0.263	0.205	0.160	0.141	0.125	0.099	0.078	0.062	0.049	0.044	0.039	0.032	0.025	0.015	0.009	0.006	0.003
15	0.861	0.743	0.555	0.417	0.315	0.239	0.183	0.140	0.123	0.108	0.084	0.065	0.051	0.040	0.035	0.031	0.025	0.020	0.011	0.006	0.004	0.002
16	0.853	0.728	0.534	0.394	0.292	0.218	0.163	0.123	0.107	0.093	0.071	0.054	0.042	0.032	0.028	0.025	0.019	0.015	0.008	0.005	0.003	0.002
17	0.844	0.714	0.513	0.371	0.270	0.198	0.146	0.108	0.093	0.080	0.060	0.045	0.034	0.026	0.023	0.020	0.015	0.012	0.006	0.003	0.002	0.001
18	0.836	0.700	0.494	0.350	0.250	0.180	0.130	0.095	0.081	0.069	0.051	0.038	0.028	0.021	0.018	0.016	0.012	0.009	0.005	0.002	0.001	0.001
19	0.828	0.686	0.475	0.331	0.232	0.164	0.116	0.083	0.070	0.060	0.043	0.031	0.023	0.017	0.014	0.012	0.009	0.007	0.003	0.002	0.001	
20	0.820	0.673	0.456	0.312	0.215	0.149	0.104	0.073	0.061	0.051	0.037	0.026	0.019	0.014	0.012	0.010	0.007	0.005	0.002	0.001	0.001	
21	0.811	0.660	0.439	0.294	0.199	0.135	0.093	0.064	0.053	0.044	0.031	0.022	0.015	0.011	0.009	0.008	0.006	0.004	0.002	0.001		
22	0.803	0.647	0.422	0.278	0.184	0.123	0.083	0.056	0.046	0.038	0.026	0.018	0.013	0.009	0.007	0.006	0.004	0.003	0.001	0.001		
23	0.795	0.634	0.406	0.262	0.170	0.112	0.074	0.049	0.040	0.033	0.022	0.015	0.010	0.007	0.006	0.005	0.003	0.002	0.001			
24	0.788	0.622	0.390	0.247	0.158	0.102	0.066	0.043	0.035	0.028	0.019	0.013	0.008	0.006	0.005	0.004	0.003	0.002	0.001			
25	0.780	0.610	0.375	0.233	0.146	0.092	0.059	0.038	0.030	0.024	0.016	0.010	0.007	0.005	0.004	0.003	0.002	0.001	0.001			
26	0.772	0.598	0.361	0.220	0.135	0.084	0.053	0.033	0.026	0.021	0.014	0.009	0.006	0.004	0.003	0.002	0.002	0.001				
27	0.764	0.586	0.347	0.207	0.125	0.076	0.047	0.029	0.023	0.018	0.011	0.007	0.005	0.003	0.002	0.002	0.001	0.001				
28	0.757	0.574	0.333	0.196	0.116	0.069	0.042	0.026	0.020	0.016	0.010	0.006	0.004	0.002	0.002	0.001	0.001	0.001				
29	0.749	0.563	0.321	0.185	0.107	0.063	0.037	0.022	0.017	0.014	0.008	0.005	0.003	0.002	0.002	0.001	0.001	0.001				
30	0.742	0.552	0.308	0.174	0.099	0.057	0.033	0.020	0.015	0.012	0.007	0.004	0.003	0.002	0.001	0.001	0.001					
40	0.672	0.453	0.208	0.097	0.046	0.022	0.011	0.005	0.004	0.003	0.001	0.001										
50	0.608	0.372	0.141	0.054	0.021	0.009	0.003	0.001	0.001	0.001												

EXHIBIT 3B
Present Value of $1 Received Annually for N Years

Years (N)	1%	2%	4%	6%	8%	10%	12%	14%	15%	16%	18%	20%	22%	24%	25%	26%	28%	30%	35%	40%	45%	50%
1	0.990	0.980	0.962	0.943	0.926	0.909	0.893	0.877	0.870	0.862	0.847	0.833	0.820	0.806	0.800	0.794	0.781	0.769	0.741	0.714	0.690	0.667
2	1.970	1.942	1.886	1.833	1.783	1.736	1.690	1.647	1.626	1.605	1.566	1.528	1.492	1.457	1.440	1.424	1.392	1.361	1.289	1.224	1.165	1.111
3	2.941	2.884	2.775	2.673	2.577	2.487	2.402	2.322	2.283	2.246	2.174	2.106	2.042	1.981	1.952	1.923	1.868	1.816	1.696	1.589	1.493	1.407
4	3.902	3.808	3.630	3.465	3.312	3.170	3.037	2.914	2.855	2.798	2.690	2.589	2.494	2.404	2.362	2.320	2.241	2.166	1.997	1.849	1.720	1.605
5	4.853	4.713	4.452	4.212	3.993	3.791	3.605	3.433	3.352	3.274	3.127	2.991	2.864	2.745	2.689	2.635	2.532	2.436	2.220	2.035	1.876	1.737
6	5.795	5.601	5.242	4.917	4.623	4.355	4.111	3.889	3.784	3.685	3.498	3.326	3.167	3.020	2.951	2.885	2.759	2.643	2.385	2.168	1.983	1.824
7	6.728	6.472	6.002	5.582	5.206	4.868	4.564	4.288	4.160	4.039	3.812	3.605	3.416	3.242	3.161	3.083	2.937	2.802	2.508	2.263	2.057	1.883
8	7.652	7.325	6.733	6.210	5.747	5.335	4.968	4.639	4.487	4.344	4.078	3.837	3.619	3.421	3.329	3.241	3.076	2.925	2.598	2.331	2.108	1.922
9	8.566	8.162	7.435	6.802	6.247	5.759	5.328	4.946	4.772	4.607	4.303	4.031	3.786	3.566	3.463	3.366	3.184	3.019	2.665	2.379	2.144	1.948
10	9.471	8.983	8.111	7.360	6.710	6.145	5.650	5.216	5.019	4.833	4.494	4.192	3.923	3.682	3.571	3.465	3.269	3.092	2.715	2.414	2.168	1.965
11	10.368	9.787	8.760	7.887	7.139	6.495	5.937	5.453	5.234	5.029	4.656	4.327	4.035	3.776	3.656	3.544	3.335	3.147	2.752	2.438	2.185	1.977
12	11.255	10.575	9.385	8.384	7.536	6.814	6.194	5.660	5.421	5.197	4.793	4.439	4.127	3.851	3.725	3.606	3.387	3.190	2.779	2.456	2.196	1.985
13	12.134	11.343	9.986	8.853	7.904	7.103	6.424	5.842	5.583	5.342	4.910	4.533	4.203	3.912	3.780	3.656	3.427	3.223	2.799	2.468	2.204	1.990
14	13.004	12.106	10.563	9.295	8.244	7.367	6.628	6.002	5.724	5.468	5.008	4.611	4.265	3.962	3.824	3.695	3.459	3.249	2.814	2.477	2.210	1.993
15	13.865	12.849	11.118	9.712	8.559	7.606	6.811	6.142	5.847	5.575	5.092	4.675	4.315	4.001	3.859	3.726	3.483	3.268	2.825	2.484	2.214	1.995
16	14.718	13.578	11.652	10.106	8.851	7.824	6.974	6.265	5.954	5.669	5.162	4.730	4.357	4.033	3.887	3.751	3.503	3.283	2.834	2.489	2.216	1.997
17	15.562	14.292	12.166	10.477	9.122	8.022	7.120	6.373	6.047	5.749	5.222	4.775	4.391	4.059	3.910	3.771	3.518	3.295	2.840	2.492	2.218	1.998
18	16.398	14.992	12.659	10.828	9.372	8.201	7.250	6.467	6.128	5.818	5.273	4.812	4.419	4.080	3.928	3.786	3.529	3.304	2.844	2.494	2.219	1.999
19	17.226	15.678	13.134	11.158	9.604	8.365	7.366	6.550	6.198	5.877	5.316	4.844	4.442	4.097	3.942	3.799	3.539	3.311	2.848	2.496	2.220	1.999
20	18.046	16.351	13.590	11.470	9.818	8.514	7.469	6.623	6.259	5.929	5.353	4.870	4.460	4.110	3.954	3.808	3.546	3.316	2.850	2.497	2.221	1.999
21	18.857	17.011	14.029	11.764	10.017	8.649	7.562	6.687	6.312	5.973	5.384	4.891	4.476	4.121	3.963	3.816	3.551	3.320	2.852	2.498	2.221	2.000
22	19.660	17.658	14.451	12.042	10.201	8.772	7.645	6.743	6.359	6.011	5.410	4.909	4.488	4.130	3.970	3.822	3.556	3.323	2.853	2.498	2.222	2.000
23	20.456	18.292	14.857	12.303	10.371	8.883	7.718	6.792	6.399	6.044	5.432	4.925	4.499	4.137	3.976	3.827	3.559	3.325	2.854	2.499	2.222	2.000
24	21.243	18.914	15.247	12.550	10.529	8.985	7.784	6.835	6.434	6.073	5.451	4.937	4.507	4.143	3.981	3.831	3.562	3.327	2.855	2.499	2.222	2.000
25	22.023	19.523	15.622	12.783	10.675	9.077	7.843	6.873	6.464	6.097	5.467	4.948	4.514	4.147	3.985	3.834	3.564	3.329	2.856	2.499	2.222	2.000
26	22.795	20.121	15.983	13.003	10.810	9.161	7.896	6.906	6.491	6.118	5.480	4.956	4.520	4.151	3.988	3.837	3.566	3.330	2.856	2.500	2.222	2.000
27	23.560	20.707	16.330	13.211	10.935	9.237	7.943	6.935	6.514	6.136	5.492	4.964	4.524	4.154	3.990	3.839	3.567	3.331	2.856	2.500	2.222	2.000
28	24.316	21.281	16.663	13.406	11.051	9.307	7.984	6.961	6.534	6.152	5.502	4.970	4.528	4.157	3.992	3.840	3.568	3.331	2.857	2.500	2.222	2.000
29	25.066	21.844	16.984	13.591	11.158	9.370	8.022	6.983	6.551	6.166	5.510	4.975	4.531	4.159	3.994	3.841	3.569	3.332	2.857	2.500	2.222	2.000
30	25.808	22.396	17.292	13.765	11.258	9.427	8.055	7.003	6.566	6.177	5.517	4.979	4.534	4.160	3.995	3.842	3.569	3.332	2.857	2.500	2.222	2.000
40	32.835	27.355	19.793	15.046	11.925	9.779	8.244	7.105	6.642	6.234	5.548	4.997	4.544	4.166	3.999	3.846	3.571	3.333	2.857	2.500	2.222	2.000
50	39.196	31.424	21.482	15.762	12.234	9.915	8.304	7.133	6.661	6.246	5.554	4.999	4.545	4.167	4.000	3.846	3.571	3.333	2.857	2.500	2.222	2.000

Full Cost Accounting

An answer to "What did it cost?" is perhaps one of the most slippery in the field of management control in both for-profit and not-for-profit organizations. Obviously, the question is rather easily answered when we are discussing the purchasing of inputs (supplies, labor, and so on) for the production or service-delivery process. Even calculating a total cost per unit produced—be it a widget or 50 minutes of psychotherapy—is relatively easy as long as the organization is producing goods or services that are completely homogeneous. Complications arise, however, when we introduce multiple goods and services into an organization, particularly when we utilize different kinds and amounts of resources to manufacture the goods or to deliver the services.

The purpose of this chapter is to address some of the key managerial decisions that are made in a cost accounting context, and to indicate the ways in which those decisions can influence the answer to "What did it cost?" As with the chapters on financial accounting, financial analysis, and financial management, this chapter is not meant to be an all-inclusive description of full cost accounting, and a bibliography is provided at the end of the chapter for individuals who wish to pursue cost accounting issues in greater depth.

OVERVIEW

An assessment of costs in health care institutions can be approached in a variety of ways, particularly if one wishes to incorporate comparisons between or among sites, as is the case for many third-party payors, policymakers, and managers. Questions of case mix, service intensity, standby capacity, teaching and research programs, referral patterns, use of ancillary services, and others add to the complexity of the cost analysis. It is in the context of this complexity that managers—either at an institutional or a regulatory level—make several important decisions that can affect the way in which information is gathered and presented for the purpose of calculating the total or "full" costs of a particular endeavor. Among these decisions are the definition of a cost objective, a selection of cost centers, a distinction between direct and indirect costs, a choice of bases for allocating overhead costs, the determination of a "stepdown" sequence, and a choice between process and job order accounting.

For these reasons and others, the literature on cost issues in health care is voluminous. Contributing to the difficulty in drawing sound conclusions from existing studies is the issue of methodology. On the one hand, there is a need to identify the individual variables which influence costs, so the effects of each may be analyzed. On the other, there are important interactions among these variables in such degree that an attempt to look at any single variable in isolation may fail to examine important interactive relationships. Additionally, to the extent that one wishes to make comparisons between or among different institutions or treatment modalities, comparability of data is essential. Comparability of data is difficult to achieve, however, when one considers the effects on costs of such variables as case mix, patient utilization patterns, mix of clinical services, managerial efficiency, and geographic differences in wages and supply prices. The difficulty is compounded when we introduce differences in cost allocation procedures, as well as the impact of teaching and research programs, on each of these variables.

To provide readers with a perspective from which to view the construction of a cost accounting system, this chapter first addresses what might be called the cost-influencing variables. Following this discussion, the chapter turns to some basic accounting decisions that must be made prior to beginning any analysis of costs. The discussion of these sets the stage for the final section, which looks at full cost accounting in the context of third-party reimbursement.

COST-INFLUENCING VARIABLES

Regardless of how costs are calculated, the fundamental issue that cost accounting is attempting to address is the *use of resources*.

Accordingly, an appropriate first set of questions to ask is, "What are these resources and how might they be defined and measured in health care settings?" Next, one must ask a somewhat more specific question: "What factors exist in health care settings which influence the use of these resources?"

At the most fundamental level, the resources used in any production effort—health care or otherwise—are the classic ones of the economist: land, labor, and capital. Of these, the most complex are labor and capital. Labor in a health care setting consists of both clinical (physician, physician extenders, nursing, and the like) and administrative personnel. Additionally, for any given department or cost center in a hospital (e.g., ambulatory care, OB/GYN, dietary), the administrative category can be subdivided into internal (i.e., within the department or cost center) and external. External administration can then be divided between support services (housekeeping, dietary, laundry, and so on) and more general administrative services (the central office staff). Although the specific categories might change, the same pattern would exist in other settings as well.

Capital can be looked at as either short-lived (used up in one year or less) or long-lived. The former category consists of supplies (syringes, pharmaceuticals, and the like); the latter of equipment and facilities. Additionally, capital can be classified as either patient-related or administratively related.

These resource distinctions, as well as the applicable cost measures, are summarized in Table 4–1. Although the terminology will change as we move from this overview to more specific cost accounting activities and decisions, this fundamental conceptual thrust remains.

While this categorization of costs provides a useful framework from which to view resource usage in health care settings, its managerial utility is limited by our incomplete understanding of the factors which influence the *use* of these resources in the service-delivery process. Further, of course, we also can expect to encounter difficulties in actually *measuring* resource usage. The first question, that of the variables which influence resource use, is an important one, since it allows us to bridge the gap between the broad overview in Table 4–1 and potential managerial action to influence and control costs. There are five variables in health care that effectively influence the use of resources:

Case mix.

Volume (number of cases of each type).

Resources used per case (medical practice).

Efficiency of resource delivery.

Cost per unit of resources.

TABLE 4–1

Resource Usage in Health Care

Basic category	Subclassifications 1	2	3	Cost measure
Land	The site	—	—	Rent/month
Labor	Clinical		MD MD extender Nursing Technicians Schedulers Administrators Etc.	Wage/encounter* ↓ Wage/procedure* Wage/month
	Administrative	Internal		
		External	Support services: Housekeeping Dietary Laundry Etc.	Wage/month
			General admin.: Administration Computer services Chaplaincy Etc.	Wage/month
Capital	Short-lived	Clinical	Patient-related supplies: Syringes Films Etc.	Price/unit
		Administrative	Admin. supplies: Stationery Etc.	Price/unit
	Long-lived	Clinical	Patient-related equipment/facilities	Depreciation per month
		Administrative	Admin.-related equipment/facilities	Depreciation per month

*Could also be wage/month, depending on the nature of compensation arrangement (salary versus fee for service) or the cost allocation procedures utilized, or both.

Table 4–2 gives examples of these variables in a hospital setting.[1]

TABLE 4–2 _____

Examples of Cost-influencing Variables

Cost-influencing variable	Example
Case type	Myocardial infarction; hypertension; appendicitis; etc.
Number of cases	10 myocardial infarctions; 50 hypertension; 30 appendicitis; etc.
Resources used per case	For myocardial infarctions: 10 days hospital care—CCU; 5 days hospital care—ward; 3 days Level III nursing care; 2 days Level II nursing care; lab; x-ray; etc.
Efficiency of resource delivery	Actual nursing hours per patient, minus standard nursing hours per patient at each level of nursing care; actual number of radiological films per procedure minus standard for procedure; actual time per lab test minus standard time for test; etc.
Cost per unit of inputs	Hourly nursing wage; hourly physician wage; price per unit of film; etc.

DECISIONS IN COST MEASUREMENT[2]

The above-discussed relationship between resources and re-source-influencing variables serves to put cost accounting in its proper perspective. Specifically, the principal objective of cost accounting is to measure as accurately as possible the consumption of resources associated with producing a particular good or service. In some instances, the measurement process is quite easy; in others, it is not. For example, an organization which produces a single good or service has little difficulty in calculating the cost of each unit. All costs associated with the organization, and hence the good or service, can be added together and divided by the number of units produced in a particular accounting cycle to arrive at a cost per unit.

> *Example:* Home Health Aides Incorporated delivers services to homebound patients. Their services include bathing, feeding as

_____

[1]See D. W. Young and R. B. Saltman, "Medical Practice, Case Mix, and Cost Containment: A New Role for the Attending Physician," *Journal of the American Medical Association*, February 12, 1982, for further discussion of this breakdown. Chapter 6 also discusses these five variables, but in a management control context.

[2]Some portions of this section appeared originally in D. W. Young, E. Socholitzky, and E. Locke, "Ambulatory Care Cost and the Medicare Cost Report: Managerial and Public Policy Implications," *Journal of Ambulatory Care Management*, February 1982.

sistance, and assistance with exercising. The cost for services is calculated on an hourly basis. Last year the organization had total
costs of $175,000 and delivered 33,000 hours of services.

Analysis: Since the unit of service is an hour, rather than a particular activity, we can say that the organization delivers a single service. Thus, its cost accounting process is quite simple: $175,000 ÷
33,000 hours = $5.30 per hour of service.

Organizations that produce a variety of goods or services, or
both, each requiring different amounts of land, labor, and capital,
will have a much more difficult time in determining the cost for
each unit sold. If, for example, the Home Health Aides agency
described above wished to distinguish among its costs for programmatic activities, such as bathing assistance, feeding assistance, and assistance with exercising, the cost accounting process
would become somewhat more complex. As described below,
these decisions and others are made in all cost accounting systems. Indeed, by design or default, the decisions discussed below
must be made to determine full cost, regardless of the complexity
of the goods or services involved.

1. The Cost Objective

The cost objective is the unit of good or service for which we wish
to know the cost. Generally, as the cost objective becomes more
specific, the methodology necessary to account for the associated
costs becomes more complex. In an acute care or a mental health
hospital, for example, the cost objective generally is a day of care.
Sometimes the day of care is "all inclusive"; that is, it includes
surgical procedures, laboratory tests, radiology exams, drug usage, and so on. In other instances, the day of care is for "routine"
costs only (i.e., room, dietary, and nursing costs). Obviously, various other combinations are possible, and even the routine distinction is not implemented in a uniform way among like insti-
tuitons. For example, nursing supplies may be classified as routine or "ancillary."

It is also possible to consider a totally different cost objective,
such as an admission or an episode of illness. If an admission is
the cost objective, we would include all costs associated with the
patient's entire stay in the hospital (i.e., for all days of care, rather
than just an average single day). If we chose an episode of illness
as our cost objective, we would then include costs for *all admissions* associated with a particular illness for a given patient.

As might be imagined, the choice of cost objectives will have a significant impact on the cost accounting methodology used in an institution. Depending on the particular cost objective, we would have a need for either different kinds of cost information or different ways of analyzing and presenting the cost information. As one might imagine, then, the choice of a cost objective can have a significant effect on the answer to "What did it cost?"

2. Choice of Cost Centers

The choice of cost centers determines the manner in which cost data will be accumulated. Again consider the organization that is producing a single good or service. The organization may wish to treat itself as one cost center, thereby creating a relatively simple cost accounting system. Alternatively, the organization may be subdivided into several cost centers, so now the cost of the good or service will be the sum of the costs attributed to it in each of the cost centers.[3]

> *Example:* Home Health Aides Incorporated is choosing between two cost center arrangements. The first possibility is to make the entire organization into one cost center; the second is to use three cost centers: depreciation, administration, and patient services. The depreciation cost is $10,000. Cost data are also available for administrative supplies ($15,000), patient-related supplies ($25,000), administrative salaries ($40,000), and professional salaries ($85,000). The agency provided 33,000 hours of service last year.
>
> *Analysis:* If we use only one cost center, our cost analysis might look as follows:

Professional and administrative salaries	$125,000
Supplies (administrative and patient-related)	40,000
Depreciation	10,000
	$175,000
Hours of service	33,000
Cost per hour	$5.30

If we were to use the three cost centers, our analysis would give the same result, but with a different structure:

---

[3]The distinction between a cost objective and a cost center is occasionally quite subtle. On occasion, both can be viewed as "purposes" for which costs are collected; for this reason, cost centers are sometimes called intermediate cost objectives. The distinction should become clearer in the pages that follow.

	Cost center			
Cost items	Depre-ciation	Adminis-tration	Patient Services	Total
Salaries		$40,000	$ 85,000	$125,000
Supplies		15,000	25,000	40,000
Depreciation	$10,000			10,000
Total	$10,000	$55,000	$110,000	$175,000
Cost per hour	$0.30	$1.67	$3.33	$5.30

Although not directly relevant to cost finding, since the total cost per hour is $5.30 in both instances, this more detailed structure may be of some use to us in comparing our costs with other agencies or in controlling our costs. A comparison between our administrative costs and those of other organizations could reveal areas of potential inefficiency, for example. In making such comparisons, however, we would need to be aware of potential comparability problems similar to those discussed in Chapter 2 (i.e., whether the organizations with which we are comparing ourselves measure their costs in the same way as we do).

Cost centers generally are divided into two basic categories: service and revenue-producing, or, occasionally, intermediate and final. Revenue-producing centers, as the name implies, are those that are reimbursed for their activities. In the above example, Depreciation and Administration would be considered service centers, while Patient Services would be a revenue center. In a larger institutional setting, housekeeping, plant maintenance, and the like are service centers, while inpatient care might constitute a single revenue-producing cost center. Alternatively, one might develop a cost accounting system which treated each individual ward as a revenue-producing center, or which separated outpatient care, inpatient care, and ancillary services into three revenue-producing centers. The cost for a given day of care would then depend on the cost center or centers in which a patient received services, and would distinguish between outpatient and inpatient costs.

Example: In addition to the cost center decision described in the last example, Home Health Aides has decided to establish a patient-education program, and to treat the program as a separate cost center. In so doing, it hired a social worker at a salary of $20,000. The supplies for the program totalled $5,000. The social worker provided 1,500 hours of education during the year.

Analysis: We now have an additional revenue-producing cost center, giving us two service centers and two revenue-producing centers. Our total costs would now look as follows:

Cost items	Cost centers Depreciation	Administration	Patient Services	Patient Education	Total
Salaries		$40,000	$ 85,000	$20,000	$145,000
Supplies		15,000	25,000	5,000	45,000
Depreciation	$10,000				10,000
Total	$10,000	$55,000	$110,000	$25,000	$200,000

At this point, our cost per hour of service becomes substantially more difficult to calculate, since it now relies on some further decisions. We will thus defer the per-unit calculations until those decisions have been discussed.

3. Distinction between Direct and Indirect Costs

A third decision inherent in a cost accounting system is the distinction between direct and indirect costs. *Direct costs* are those costs unambiguously associated with, or physically traceable to, a specific cost objective or cost center; *indirect costs* are those costs which apply to more than one cost objective or cost center. Again, under the simplest of circumstances, where an organization produced one product in one cost center, there would be no indirect costs, since it would not be possible to have costs which applied to more than one cost center. The creation of multiple cost centers, however, implies that some costs become indirect, thereby necessitating their assignment to the cost centers to which they apply. This assignment can be carried out in one of two ways: (1) developing improved measurement techniques, which effectively convert indirect costs into direct ones; or (2) establishing assignment formulas, which distribute indirect costs as fairly as possible into the appropriate cost centers.

> *Example:* The social worker in the patient education program at Home Health Aides is supervised by one of the Aides supervisors whose salary at present is included in the Patient Services cost center.
>
> *Analysis:* The salary of the Aides supervisor is an indirect cost, since it applies to activities in both the Patient Services and Patient Education cost centers. There are several possibilities for assigning the salary to the two centers. We might, for example, ask the supervisor to maintain careful time records, which then could be used to distribute the salary. If we were to do this, we effectively would have converted the indirect cost into a direct cost, since we would have created a situation in which the cost (time) is physically traceable.
>
> Alternatively, we might simply establish an assignment formula, using, say, relative hours of service or number of personnel in each

cost center as the assignment mechanism. Assume we decide to use relative hours of service, and that the supervisor's salary is $25,000. We could then perform the following calculations:

Cost centers	Hours of service	Percent	Assigned supervisor's salary	Percent
Patient Services	33,000	96%	$24,000	96%
Patient Education	1,500	4	1,000	4
Total	34,500	100%	$25,000	100%

Our cost centers would then have the following costs:

Cost centers	Cost	
Depreciation	$ 10,000	
Administration	55,000	
Patient Services	109,000	(i.e., 110,000 − 1,000 for supervisor)
Patient Education	26,000	(i.e., 25,000 + 1,000 for supervisor)
Total	$200,000	

4. Allocation of Overhead

The fourth step in the cost accounting process is the allocation of service center costs to revenue-producing centers. Here, the principal choice concerns the *bases of allocation,* where a number of alternatives are possible. In general, an attempt is made to determine a basis of allocation for each service center that most accurately measures its use by the remaining cost centers.

In this context, it is important to clarify the distinction between "assignment" and "allocation." The assignment process discussed above takes place before allocation, and serves to distribute costs into both service-producing and revenue-producing cost centers. Costs that are direct for a given cost center need not be assigned, while indirect costs (i.e., those applying to more than one cost center) must be assigned to the centers to which they apply. *Allocation* is the process of distributing service center costs to revenue-producing centers to determine the full cost of each revenue-producing center.[4]

> *Example:* If we are to determine the full cost for each of our revenue-producing cost centers at Home Health Aides Incorporated, we must (1) determine the direct costs of each cost center, (2) assign indirect costs to the cost centers where they apply (which we have already done), and (3) allocate our service center costs (depre-

---

[4]To make matters even more complicated, allocation is sometimes called apportionment.

ciation and administration) to the revenue-producing centers. Depreciation might be allocated on the basis of square feet of floor used by each cost center, and the following information is available to us:

Cost center	Square feet
Administration	3,000
Patient Services	3,000
Patient Education	500
Total	6,500

Administration might be allocated using several alternative bases, such as number of personnel, salary cost, or number of visits. Assume we decide to use salary cost, and that the following information is available to us:

Cost center	Initial salary costs	With supervisor assignment	
Administration	$ 40,000	$ 40,000	
Patient Services	85,000	84,000	(1,000 removed for supervisor)
Patient Education	20,000	21,000	(1,000 added for supervisor)
Total	$145,000	$145,000	

Analysis: Depreciation can be allocated on the basis of $1.54 per square foot (10,000 ÷ 6,500). Administration is somewhat more complicated, since total costs in the administrative cost center will not be known until depreciation has been allocated, and since administrative salaries themselves cannot be used in the denominator of the calculation.[5] This dilemma will be resolved once we have discussed some additional cost accounting decisions.

In the context of deciding on allocation bases, we should note that, generally, one can achieve increased precision at increased cost. For example, in a hospital setting the allocation of housekeeping costs frequently is done on the basis of square feet. Alternatively, and more accurately, it could be allocated on the basis of hours of service. Clearly, although hours of service is a more accurate base, and thus would give us more accurate full cost data, its use requires a possibly costly compilation of the necessary data. The choice of using the more accurate basis, then, depends in large part on the uses management might make of the

---

[5]This is a subtle point, but, as the reader will see later, to include administrative salaries in the denominator would not allow us to fully allocate the costs in the "Administration" cost center.

information. In some instances, the information can improve pricing decisions; in others, it will have an effect on the institution's reimbursement from third-party payors; in still others, it may influence the motivation of people responsible for managing the "cost centers." These and other similar considerations will determine whether a more accurate—and generally more costly—allocation basis should be used.

In sum, the more precise the assignment and allocation processes, the more accurately one captures true resource consumption. Exact measurement of resource use can be a time-consuming and complicated process, however, and thus less accurate measurement procedures often are adopted in response to time, manpower, and technical constraints. As indicated in the housekeeping example discussed above, a typical basis of allocation is square feet of floor space in each cost center receiving housekeeping services. If the square footage for all cost centers is known, the total housekeeping costs can be distributed quite easily in proportion to the square feet in each center. This less precise method, while easier to apply, obviously can lead to over- or under-representation of the actual use of housekeeping services received by a given cost center.[6]

5. The Stepdown Sequence

Although several methods of varying complexity and accuracy are available for allocating service center costs to revenue centers, the *stepdown* method is the most commonly used. Its use is based not only on its relative ease of application but the fact that it traditionally has been the method preferred by the American Hospital Association (AHA). As a consequence, it is required by many third-party reimbursers for institutions with multiple-cost centers. The *Medicare Cost Report*, which may be familiar to many readers, requires the use of the stepdown method.

The stepdown procedure is basically a method of sequentially "trickling down" the costs of the service cost centers to the revenue-producing centers. This stepping down process, simplified in Table 4–3, typically begins with the service center serving the most cost centers in the institution, spreading its costs over both the remaining service centers as well as the revenue-producing ones.

> *Example:* Home Health Aides Incorporated has decided to use the stepdown method to allocate its service center costs.
>
> *Analysis:* The process would be performed as follows:

---

[6]See Young, Socholitzky, and Locke, "Ambulatory Care Cost," for a description of this effect in one institution.

TABLE 4-3
The Stepdown Procedure*

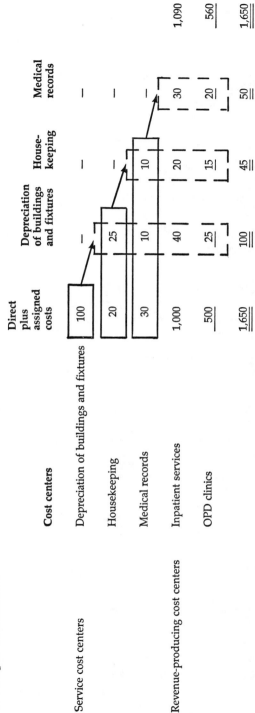

Cost centers	Direct plus assigned costs	Depreciation of buildings and fixtures	Housekeeping	Medical records	
Service cost centers					
Depreciation of buildings and fixtures	100	—	—	—	
Housekeeping	20	25	—	—	
Medical records	30	10	10	—	
Revenue-producing cost centers					
Inpatient services	1,000	40	20	30	1,090
OPD clinics	500	25	15	20	560
	1,650	100	45	50	1,650

*The three solid horizontal bars contain the direct and assigned costs to be allocated plus, in the cases of housekeeping and medical records, those amounts allocated from the previous cost centers. The three dotted vertical bars contain the individual amounts allocated to each cost center from the three service cost centers. Note that, as the arrows indicate, the total amount in each horizontal bar has been redistributed within a vertical bar. This redistribution is done in accordance with the chosen allocation basis (e.g., by square feet for housekeeping).
Source: Edward Locke (a personal communication).

		Allocation bases		
Cost center	Direct plus assigned costs	Deprecia-tion (square feet)	Adminis-tration (salary dollars)	Total
Depreciation	$ 10,000	—		
Administration	55,000	$ 4,620 (a)		
Patient Services	109,000	4,620 (a)	$47,696 (c)	$161,316
Patient Education	26,000	760 (b)	11,924 (c)	38,684
Total	$200,000	$10,000	$59,620	$200,000

a. $1.54 per square foot × 3,000 square feet
b. $1.54 per square foot × 500 square feet
c. Administration costs = $59,620 ($55,000 + $4,620)
   Salary dollars of two remaining departments = $105,000 ($84,000 + $21,000).
   Administration costs per salary dollar = $.568 ($59,620 ÷ 105,000)
   Administration cost for Patient Services = $47,696 ($.568 × $84,000)
   Administration cost for Patient Education = $11,924 ($.568 × $21,000)*
   *See text footnote 5. Note that to include the $40,000 of administrative salaries in the denominator of the calculation would result in our not fully allocating the costs of the Administration cost center.

Although the effect of different stepdown sequences typically is minimal, it nevertheless is important to note that the choice of a sequence usually will have some influence on the costs allocated to any given revenue-producing department.

Example: We wish to change the sequence for Home Health Aides, allocating Administration first and Depreciation second.

Analysis:

		Allocation bases		
Cost center	Direct plus assigned costs	Adminis-tration (salary dollars)	Depre-ciation (square feet)	Total
Administration	$ 55,000			
Depreciation	10,000	—		
Patient Services	109,000	$44,000 (a)	$ 8,571 (b)	$161,571
Patient Education	26,000	11,000 (a)	1,429 (b)	38,429
Total	$200,000	$55,000	$10,000	$200,000

a. $55,000 ÷ 105,000 = $.524
   $.524 × $84,000 = 44,000
   $.524 × $21,000 = 11,000
b. $10,000 ÷ 3,500 = $2.86 per square foot. (The 3,000 square feet in Administration cannot be included since we have completed allocation for that cost center.)
   $2.86 × 3,000 = $8,571
   $2.86 × 500 = $1,429

As the last two examples indicate, changing the stepdown sequence can have an effect on the costs allocated to revenue-producing cost centers. The magnitude of the effect will depend on the extent to which the service cost centers "use" the services of each other.

> *Example:* Assume that Patient Services uses 90 percent of Administration and that Patient Education uses the remaining 10 percent. Assume also that Administration occupies 80 percent of the square feet of the building. Patient Services, 5 percent, and Patient Education, 15 percent.

> *Analysis:* If administration is allocated before depreciation, we cannot allocate any depreciation to administration. Therefore, all depreciation must be divided between Patient Services and Patient Education. Let us now examine what happens under the two possible stepdown sequences:

Sequence 1:

Cost center	Direct plus assigned costs	Depre-ciation	Adminis-tration	Total
Depreciation	$ 10,000			
Administration	55,000	$ 8,000 (*a*)		
Patient Services	109,000	500 (*a*)	$56,700 (*b*)	$166,200
Patient Education	26,000	1,500 (*a*)	6,300 (*b*)	33,800
Total	$200,000	$10,000	$63,000	$200,000

a. Administration = 80% of $10,000 = $8,000
 Patient Services = 5% of $10,000 = $500
 Patient Education = 15% of $10,000 = $1,500
b. Patient Services = 90% of Administration ($55,000 + $8,000) = $56,700
 Patient Education = 10% of Administration ($55,000 + $8,000) = $6,300

Sequence 2:

Administration	$ 55,000			
Depreciation	10,000			
Patient Services	109,000	$49,500 (*a*)	$ 2,500 (*b*)	$161,000
Patient Education	26,000	5,500 (*a*)	7,500 (*b*)	39,000
Total	$200,000	$55,000	$10,000	$200,000

a. 90% of $55,000 = $49,500
 10% of $55,000 = $5,500
b. Cannot use Administration floor space. Since Patient Services = 5% and Patient Education = 15% of floor space, the former receives 25% of Depreciation, the latter, 75%

Note that a much more sizable shift in total costs has taken place than with the previous example. This is because, when depreciation is allocated first, most of it enters administration. When administration subsequently is allocated, it "carries with it" a great deal of depreciation. Since Patient Services receives 90 percent of administration, it also receives 90 percent of the depreciation which previously had been allocated into administration. Thus, even though it occupies only 5 percent of the floor space, Patient Services receives a great deal of depreciation.

When administration is allocated first, it carries no depreciation with it, and depreciation must be divided between Patient Services and Patient Education. Patient Education, with three times the floor space of Patient Services (15 percent versus 5 percent), thus receives three times as much depreciation.

In sum, with Sequence 1, Patient Services received $7,700 of depreciation (500 + .9 × 8,000). With Sequence 2, it received only $2,500. The difference of $5,200 (7,700 − 2,500) shifts from Patient Services into Patient Education.

An obvious question which arises is, "Which is better?" Clearly, this is difficult to answer; but, in general, the principle of first allocating those service centers which are used the most by all other service centers seems the most appropriate. This would lead us to use Sequence 1 in the last example, since administration "uses" some depreciation while "depreciation" uses no "administration." Patient services, which uses a lot of administration, thus uses a great deal of depreciation, too, albeit in a "secondary" or "lagged" fashion.

In summary, to carry out the stepdown process, a "basis of allocation" is chosen for each cost center which attempts to reflect and measure the usage of that cost center by the others. For example, "pounds of laundry" frequently is used as the basis of allocation of the costs of the laundry cost center; thus, each cost center would receive a portion of the institution's laundry costs in accordance with its proportion of the total pounds of laundry processed. The total costs in the revenue-producing departments, then, are a function of their direct and assigned costs, as well as those costs allocated to them from the service centers.

Health care institutions continually make trade-offs between accuracy of data available to carry out the stepdown and the cost of obtaining greater accuracy. Additionally, the choice of allocation bases is affected by such concerns as reimbursement requirements, overall financial implications arising from choices of different allocation bases, and the costs, availability, and accuracy of data used in carrying out the allocation process.

In the absence of cost-based reimbursement, one might expect that, where feasible, a basis of allocation would be chosen for each service center which most accurately measured the use of that service center by both revenue-producing centers and other service centers. A decision to use a more accurate allocation basis is influenced by more than just the act of gathering the necessary information, however, since the increased accuracy quite likely will affect the institutions's total Medicare reimbursement, as well as all other "cost-based" reimbursements. Thus, the decision has important financial consequences. In some instances, greater accuracy may help to increase the reimbursement for a given revenue-producing cost center, to such an extent that institutions with similar service center costs may, by choosing different bases of allocation, distribute these costs in different proportions to their revenue-producing cost centers. Conversely, institutions with different service center costs may have similar allocated costs in some of their revenue-producing cost centers as a result of their choices of bases of allocation, or the chosen stepdown sequence.

6. Process versus Job Order

A final decision in a full cost accounting system concerns the way in which cost center costs are distributed to an organization's cost objective. Here a range of choices present themselves; but, for purposes of discussion, we will look at only the two extreme ends of the spectrum. At one end is a process method, which typically is used when all units of output are roughly identical. The production of chairs, plastic cups, and so on—an activity often performed by a production line—usually calls for a process method of cost accounting. All production-related costs for a given accounting period are calculated and then divided by the total number of units produced to give an average cost per unit.

At the other end of the spectrum is a job order method, which typically is used when the units of output are quite different. A good example is an automobile repair garage, where adding all costs for a given accounting period, such as a day, and dividing by the number of cars repaired, to determine an average cost per unit, almost certainly would be quite misleading. Instead, the cost accounting system utilizes a "job ticket" on which the time and parts associated with each repair effort are recorded separately, and then are costed out by means of hourly wage rates, unit prices, and so on.

> *Example:* The Home Health Aides Incorporated agency currently bills its patients on the basis of number of hours spent with the patient. It is considering using a different rate for Patient Education than for Patient Services.

> *Analysis:* If the agency simply added all its costs and divided this amount by the total number of hours of care, it would be using a process method in which it assumed that each hour cost the same:

Total costs = $200,000

Total hours = 34,500 (33,000 Patient Services + 1,500 Patient Education)

Average cost
per hour = $5.80 ($200,000 ÷ 34,500)

If, on the other hand, it decided to use different rates for Patient Services and Patient Education, its cost per hour would look as follows:

Program	Total cost	Number of hours	Cost/hour
Patient services	$161,316	33,000	$ 4.89
Patient education	38,684	1,500	25.79

It has now moved along the spectrum toward a job order method. Further movement along the spectrum could take place by incorporating travel time into the number of hours, thereby reflecting a higher cost for patients who live farther away, or by calculating different costs for different categories of employees within each program. If, for example, Patient Services included both Senior Aides, who handle more difficult cases, and Junior Aides, who handle the easier cases, the agency might wish to distinguish between the cost of these two categories of employees.

Per-diem reimbursement methods in hospitals, particularly ones that use an *all inclusive* per diem, use a process costing method in which total inpatient care costs are divided by total inpatient days to give a rate per day. Alternatively, a hospital's billing department, which accumulates the various services received by a patient (medications, special dietary services, operating room usage, ancillary usage, special nursing care, ICU usage, and so on), is approximating a job order costing method. In choosing between methods of this sort, one frequently is weighing the costs associated with the increased reporting and processing effort of the job order method with the managerial benefits (e.g., competitive pricing needs, management control potential) which such a system provides. As with many other managerial activities, the choice between the two methods—or among a variety of methods on the spectrum possessing some characteristics of both job order and process—is rarely a completely clear one.

7. Summary

As the above discussion indicates, the managerial choices involved in developing a cost accounting system frequently are quite difficult. Moreover, they are highly interdependent. The choice of cost centers, as indicated, will influence the distinction between direct and indirect costs. The choice of a particular cost objective frequently will require the use of certain kinds of cost centers. Allocation of service-center costs to revenue producing centers will be determined, in part, by the choice of the service centers themselves and by the assignment process followed. And so on.

In this context, it is important to note that any changes in the cost of one cost center always are accompanied by changes in another direction to other cost centers. That is, since the total costs of operating the institution have been incurred at the time a cost report is prepared, they will always remain the same on any given cost report. Thus, the effect of any change in methodology is solely one of making shifts among cost centers. In some instances, changes in cost accounting definitions and techniques can have a significant effect upon the costs associated with a given cost center or cost objective.

FULL COST ACCOUNTING AND THIRD-PARTY REIMBURSEMENT[7]

Although full cost accounting is a management accounting activity in almost all organizations, with full cost data rarely if ever presented to outsiders, this is not the case in health care. To receive third-party reimbursement from Medicare, Medicaid, and many Blue Cross plans, hospitals must comply with a variety of requirements related to the full cost accounting process. These reimbursement requirements include an accounting for both direct and indirect costs, as well as an allocation of service center costs to revenue-producing centers. Further, most third-party payors require that hospitals and other organizations reimbursed by them prepare cost reports on a regular basis. These cost reports, thus, contain information that is perhaps more useful to "outsiders" than to "insiders."

Regardless of the end users involved, it is important to note that the methodology necessary for calculating the costs of each patient service department (or revenue center) requires a decision be made in each of the six areas described in the previous section. Thus, the methodology includes the determination of a cost objective, a structuring of the revenue-producing and service cost

---

[7]The appendix on hospital reimbursement systems, at the end of this chapter, gives the interested reader additional details on third-party payment systems and their role in the health care system.

centers, a distinction between the direct and indirect costs of each, a choice of allocation bases, and the determination of the stepdown sequence in allocating the general service cost center totals to the revenue cost centers. Finally, all of these activities are influenced by the nature of the costing method: job order versus process.

In the case of third-party reimbursement, some of an individual institution's cost accounting decisions are constrained or eliminated. Medicare, Medicaid, and Blue Cross frequently dictate or strongly recommend which cost centers the health care organizations should use, as well as the cost objectives, allocation bases, and stepdown sequence. The direct/indirect distinction, on the other hand, is a choice which institutions generally must make themselves, and frequently a choice is allowed between two different bases of allocation for each general service center.

As a result of this constrained decision-making ability in the full cost accounting process for external purposes, the cost reports which emerge for third-party payors frequently do not represent the "full cost" of a particular activity as accurately as might be desired for internal purposes. It is obvious, for example, that significant changes can occur in the costs of a particular cost center as a result of modifications in the cost accounting methodology used for the *Medicare Cost Report*. As a result, similar cost centers of different institutions, delivering similar services, will have different costs, not because of variations in resource consumption but because of variations in reimbursement methodologies. Consequently, attempts to make cost center comparisons among institutions, based on these reports, should be viewed with some skepticism.

Thus, while the principal purpose of full cost accounting is to assist management in the accurate measurement of the resources devoted to a particular cost objective, and to use that information internally for pricing, profitability analysis, or control,[8] this generally is not the case in health care. As a consequence, the cost reports prepared for third-party payors are not particularly valuable as management tools; nor are they useful for a variety of cost-related decisions, such as alternative choice decisions, which managers of health care organizations frequently must make. For this reason, a portion of the next chapter is devoted exclusively to the effect of cost-based reimbursement on alternative-choice decisions.

---

[8]Use of this kind of information for control purposes will be discussed in Chapter 6.

MANAGERIAL CHECKLIST

1. What are our cost objectives? What optional cost objectives could we use? What is the rationale behind the choice?

2. What are our cost centers? What additional effort would be necessary to expand the number of cost centers? What management benefits might result?

3. Which of our indirect costs could be physically traced to the cost centers where they apply? What additional efforts (e.g., time sheets, supply requisitions, and so on), would be necessary to do so? Would the effort significantly improve the accuracy of the cost report, and, if so, what management decisions would be improved as a result of the additional accuracy?

4. What are our bases of allocation? How many have been established by our third-party payors, and with which do we have some latitude? What costs would be necessary to develop and use more accurate bases? Would the additional accuracy improve our reimbursement from third parties? Would it improve any of our managerial decision making?

5. What optional stepdown sequences are available to us, and what would their effect be on reimbursement?

6. Where do we stand on the spectrum from process to job order cost accounting systems? To what extent is our position on this spectrum a result of third-party requirements? Would a move toward the job order end of the spectrum be possible, and, if yes, would it so improve the information available to management that better management decisions might take place?

Bibliography

Anthony, R. N., and G. A. Welsch. *Fundamentals of Management Accounting.* Homewood, Ill.: Richard D. Irwin, 1981.

Anthony, R. N., and D. W. Young. *Management Control in Nonprofit Organizations.* Homewood, Ill.: Richard D. Irwin, 1984.

Bennington, J. L., et al. *Management And Cost Control Techniques for the Clinical Laboratory.* Baltimore: University Park Press, 1977.

Coyne, J. S. "Multihospital System Types: Comparing Costs and Occupancy." *Hospital Progress,* January 1980.

Dearden, J. *Essentials of Cost Accounting.* Reading, Mass.: Addison-Wesley Publishing, 1969. A programmed text.

Goggans, T. P. "Cost Allocation for LTC Facilities." *Contemporary Administrator,* May 1980.

Griffith, J. R., et al., eds. *Cost Control in Hospitals.* Ann Arbor, Mich.: Health Administration Press, 1976.

Horngren, C. T. *Introduction to Management Accounting.* Englewood Cliffs, N.J.: Prentice-Hall, 1978.

Kaufman, S. L., and D. S. Shepard. "Costs of Neonatal Intensive Care by Day of Stay." *Inquiry,* Summer 1982.

Lohmann, R. A. *Breaking Even: Financial Management in Human Service Organizations.* Philadelphia: Temple University Press, 1980.

Suver, J. D., and B. R. Neumann. *Management Accounting for Health Care Organizations.* Oak Brook, Ill.: Hospital Financial Management Association, 1981.

Tribles, R. J. "Managing *with* Accounting." *Hospital Financial Management,* November 1977.

Watts, C. A., and T. D. Clastorin. "The Impact of Case Mix on Hospital Costs: A Comparative Analysis." *Inquiry,* 1980.

Wood, C. T. "Relate Hospital Charges to Use of Services." *Harvard Business Review,* March–April 1982.

Young, D. W.; E. Socholitzky; and E. Locke. "Ambulatory Care Cost and the Medicare Cost Report: Managerial and Public Policy Implications." *Journal of Ambulatory Care Management,* February 1982.

APPENDIX: Hospital Reimbursement Systems[9]

INTRODUCTION

Much of the discussion concerning full costs, in Chapter 4, was built around the notion of decisions (i.e., that the full cost accounting effort taking place in an organization can be characterized in terms of a variety of decisions concerning the cost objective, cost centers, allocation bases, and the like). In many health and human service organizations, several of these decisions are made by regulators, rather than by managers. Indeed, in some instances, third-party reimbursement systems dictate much of the analytical effort in cost accounting, leaving little to the discretion of the organization's managers. What discretion exists frequently is focused on maximizing the organization's reimbursement,

[9]Adapted from M. J. Connelly and D. W. Young, *Note on Prospective Reimbursement Systems: Structure and Process Considerations* (Boston: Intercollegiate Case Clearing House), 9–180–510.

rather than using the cost accounting system for internal management purposes.

Since third-party reimbursement systems play such an important role in the lives of many health and human service organizations, particularly hospitals, and since many readers may not be familiar with these systems and their characteristics, it is important to provide a general overview. This is particularly important because, over the past several years, the process by which hospitals are reimbursed for services they provide has grown increasingly complex. Current reimbursement systems encompass a variety of prospective rate-setting mechanisms, certificate of need criteria, peer review procedures, and many other processes and mechanisms. The purpose of this appendix is to describe these issues by looking at nine components of a hospital reimbursement system: reimbursement entity, payment unit, incentives, participation, coverage, system objectives, payment timing focus, payment setting methods, and payment source. The latter two of these components are examined in some depth.

The Reimbursement Entity

The reimbursement entity is the individual or organization that is reimbursed by the system. Three of the most frequently used entities are the hospital, the physician, and the patient. The discussion in this appendix will be concerned only with reimbursement systems directed toward hospitals.

The Payment Unit

In the terminology of Chapter 4, the payment unit is the cost objective (i.e., the "output measure") for which payment is made. William Dowling has identified seven such units: capitation, apportionment of total budget, apportionment of department budgets, per-diem cost (patient day), specific services, case, and episode of illness.[10] These units are defined in Table 4A–1. Although "retrospective" and "prospective" distinctions frequently are made (and will be discussed later), it is important to note that these seven units can be classified into two fundamental categories: anticipated use and actual use. The first three of those listed above (capitation, apportionment of total budget, and apportionment of department budgets) fall into the *anticipated use* category; the remaining four fall into the *actual use* category.

---

[10]W. L. Dowling, "Prospective Reimbursement of Hospitals," *Inquiry*, September 1974, pp. 163–79.

TABLE 4A–1

Payment Units

Capitation[1]

A method of payment for health services in which an individual or institutional provider is paid a fixed, per-capita amount for each person served without regard to the actual number or nature of services provided to each person. . . .

Per-Diem Cost[1]

Literally cost per day. Refers, in general, to hospital or other *inpatient* institutional costs per day or for a day of care. Hospitals occasionally *charge* for their services on the basis of a per-diem rate derived by dividing their total costs by the number of inpatient days of care given. Per-diem costs, therefore, are averages and do not reflect true cost of each patient. . . .

Apportionment of Total Budget[5]

Determined by means of first negotiating a hospital's total budget, usually in conjunction with some rate-setting agency or program. Once negotiated, the total budget amount would be divided among the various third-party payors using some agreed-upon basis, such as admission or patient days. Each third party would be obligated to pay its share of budgeted costs, regardless of the costs actually incurred by the hospital during the year. Fixed payments would be made to the hospital by each third party on a regular basis (such as monthly), which would sum to the total amount apportioned for the year.

Apportionment of Departmental Budgets[2]

A refinement of the apportionment of total budget, but with cost figures set for individual departments. Each third-party's payment responsibility would be determined by the proportion of each department's services going to its patients.

Specific Services[2]

The payment for a given service at a set amount.

Case[3]

An average amount per diagnosis, which is established by prospective budget negotiations.

Episode of Illness

Although the definition of this unit seems intuitively obvious, it is not easily translated into terminology that can be readily agreed upon by providers and third parties. Dowling,[3] in presenting it as a potential payment unit states:

> The problem of defining episodes of illness is substantial, however, and although included here for completeness, this payment unit has not been operationalized.

[1]*A Discursive Dictionary of Health Care Staff,* Subcommittee on Health and the Environment, Committee of Interstate and Foreign Commerce House, February 1976.

[2]Based on William L., Dowling, "Prospective Rate Setting: Concept and Practice," *Topics in Health Care Financing,* Winter 1976.

[3]William L. Dowling, "Prospecitve Reimbursement of Hospitals," *Inquiry,* September 1974, p. 168.

Incentives

All reimbursement systems have incentives, or motivating factors, of some sort incorporated into their design; sometimes these are stated explicitly, sometimes they are implicit. At the most general level of analysis, there are two types of incentives: positive (rewarding) and negative (punishing). In reimbursement systems, the incentives generally are of a financial nature. For example, when reimbursement is based on cost, the implicit (and positive) incentive is to spend, since cost increases are rewarded by increases in reimbursement. On the other hand, when reimbursement is based on a capitation fee, the incentive is to maintain the average cost per enrolleee at an amount less than or equal to the capitation fee, since excess expenditures are not reimbursable and, hence, the organization is penalized financially for excessive spending.

Participation

Participation refers to the question of whether a hospital has the option of being a part of the reimbursement system. At the present time, membership in some reimbursement systems is voluntary, although a number of quasi-voluntary (i.e., just short of mandatory) systems exist. An example of the latter type is a state-run system, in which a hospital that does not participate is unable to obtain reimbursement for its Medicaid patients (i.e., those patients whose care is funded in part by the state).

Coverage

Most systems are not liable for all aspects of health care. Coverage, thus, refers to the liability of the system (i.e., the specific services, sets of circumstances, and groups of people for which payment will be made). Coverage can range from being all-inclusive to very narrowly defined. Additionally, some systems specify certain costs as "allowable" or "reasonable." Clearly, in these systems, definitions of allowability and reasonability become extremely important.

System Objectives

There are many goals or objectives that a reimbursement system can have, including: guaranteeing a high quality of care for some specific target group, such as the elderly; assuring adequate care for all individuals; reducing the cost of medical care while maintaining satisfactory access and quality; containing the cost of medical care while increasing coverage; and so on. It is important to realize that these goals can overlap or contradict each other, so trade-offs frequently are necessary. In some instances, the system's designers specify the nature of the trade-offs; in others, they are not made explicit.

Payment Timing Focus

This component of a reimbursement system refers to the time of final determination of the reimbursement amount, which can be either prior to the fiscal year in question or after it (i.e., before the expenses are incurred or afterwards).[11] A *retrospective focus* uses the costs incurred in the delivery of a service as a base for the determination of the level of reimbursement. This focus is characterized by its use of *actual* costs for the period covered (usually a fiscal year), which means that the level of the reimbursement is determined *after* the services have been provided.

   With a *prospective focus,* the level of reimbursement is determined all or in part *before* the services have been provided. Frequently, the costs of a prior period are used as a base and transformed by a projection process to determine the level of reimbursement for the payment period. Thus, the level of reimbursement or, as a minimum, the reimbursement *rate* is determined prior to the actual provision of services. To the extent that retrospective adjustments are made, however, the system is not truly prospective. Retrospective adjustments can include "base-year lags" (which put actual costs for one year into the prospective rate of another), volume adjustments, and adjustments for "costs beyond control." One important implication of a retrospective adjustment is that it changes the incentives of the reimbursement entity, making it less desirable to contain costs as much as possible. This may or may not be desirable, depending on the system's objectives.

Payment Setting Methods

A variety of methods can be used to determine the amount of payments made to the entity. Although some payors determine their payments as based upon a hospital's charges, most utilize cost as the basis of payment. The question then becomes how "cost" is adjusted for payment purposes. Essentially, two meth-

---

[11]Note that it does not refer to the timing of the actual payment (i.e., how soon payments are received after the submission of invoices) but rather to the nature of the costs that are to determine the level of reimbursement.

ods can be identified: (1) actual costs incurred: and (2) those projected to be incurred by a variety of mechanisms, including formulas and budget review. In this context, the terms *cost, charges, formulas,* and *budget review* take on special significance.

Cost. For reimbursement systems, the word *cost* generally is used in one of two ways: "allowable" and "reasonable." An *allowable cost* is one for which a payment source will reimburse a provider. The term *reasonable cost* came into being through the Medicare/Medicaid legislation of the mid-1960's, and was further refined through amendments to that legislation during the 1970's. According to Section 1861(v) of Public Law 89-97 (the 1965 law which established Medicare), the Secretary of Health and Human Services is responsible for determining reasonable cost. This determination must consider several interrelated items: (1) principles generally applied by national organizations or by established prepayment organizations; (2) the most appropriate payment unit, including the use of different methods under different circumstances; (3) the use of charges when they reasonably reflect costs; (4) the direct and indirect costs of providers of services; (5) the minimization of cross-subsidization between insured and uninsured individuals; and (6) a provision for "suitable retroactive corrective adjustments" when ". . . the aggregate reimbursement produced by the methods of determining costs proves to be either inadequate or excessive."[12]

To determine its level of reimbursement, a hospital generally must go through a process called cost finding. The nature of this process was described in Chapter 4, in the section entitled Decisions in Cost Measurement. Once computed, the full costs of each revenue center or department are then used in the per-diem (or other payment unit) calculations. Specifically, total allowable costs for a department (which were determined in the cost-finding process) are divided by the total number of payment units (e.g., inpatient days) to give the per-unit reimbursement amount. To determine the total amount of reimbursement from a given source, the resulting departmental rates are multiplied by the number of payment units in each department that are covered by that source.

Although it follows the same general format, the cost-finding procedure under Medicare is somewhat different from that described above. Once service center costs have been allocated, the next step is to determine the portion of those costs attributable to Medicare-covered patients. Two methods can be used for this cost

---

[12]Public Law 89–97, Title XVIII, Sec. 1861 (v) (1).

apportionment process: departmental and combination, with
hospital size being the determining factor. Specifically, the departmental method is for hospitals of 100 beds or more, and the combination method for those with fewer than 100 beds.

When using the departmental method, the cost of services of
each ancillary department is calculated by taking the ratio of Medicare charges to total patient charges and multiplying that figure
by the total department costs. This is the "ratio of charges to
charges to cost" (RCCC) method. Once these costs have been determined, they are added to (1) the cost of the routine services,
based on the average per-diem cost for routine general service
(i.e., the room, board, and nursing provided the patient), and (2)
a separate per-diem cost for the various specialized care units
(e.g., intensive care units, coronary care units, and the like).

By contrast, the combination method allows the "lumping" of
all ancillary services for the calculation of their cost. That is, the
cost of ancillary services for Medicare purposes is determined by
taking the ratio of the total Medicare charges for ancillaries to total
patient charges for ancillaries and multiplying the result by the
total cost of all ancillaries.[13] As with the departmental method, the
per-diem cost of routine care and specialized unit care is then
added to that amount.

When reimbursement is based on cost, as it is for departmental
and the combination methods, the payment timing focus is usually retrospective.

Charges. A charge can be defined most simply as the price of a
particular hospital service. In a profit-seeking setting, this price or
charge frequently is based on the full cost of providing the service
plus a margin for profit. The desired profit margin, generally, is
based on an analysis of the organization's required rate of return
on investment, juxtaposed with its asset base and its projected
unit volume of sales. This process, described briefly in Chapter 3,
explains why supermarkets have low markups or profit margins,
for example, and why heavy equipment manufacturers have high
markups. In the former instance, the high sales volume and comparatively small asset base create a high asset-turnover ratio,
thereby generating an acceptable return on assets; while in the
latter, the low volume of sales, coupled with a large base of fixed
assets (i.e., a low asset-turnover ratio), creates a need for a high
profit margin if the same return on assets is to be achieved.

Hospitals, rather than following a process of analysis such as
the above in setting prices, appear to have utilized a less rigorous

---

[13]It should be noted that delivery room charges are excluded from these
calculations, since delivery room services are rarely utilized by Medicare patients.

approach. Generally, hospital charges reflect their historical levels, with increases for inflation. Some hospitals utilize a ratio of costs to charges (RCC) as a basis for price setting, so charges tend to remain at a fixed percentage over costs for each department. As Chapter 3 argued, however, the need for more rigorous financial management is becoming increasingly apparent in health care, and, consequently, one might expect to see more precise charge-setting measures being developed in the future.

The payment timing focus for the charge method can be either retrospective or prospective. Where cost information is used in conjunction with a RCC to develop the price for each department, the focus generally is prospective, based on projected costs.

Formulas. The formula method for determining the level of reimbursement was first developed by Blue Cross in New York in the early 1970s. Typically, formulas are used to project costs based on (1) group cost levels and trends, where hospitals are grouped by characteristics such as numbers of beds, types of services offered, physician mix, and so on; (2) economic indices; (3) normative standards; or (4) some combination of the above.[14] They usually include a base cost and a calculation process necessary to adjust the base to a level for the year in question. The base cost uses a definition of allowable and reasonable, just as with Medicare. (In fact, Medicare definitions generally are used.)

Occasionally, the amount determined by the formula is supplemented by an appeal process and pass-through items. Pass-through items are those costs that a hospital incurs in a period but which the hospital cannot determine or control. Generally, these costs are not used to determine the reimbursement rates but are added to the final reimbursement amount, instead. An example is malpractice insurance premiums.

The payment timing focus under formula plans allegedly is prospective, with the rate of reimbursement determined in advance of the year in which services are delivered. The fact that most formula systems use a "rolling base" means a lagged adjustment for actual costs incurred, however, thereby giving the systems a retrospective flavor. Further, the introduction of generous appeal procedures or the allowance of extensive pass-throughs can give a formula system an even more pronounced retrospective character, thereby mitigating its effectiveness in controlling costs.

Budget Review. In a budget review method of payment setting, the rate-setting authority, the hospital, and the third-party payors negotiate in advance the payment unit and the rate of reimburse-

---

[14]W. L. Dowling, "Prospective Rate Setting: Concept and Practice," *Topics in Health Care Financing/Prospective Rate Setting* 3:2, pp. 132–46.

ment per payment unit for the coming fiscal year. Four types of review may be used: (1) comparison of budgeted costs to costs for prior years; (2) comparison of budgeted costs to peer group costs; (3) comparison of budgeted costs to normative cost standards; or (4) some combination of the above, including the use of a formula supplemented by negotiated changes to the formula.[15] The review may be based either on a line-item analysis or on the "bottom line" only. The payment timing focus for the budget review method generally is prospective, and only becomes retrospective if a "settling up" process takes place at the end of the year—or if the base year eventually reflects the actual costs of a prior "prospective" year.

Payment Source

The payment source is the payor. Five major sources are to be considered in analyzing reimbursement systems: (1) self-pay, (2) Blue Cross, (3) commercial insurers, (4) Medicare, and (5) Medicaid.

Self-Pay. The self-pay source refers to the patient who is not covered by a third-party payor, and, therefore, pays his or her own hospital bill. The payment setting method is charges, and the payment timing focus is prospective. In general, only a small percentage of a hospital's revenue (but a large portion of its bad debt) comes from this source.

Blue Cross. Blue Cross is a nonprofit insurer founded by hospital groups during the Great Depression. The Baylor Plan, founded by Dr. Justin Ford Kimball in 1929, is considered the "Father of Blue Cross."[16] A close association between Blue Cross and the founding hospitals continued until 1972, when Blue Cross became a more independent organization. There are currently over 70 Blue Cross plans in operation in the United States. Each plan is a separate entity and determines its own method for reimbursing providers.

Because each plan is able to determine its own methodology for reimbursing providers, all four payment methods are used by various plans, with both prospective and retrospective timing foci. The majority of plans use either cost, charges, or a combination of the two (i.e., the lower of cost or charges), although formulas and budget review methods are on the increase.

---

[15]Dowling, "Prospective Rate Setting."

[16]S. A. Law, *Blue Cross: What Went Wrong?*, 2d ed. (New Haven, Conn.: Yale University Press, 1976).

Commercial Insurers. Commercial insurers are for-profit, private insurance companies that most often reimburse on the basis of charges up to the limit of their liability as outlined in a subscriber's contract. The contract is only between the insurer and the subscriber. Payment is made either to the hospital (if the benefits have been assigned by the subscriber to the hospital) or directly to the subscriber. The subscriber is responsible for the total charge (if assignment is not made) or for the difference between the benefits allowed under his or her contract and the hospital's charges (if there is assignment).

Medicare. The Medicare program is funded and administered by the federal government and is designed to meet the health care needs of the aged (over 65), of certain disabled individuals, and of individuals with chronic renal disease. Each state selects an intermediary, which handles the processing and payment of claims. Blue Cross frequently is the intermediary chosen, although commercial insurers are used in some states. The level of reimbursement for Medicare is based on "reasonable" costs, and the timing focus is retrospective.[17]

Medicaid. Medicaid is a publicly sponsored program designed to provide medical care for the indigent, disabled, and elderly (supplementing Medicare coverage when necessary). Historically, funds for reimbursement have been supplied by the federal and state governments in varying amounts, ranging from 20 to 50 percent state participation, based on a per capital income formula. Each state determines both the services which will be provided and the individuals who will be eligible (subject to minimum federal guidelines), as well as the reimbursement rates for those services. The federal guidelines, as outlined by the staff of the Senate Finance Committee, give substantial latitude to the states, although each state's definitions of "eligibility" and "reasonable costs" are subject to the approval of the Secretary of HHS.[18]

Since each state's plan is unique, it is not possible to describe all Medicaid plans within the limits of this appendix. It should be noted, however, that providers generally bill Medicaid and are reimbursed on the basis of these statements. Reimbursement for services rendered under Medicaid frequently is delayed many months, with the delays compounded by retroactive changes in eligible services and by claim denials.

---

[17]The federal government has granted Medicare waivers to a few states. These states have changed cost definitions and have initiated prospective reimbursement for Medicare.

[18]Staff of Senate Finance Committee, 91st Congress, 1st Session, Report: Medicare and Medicaid: Problems, *Issues and Alternatives* 46 (1970).

SUMMARY

The last three reimbursement system components, which have been discussed above—the payment timing focus, the payment setting method, and the payment source—are clearly highly interrelated. The nature of the relationship among the three can be viewed most clearly in terms of Figure 4A–1.

Although Figure 4A–1 shows a variety of possible combinations, it should be noted that not all combinations are currently in use. Specifically, (1) the retrospective-charge Medicare branch, (2) the prospective-formula Medicaid branch, and (3) the prospective-charge Medicaid branches are not in use at present.

Looked at somewhat more broadly, the total amount paid by a given source to a given organizational unit is determined by a combination of (1) the payment unit, (2) the coverage, (3) the payment timing focus, (4) the payment setting method, and (5) the quantity of care provided (or the number of enrollees, and so on). Further, however, the interactive effect of all nine components will determine whether and to what extent a reimbursement system achieves its objectives.

FIGURE 4A–1 _____

Relationships among Payment Timing Focus, Payment Setting Method, and Payment Source

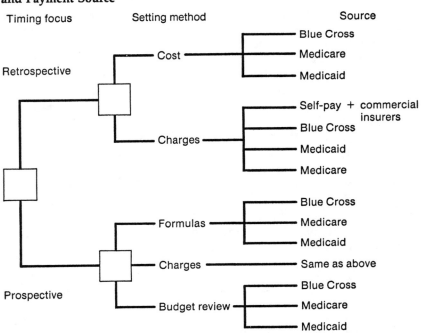

5

Differential Cost Accounting

One of the most significant principles of cost accounting is the notion that "different costs are used for different purposes." The full cost accounting principles discussed in Chapter 4, while valuable for such activities as pricing and reimbursement, have some important limitations. Specifically, they are not appropriate for several types of decisions that frequently are made in health care and other organizations, such as (1) add or drop a product or service, (2) contract out for services, (3) accept or reject a special request (e.g., by a health maintenance organization (HMO) to use a certain amount of a hospital's capacity), or (4) to sell obsolete supplies or equipment. For these types of decisions, the appropriate information is *differential costs*.

The key question asked in the context of the above types of situations is, "How will costs (and revenues) change under the new set of circumstances?" (In essence, "What costs and revenues will be different?") In both the add/drop and contract-out decisions, for example, certain costs will be eliminated and other costs will be incurred. In the special request or obsolete asset situations, certain revenues will be received; but costs will not change in accordance with the indications of a full cost analysis. As this chapter explains, to utilize full cost information as a basis for deciding which costs will change or how costs will change under alternative sets of circumstances can be extremely misleading, and, indeed, can lead to decisions which will be more, rather than less, costly for the organization.

The process of differential cost analysis in health care organizations varies, depending on the type of organization in which the analysis is taking place. Organizations that are paid according to charges, or which operate with an essentially fixed budget (such as health maintenance organizations, Veterans Administration hospitals, Public Health hospitals, and so on), typically will undertake the same sort of differential cost analysis that is used in for-profit organizations. Health care organizations that have a percentage of their revenue from cost-based reimbursement will find it necessary to undertake a different form of differential cost analysis, however. To illustrate the differences as clearly as possible, this chapter first addresses the nature of costs, followed by a discussion of the normal process of differential cost analysis as performed in for-profit organizations, including illustrations of the concepts of "contribution" and "sunk costs." Once terms and concepts have been defined, the subject of breakeven analysis, a special form of differential cost analysis, can be taken up. Finally, the more complex process of differential cost analysis under cost-based reimbursement is discussed.[1]

THE NATURE OF COSTS

Fundamental to any discussion of differential cost analysis is the question of cost behavior. Readers will recall that Chapter 4 identified the distinction between direct and indirect costs. Differential cost analysis relies on a different view of costs, dividing them between fixed and variable. Although the analysis of differential costs would be simplified if, as occasionally is assumed, all indirect costs were fixed and all direct costs were variable, this unfortunately is not always the case. Figure 5–1 contains an illustration of four different cost types and their fixed/variable and direct/indirect distinctions.

In analyzing costs for purposes of differential cost analysis, it is preferable to utilize the fixed/variable distinction, since this lets us see more clearly how a change in the volume of activity of a given cost center will affect cost behavior. In fact, it is useful to include the refinement of *semi*-fixed costs as well. A discussion of each cost type follows.

Fixed costs can be defined as those costs that remain at the same level regardless of the number of units of service delivered. While

---

[1] Some forms of differential analysis do not look at cost behavior in relation to changes in volume, but these situations are infrequent. Thus, the discussion in this chapter will focus exclusively on cost-volume relationships.

FIGURE 5–1

Cost Examples: Fixed/Variable versus Direct/Indirect

	Fixed	Variable
Direct	Supervisor's salary in dialysis unit.	Saline solution in dialysis unit.
Indirect	Portion of supervisor's salary in housekeeping department that is allocated to the dialysis unit.	Cleaning solutions in housekeeping department that are allocated to dialysis unit.

no costs are fixed if the time period is long enough, the "relevant range" for fixed costs (i.e., the span of units over which they remain unchanged), or the time period within which they are considered, is generally quite large, so they can be viewed graphically as follows:

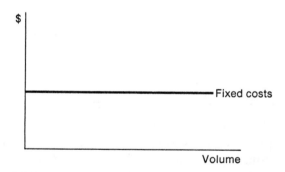

A good example of a fixed cost in most organizations is rent. Regardless of the number of patient days of care, patient visits, and the like, the amount of rent the organization pays will remain the same.

Semi-fixed costs are similar to fixed costs in nature, except they have a much narrower relevant range. As such, they do not change in a smooth fashion, but are usually added in "lumps." The result is that, graphically, they take on the form of a step function as shown on the following page.

A good example of semi-fixed costs in most organizations is supervision. As the number of nurses, social workers, and the like increases, supervisory personnel must be added. Since it is difficult for most organizations to add part-time supervisory help, the cost function for the supervisor will behave in a semi-fixed fashion.

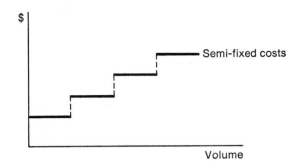

Volume

Variable costs are those costs that behave in a roughly linear fashion in accordance with changes in volume. The principle is that, as volume increases, total variable costs will increase in some constant proportion. The result is a sloped line, the increase of which is determined by the amount of variable costs associated with each unit of output, as follows:

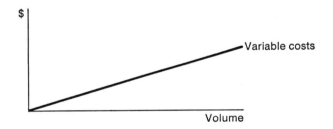

Volume

An example of variable costs is medical supplies and pharmaceuticals. Some organizations will have relatively high variable costs per unit, resulting in a line that slopes upward quite steeply; while other organizations have variable costs that are relatively low for each unit of output, so the variable-cost line slopes upward more slowly.

Example: The Hawthorne Community Health Center delivers 2,000 patient visits each month. At this level of care it incurs the following costs:

Provider personnel	$11,000
Supervisory personnel	3,000
Medical supplies	4,000
Pharmaceuticals	3,000
Administrative supplies	2,000
Utilities	1,000
Rent	3,000
Other costs	4,000
Total	$31,000

The administration estimates that medical supplies and pharmaceuticals are variable costs, and that rent, utilities, and "other costs" are fixed as long as the number of patient visits does not exceed 10,000. Administrative supplies will increase to $3,000 when the number of patient visits reaches 5,000, and will go up to $4,000 when patient visits increase to 10,000. The five provider personnel can each deliver 20 patient visits a day, or 400 a month. Ideally, one supervisor is needed for each five providers, but a new supervisor will not be hired until the number of providers reaches eight. What will the organization's costs be at 5,000 patient visits? At 10,000 patient visits?

Analysis: Medical supplies and pharmaceuticals are variable costs, which increase at a rate of $3.50 per visit [(4,000 + 3,000) ÷ 2,000]. Provider personnel are *essentially* variable, as well, although we would probably "stretch" our current providers up to, say, 25 visits a day before hiring a new provider. But, for all intents and purposes, a provider can deliver 400 visits a month. Therefore, since our current providers are fully utilized, the provider cost will be $5.50 a visit (11,000 ÷ 2,000).

Both administrative supplies and supervisory personnel costs are semi-fixed. The behavior of administrative supplies has been described above. Supervisory personnel cost behavior is somewhat more complicated. At 5,000 patient visits per month, we will need 12 providers (5,000 ÷ 400 = 12.5), and at 10,000 patient visits, 25 providers (10,000 ÷ 400). With 12 providers we will need two supervisors, at a monthly cost of $6,000 ($3,000 × 2), and, at 25 providers, we will need 5 supervisors (we could "get along" with four) at a monthly cost of $15,000.

Summary

	2,000 Visits	5,000 Visits	10,000 Visits	Type of cost
Provider personnel	$11,000	$27,500	$55,000	Variable $5.50/visit
Supervisory personnel	3,000	6,000	15,000	Semi-fixed
Medical supplies and pharmaceuticals	7,000	17,500	35,000	Variable $3.50/visit
Administrative supplies	2,000	3,000	4,000	Semi-fixed
Utilities	1,000	1,000	1,000	Fixed
Rent	3,000	3,000	3,000	Fixed
Other costs	4,000	4,000	4,000	Fixed
Total	$31,000	$62,000	$117,000	
Cost per visit	$15.50	$12.40	$11.70	

The fact that the per-visit cost declines, as the number of visits increases, is indicative that all costs do not increase proportionate to volume. In fact, as indicated in the last column, costs behave as follows:

Cost Type

Variable:	Provider personnel (PP)	$5.50/visit
	Medical supplies and pharmaceuticals (MSP)	$3.50/visit
Semi-fixed:	Supervisory personnel (SP)	1 supervisor for every 5 providers Up to 8 providers for 1 supervisor
	Administrative supplies (AS)	$2,000 at 2,000 to 4,999 patient visits $3,000 at 5,000 to 9,999 patient visits $4,000 at 10,000 patient visits
Fixed:	Utilities (U)	$1,000 at 2,000 to 10,000 patient visits
	Rent (R)	$3,000 at 2,000 to 10,000 patient visits
	Other costs (OC)	$4,000 at 2,000 to 10,000 patient visits

Graphically, the costs behave as shown in Figure 5–2.

Note that the variable-cost line for medical supplies and pharmaceuticals slopes upward more slowly than that for provider personnel ($3.50 per visit versus $5.50 per visit) and that the "jump" in semi-fixed costs takes place at different visit levels for different categories of costs. For example, in the case of the SP (supervisory personnel) line, one supervisor is hired for every five providers,

FIGURE 5–2

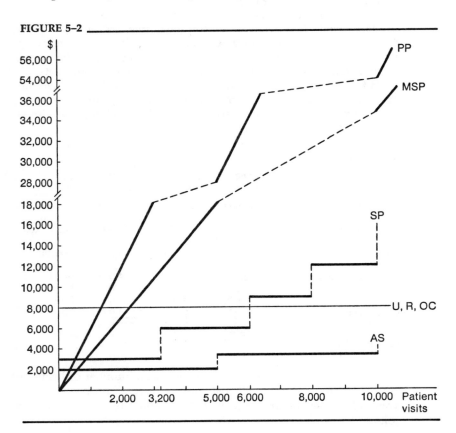

but a supervisor can cover up to eight providers before another supervisor is hired. Therefore:

$$5 \text{ providers } = 2,000 \text{ visits } = 1 \text{ supervisor}$$
$$8 \text{ providers } = 3,200 \text{ visits } = 2 \text{ supervisors}$$
$$15 \text{ providers } = 6,000 \text{ visits } = 3 \text{ supervisors}$$
$$20 \text{ providers } = 8,000 \text{ visits } = 4 \text{ supervisors}$$
$$25 \text{ providers } = 10,000 \text{ visits } = 5 \text{ supervisors}$$

Thus, for this cost item the jumps take place at visit levels of 2,000; 3,200; 6,000; 8,000; and 10,000.

THE DIFFERENTIAL COST CONCEPT

With an understanding of cost behavior according to the fixed, semi-fixed, or variable nature of costs, we are in a position to undertake differential cost analysis. Effectively, differential cost analysis attempts to identify the behavior of an organization's costs under different sets of strategic assumptions, relating cost behavior principally to the type of differential decision.

Example: Clearwater Ambulance Service operates a fleet of two ambulances. It charges 50 cents a mile for each "service mile" driven. Ambulance 1 drives 60,000 service miles a year; Ambulance 2 drives 30,000 service miles a year. The variable cost per mile for each ambulance is 20 cents. The organization's revenues and costs are as follows:

Item	Ambulance 1		Ambulance 2		Total
Revenue	.50 × 60,000 = $30,000		.50 × 30,000 = $15,000		$45,000
Expenses:					
Variable costs	.20 × 60,000 =	12,000	.20 × 30,000 =	6,000	18,000
Drivers		5,000		5,000	10,000
Indirect costs (rent and administration)		10,000		5,000	15,000
Total		27,000		16,000	43,000
Profit (loss)		$ 3,000		$(1,000)	$ 2,000

Question: Would the profitability of Clearwater Ambulance Service be improved if Ambulance 2, which is losing money, were discontinued?

Analysis: An answer to the above question must be structured in terms of differential costs. The question is not whether Ambulance 2 is losing money on a *full cost* basis, but rather the nature of its differential costs and revenues; that is, what revenues and costs would be eliminated if Ambulance 2 were discontinued? and what revenues and costs would remain? Although the data are perhaps not as good as we would like, it does appear that, if we eliminate Ambulance 2, we discontinue its revenue and its variable costs and the fixed cost of the driver. From all indications, however, the rent and administrative costs will continue (i.e., they are nondifferential). The result is a shift from a profit of $2,000 to a loss of $2,000— as the analysis below indicates:

	Ambulance 1
Revenue	$.50 \times 60,000 = \$30,000$
Expenses:	
Variable costs	$.20 \times 60,000 = $ 12,000
Driver	5,000
Indirect costs	
(rent and administration)	15,000
Total	$32,000
Profit (loss)	$ (2,000)

This example and its accompanying analysis illustrates several important principles. First, the kind of information available from most full cost accounting systems can produce highly misleading results if used for differential cost decisions, in this instance an add/drop decision. In the Clearwater case, the full cost data would seem to indicate that we could increase profits by dropping Ambulance 2; but this clearly was not the case.

Second, although initially counterintuitive, it is important to recognize that differential costs can include *both* fixed *and* variable costs. In the above example, the driver generally would be considered a fixed cost of Ambulance 2, and yet the elimination of Ambulance 2 eliminates this fixed cost. The key point here is that, as long as we operate the ambulance, we have the fixed cost of the driver's salary; it does not fluctuate in accordance with the number of miles driven, within the relevant range. But, when we eliminate the ambulance, we also eliminate this cost in its entirety; thus, it is differential in terms of the decision we are analyzing.

A third principle is that differential cost analysis invariably requires *assumptions*. Since we do not have perfect knowledge of the future, we must make some guesses about how costs will behave. In this example, there are two important assumptions: (1) the number of miles driven by Ambulance 1 will not increase with the elimination of Ambulance 2, and (2) we will not be able to reduce or eliminate any indirect costs with the elimination of Ambulance 2. Changes in these assumptions clearly would have an impact on the new profit (loss) figure, and might, in fact, actually make it profitable to eliminate Ambulance 2. It is important, therefore, in undertaking any form of differential cost analysis both to clarify the assumptions one is making and to explore how changes in these assumptions would affect the conclusions of the analysis. This latter activity generally is called sensitivity analysis.

The final principle illustrated by this example is that of the importance of structuring information for purposes of decision making. One way of structuring the information is the table shown in the *Analysis* section above. Another way of structuring differential cost information is in terms of *contribution*.

THE CONCEPT OF CONTRIBUTION

As the above example indicated, a key question in differential cost analysis is the behavior of indirect or overhead costs. In the example, a key assumption was that indirect costs (rent and administration) for the ambulance service would not be reduced if the second ambulance were eliminated. As indicated above, and as will be discussed in greater detail later in the chapter, an assumption of this sort is not necessarily valid under all sets of circumstances. Nevertheless, in most instances, an analysis of differential costs is most easily performed when the direct fixed and variable costs of the particular activity itself are analyzed separately from the indirect costs of the organization. Such an analysis can be structured in terms of the *contribution* of the particular product or service to the organization's indirect costs. By "contribution" we mean the amount that each program in an organization contributes to the recovery of indirect costs. More specifically, a program (an ambulance in this case) provides some revenues and incurs some direct costs. The difference between the revenue provided and the direct costs (both fixed and variable) is the *contribution* of that program to the organization's indirect costs.

Returning to the above example, the cost data for the ambulance service could be structured in the following way:

Item	Ambulance 1	Ambulance 2	Total
Revenue	$30,000	$15,000	$45,000
Variable costs	12,000	6,000	18,000
Margin (for fixed and indirect costs)	18,000	9,000	27,000
Fixed costs (drivers)	5,000	5,000	10,000
Contribution (to indirect costs)	13,000	4,000	17,000
Indirect costs	10,000	5,000	15,000
Profit (loss)	$ 3,000	$(1,000)	$ 2,000

What this example indicates is that both Ambulance 1 and Ambulance 2 are *contributing* to the coverage of indirect costs. Consequently, an elimination of either ambulance will reduce the total contribution to indirect costs and, thus, either reduce the organization's profit or increase its loss. In fact, it was the $4,000 that Ambulance 2 was contributing that led to the change from a $2,000 profit to a $2,000 loss.

THE CONCEPT OF SUNK COSTS

One of the most difficult aspects of differential cost analysis concerns the concept of sunk costs. A differential cost analysis always looks toward the future, rather than the past, so our focus is on how costs will be affected in the future. Since full cost analyses typically rely on historical data, we have still another reason why such costs are inappropriate for differential cost analysis. Nevertheless, even when we confine our analytical effort to the future, we frequently are plagued by history, particularly when it presents itself in the form of sunk costs.

The term *sunk costs* is used to refer to those expenditures which have been made in the past, which appear on a full cost report, but which, because they have already been incurred and the decision cannot be changed, are inappropriate for future considerations. Consequently, they should not be incorporated into a differential cost analysis, which is concerned only with the future. In a very real sense they are costs which are *sunk*. The classic example of a sunk cost is depreciation which, as the reader will recall from Chapter 1, is an accounting technique used to spread the costs of an asset over its useful life. Thus, although depreciation will appear on a full cost report, it is inappropriate for differential cost analysis, since it will not change regardless of the alternative chosen for the future.

> *Example:* Assume we have a machine for which the book value is 4,000 and that we are depreciating at a rate of $1,000 per year. Assume also that our surplus before depreciation is $10,000 and that we are faced with an opportunity to subcontract all the work being done on the machine. Is the book value of the machine a relevant cost to consider?
>
> *Analysis:* The answer is no, since the cost is the same regardless of whether we accept the subcontractor's offer or not. If we do accept the offer and throw the machine out (i.e., receiving nothing for it), we would no longer have any depreciation on it, and our income

statements for the next four years would be something like the following:

	Year				Total
	1	**2**	**3**	**4**	
Surplus before depreciation	$10,000	$10,000	$10,000	$10,000	$40,000
Depreciation	0	0	0	0	0
Surplus before extraordinary gains (losses)	10,000	10,000	10,000	10,000	40,000
Loss on sale of machine	4,000	0	0	0	0
Net surplus	$ 6,000	$10,000	$10,000	$10,000	$36,000

If we reject the offer, we would have an entry, such as the following, for each of the four years of the remaining life of the machine:

	Year				Total
	1	**2**	**3**	**4**	
Surplus before depreciation	$10,000	$10,000	$10,000	$10,000	$40,000
Depreciation	1,000	1,000	1,000	1,000	4,000
Surplus before extraordinary gains (losses)	9,000	9,000	9,000	9,000	36,000
Loss on sale of machine	0	0	0	0	0
Net surplus	$ 9,000	$ 9,000	$ 9,000	$ 9,000	$36,000

In either case, for the four-year period, net surplus is $36,000 and the machine expense is $4,000. The only difference is that, in the first alternative, we incur the expense in a single year, whereas in the second alternative the expense is spread over four years.[2]

If, however, we can sell the machine today for, say, $1,500, then that $1,500 "salvage value" *is* a differential item; it is cash that will be received if the subcontractor's offer is accepted that would not have been received otherwise. Our income statements would then look as shown on the top of the next page.

The fact that we have received something for the machine changes the impact of the transaction on net surplus, but it does

---

[2]In a for-profit context, we would consider the time value of the cash generated from an earlier reduction in income taxes in the first alternative, and this *would be* a differential item.

	Year				
	1	**2**	**3**	**4**	**Total**
Surplus before depreciation	$10,000	$10,000	$10,000	$10,000	$40,000
Depreciation	0	0	0	0	0
Surplus before extraordinary gains (losses)	10,000	10,000	10,000	10,000	40,000
Loss on sale of machine (1,500 − 4,000)	2,500	0	0	0	2,500
Net surplus	$ 7,500	$10,000	$10,000	$10,000	$37,500

not change the fact that we reduced the value of the machine in our accounts by $4,000. This is the sunk cost.

The above example has some important implications for differential cost analysis: Specifically, in analyzing the make/buy decision (i.e., whether to accept the subcontractor's offer in this case), the $4,000 is not a relevant item inasmuch as it would be the same whatever we do. The $1,500 we receive for the machine is a relevant item, however, since it occurs only if we accept the subcontractor's offer.[3]

Conceptually, then, the $1,500 might be thought of as the portion of the machine cost that is recovered if we accept the subcontractor's offer. Thus, in assessing the offer, we look at both the costs to be avoided and the costs which would be incurred if the work is subcontracted, as well as any revenue received as a result of an action, such as selling the piece of equipment. In the category of avoided costs, we would include all variable costs, including such items as variable labor and supplies. In the category of revenue, the $1,500 scrap value of the machine is relevant, since it is differential; it effectively serves to reduce the cost of the contract.

In sum, the amount for which we can sell the machine becomes a relevant differential cost in evaluating the subcontractor's offer, but the *book value of the machine* (i.e., the $4,000), since it is *sunk*, is *not* a relevant consideration. This same principle can be applied to any other asset we would dispose of if we accept a subcontractor's offer. Specifically, in all cases the book value of the asset is a sunk cost and is irrelevant; but the scrap value (i.e., the revenue from its sale) is a differential item and, therefore, *is* relevant. Of course, it is a one-time item, as contrasted with most other items in a differential analysis, which are ongoing.

---

[3]Assuming we would not dispose of the machine *unless* we accepted the offer.

BREAKEVEN ANALYSIS

One important technique used in differential cost situations is that of breakeven analysis. The intent of breakeven analysis is to determine the volume of activity at which the total revenue for an organization will equal its total costs. A breakeven analysis thus begins with the fundamental equation:

Total revenue (TR) = Total costs (TC)

Total revenue for many activities is quite easy to calculate. If we assume that an organization's charge per unit or price is represented by the letter p and its volume by the letter x, then, total revenue is price times volume, or:

TR = px

Total costs, however, are somewhat more complicated. Breakeven analysis requires a recognition of the previously discussed three types of cost behaviors in an organization: fixed, semi-fixed, and variable. Let us begin with the simplest of cases, in which there are no semi-fixed costs. In this instance, the formula would be quite simple:

Total revenue = Fixed costs + Variable costs

Fixed costs generally are represented by the letter a and variable costs *per unit* by the letter b. Thus, total variable costs can be represented by the term bx where, as before, x represents volume. The resulting breakeven formula can be shown as follows:

px = $a + bx$

Graphically we can represent the formula as shown below. Point x_1 where $px = a + bx$ is, therefore, the breakeven volume (i.e., it is the point at which total revenue, px, equals total costs, $a + bx$). Thus, if we know price, fixed costs, and variable costs per unit, we can solve the formula algebraically for x, which would be our breakeven volume.

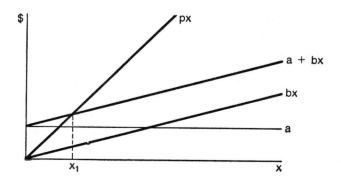

Example: The Littleton Home Health Agency has fixed costs of $10,000, variable costs per visit of $18, and it charges $38 per visit. What is its breakeven volume (number of visits)?

Analysis:

$$px = a + bx$$
$$38x = 10,000 + 18x$$
$$20x = 10,000$$
$$x = 500$$

Breakeven, thus, would be 500 visits. To confirm:

Revenue:	$38 (500) =	$19,000
Costs:		
Variable:	$18 (500) =	9,000
Fixed:		10,000
Total		$19,000

The introduction of semi-fixed costs is conceptually more difficult than it might first appear. Ideally, we would like to be able to assume that, for any given relevant range, we could simply add together the semi-fixed costs and the fixed costs to give us the total applicable fixed costs. We then could utilize the formula as described above. Unfortunately, the process is not quite that simple—as the following example illustrates.

Example: In addition to the $10,000 in fixed costs stipulated in the previous example, Littleton also has supervisory costs, which behave as follows:

Visits	Costs
0– 500	$ 5,000
501–1,000	10,000
1,001–1,500	15,000
1,501–2,000	20,000

If we attempt to solve the breakeven formula at the first level of fixed costs, we have the following equation:

$$38x = 10,000 + 5,000 + 18x$$
$$20x = 15,000$$
$$x = 750$$

The problem, of course, is that, while the breakeven volume is 750 visits, the relevant range for the semi-fixed costs was only 0–500 visits. Thus, the solution is unacceptable and we must move to the next step on the step function, which gives us the following equation:

$$38x = 10,000 + 10,000 + 18x$$
$$20x = 20,000$$
$$x = 1,000$$

This solution is within the relevant range for step 2 and, therefore, is acceptable.

The conclusion we must draw is that the incorporation of semi-fixed costs in the breakeven formula requires a trial-and-error process to reach the breakeven volume.

SUNK COSTS AND BREAKEVEN ANALYSIS

The fact that depreciation is a sunk cost does not necessarily mean that it or any other sunk cost should be excluded from *all* differential cost analyses. The decision whether to include it in a differential cost analysis will depend on the focus of the analysis. If, for example, one is looking at a breakeven situation, or at an analysis of contribution, and the focus is the continuation of a particular program or activity over some indefinite time period, it would be quite appropriate to include depreciation, since the continuation of the activity or program requires eventual replacement of the machines or other assets that are being depreciated. Thus, if the analysis is to show whether the program or activity is breaking even when all costs are considered, depreciation is a relevant cost to include.

However, if one is simply looking at whether a particular activity or program should be phased out immediately, because it is a clear "money loser," the appropriate question is whether the program is breaking even or making a positive contribution when *only* its out-of-pocket costs are considered. The question then becomes, "If we do away with the program, what costs and what revenues do we do away with?" Here, such sunk costs as depreciation are irrelevant, since they will not change if the program is discontinued. In effect, the expenditure that is represented by depreciation has already been made. Under this circumstance, depreciation is an irrelevant consideration and should not be included in the differential cost analysis.

Example: Lakeside hospital has a dialysis unit with 12 machines. Total depreciation on the machines is $120,000 per year. At present, the unit performs 10,000 procedures a year at a price of $140 per procedure. Fixed costs, excluding depreciation, are $830,000 per year. Variable costs are $55 per procedure. The administrator reasons that the unit should be discontinued, since it is losing $100,000 a year:

Revenues (10,000 × $140)		$1,400,000
Variable costs (10,000 × $55)	$550,000	
Depreciation	120,000	
Other fixed costs	830,000	
Total costs		1,500,000
Profit (loss)		$ (100,000)

Analysis: If the time perspective is a relatively long one, and if the "other fixed costs" are all associated with the dialysis unit, the administrator is correct that the unit is losing money. And unless strategic reasons dictate its continuation in the hospital, it should at least be evaluated against other activities, which might either lose less or produce a gain for the hospital.

If, however, the time perspective is a short one—in this case, one in which the current machines can continue to be used without the need for replacement—then the dialysis unit is making a positive contribution to the hospital, as follows:

Revenues		$1,400,000
Variable costs	$550,000	
Fixed costs (other than depreciation)	830,000	
Total out-of-pocket costs		1,380,000
Contribution to hospital overhead		$ 20,000

This situation arises because, as discussed, depreciation is a sunk cost—it already has been incurred and there is nothing we can do to change that fact—and, hence, is irrelevant for the decision to discontinue the dialysis unit in the short run.

THE DIFFERENTIAL CONCEPT UNDER COST-BASED REIMBURSEMENT

Recognizing that differential costs are the proper costs to use for add/drop, contract-out, special request, or obsolete asset decisions is sufficient to provide a focus for the analytical efforts involved in such decisions; but it by no means makes either the decisions themselves, or the analytical efforts which underlie them, easy. Indeed, as suggested above, a variety of strategic aspects to these decisions go beyond the financial analysis and create highly complex situations. Adding to this complexity in health care—more so than in most organizations—is the presence of cost-based reimbursement. The following example illustrates this complexity:

Example: Longwood Hospital is considering contracting out its laundry services with a private vendor. At present, the direct cost of the laundry department (all of which is differential) is $100,000, consisting of salaries, supplies, water, and electricity. There is no depreciation cost, since all equipment is fully depreciated. Eighty percent of the hospital's patients are covered by cost-based payors. A private firm has offered to contract with the hospital to do its laundry for $90,000 a year. The amount of laundry is expected to remain relatively constant over the next several years.

Analysis: Although it would first appear that the hospital can save a total of $10,000 by contracting out for laundry, this is not the case. Instead, since the hospital's costs are reduced by $10,000, those third-party payors who pay costs will reduce their payments, accordingly. The result is that, while the hospital's costs fall by $10,000, its revenue falls by $8,000 ($10,000 × .8). Thus, the net savings to the hospital is only $2,000, a relatively small amount, given the uncertainty of the projections and the strategic considerations.[4]

This analysis, although oversimplified, nevertheless illustrates an important concept about differential cost analysis in a setting in which an institution's revenues come from payors who pay on a cost basis. Specifically, any projected savings to the institution from a contract-out or add/drop decision must be reduced by the percent of cost-based payors to arrive at the savings to the institution itself. Or, alternatively, the institution's savings equal the projected savings multiplied by the percent of charge-based payors. In the above example, the hospital's savings = $10,000 × .2 = $2,000.

Further complexities are introduced into the differential cost analysis when indirect costs are associated with a particular effort for which the differential analysis is to be made. This complexity can be viewed along three important dimensions. First, as indicated in Chapter 4, the bases of allocation used in the full cost accounting effort do not necessarily reflect actual use by revenue-producing or service cost centers. Thus, if the costs of a particular revenue-producing cost center are reduced, one result may be that the indirect costs *allocated* to that center will be reduced; but it is quite likely that these costs will be allocated to other cost centers and not necessarily eliminated for the institution as a whole. Correspondingly, while some indirect costs may actually be re-

---

[4]See the appendix to Chapter 4 for a discussion of cost-based reimbursement. Obviously, there would be a $10,000 savings to the *health care system* as a result of contracting out the laundry service; but the bulk of the savings ($8,000) would accrue to the third-party payors, not to the hospital.

duced as a result of reduced activity in a given revenue-producing cost center, the reduction may not accrue to that revenue center, since the allocation basis may not change.

A good example of the first instance is administration and general (A&G). A reduction of staff in a given revenue center will lead to a reduction in total salaries in the center. If A&G costs are allocated according to salary dollars, there will be a reduction in the amount of A&G allocated to the center. It is highly unlikely, however, there will be any reduction in the staff or in other costs associated with the A&G service cost center. Thus, total indirect costs will not be reduced, but only be redistributed to other cost centers.

An example of the second instance is housekeeping. While a reduction in effort in a given revenue-producing cost center may reduce the need for housekeeping services, the cost report, which allocates housekeeping on a square-footage basis, will not indicate this reduction unless the space utilized by the revenue center also is reduced. While costs allocated to the revenue center will fall, as a result of the lower amount of housekeeping costs overall, the *indicated* reduction on the full cost report will be much less than the *real* reduction that took place.

The second dimension of complexity arises because of the nature of the stepdown. Since each service cost center is allocated to all remaining cost centers as one moves down the steps in the stepdown, those service centers farthest down in the report will have portions of the cost centers above them included in their totals. That is, the total to be allocated from each service center includes both its direct costs and the costs that have been allocated to it from previous "steps" in the stepdown. For example, if social service is far down on the list, the total social service costs allocated to a particular revenue center will have a significant allocated component (e.g., administration, housekeeping, laundry and linen, and so on). While it may be possible to reduce the use of social workers in a revenue center by reducing the number of patients treated, the full impact of that reduction on the costs in the social services cost center will be overstated if one uses the fully allocated social service totals (including both direct *and* previously allocated costs), since the allocated component contains costs from a variety of other cost centers that may not be affected at all by the reduction in patient volume.

Finally, to the extent that a cost reduction in a given revenue center results in real cost reductions in some of the service cost centers, fewer dollars will be allocated to other revenue-producing cost centers. This will lower the cost of those cost centers and, in accordance with the process of cost-based reimbursement discussed above, will result in a reduction in their reimbursement from cost-based payors. Thus, once again, a cost-cutting effort is accompanied by a reduction in revenue.

Recognizing these complexities and incorporating them into analytic efforts is one of the most challenging aspects of differential cost accounting in health care. Determining which costs are indeed differential, the extent of their differential nature, and the impact of cost-based reimbursement on an institution's revenue are all extremely difficult, particularly when a cost report (step-down) is the principal source of information. There are no easy answers to this dilemma, just a great deal of hard work.

MANAGERIAL CHECKLIST

1. What kinds of differential cost decisions (add/drop a service, contract-out, accept or reject a special request, or sell obsolete supplies or equipment) have we made recently? What were the cost analyses that underlay those decisions? Did they adequately consider the true differential nature of our costs, or were they based on a full cost report?

2. What is the contribution of each program/department to the institution's indirect costs? Why are those programs that have a negative contribution being continued (i.e., are there good strategic reasons)?

3. What is the breakeven volume in each of our programs/departments? Has this analysis given adequate consideration to the behavior of the semi-fixed costs?

Bibliography

Anthony, R. N., and G. A. Welsch. *Fundamentals of Management Accounting.* Homewood, Ill.: Richard D. Irwin, 1981.

Bennington, J. L., et al. *Management and Cost Control Techniques for the Clinical Laboratory.* Baltimore: University Park Press, 1978.

Demone, H., and Z. Z. Gibelman, eds. *Purchasing Human Services: Policies, Programs and Procedures.* New York: Human Sciences Press. Forthcoming.

Horngren, C. T. *Introduction to Management Accounting.* Englewood Cliffs, N.J.: Prentice-Hall, 1978.

Hospital Research and Educational Trust. *The Nature of Hospital Costs: Three Studies.* Chicago: The Hospital Research and Educational Trust, 1976.

Young, D. W., "Contracting Out of Services: A Researcher's Perspective." In *Human Services Management: Priorities for Research,* eds. M. J. Murphy and T. Glynn. Washington, D. C.: International City Management Association, 1978.

6

Management Control Systems[1]

As previous chapters have described, health care institutions prepare a variety of routine information, such as financial statements and full cost reports for use by outsiders, and frequently undertake ad hoc analyses of cost data—usually of a differential nature—for internal use by managers in making alternative-choice decisions. While the preparation of both routine reports and ad hoc analyses are necessary management activities to assure the viability of the organization, a third kind of information is necessary to assist in the ongoing management of the organization. This is the information that is generated and provided to managers via the management control system.

Although management control systems generally are thought of only in terms of the information they provide, they include much more. Indeed, as with any system, a management control system consists of both structure and process, analogous to anatomy and physiology in the human body's system. The purpose of this chapter is to look at management control systems from both a structure and process perspective. The chapter begins with a discussion of the relationship between full cost accounting and management control. Next, we look at the structural issues and decisions inherent in management control systems, followed by a consideration of process issues. Finally, the topic of budgeting is

---

[1]Portions of this chapter have been adapted from D. W. Young and R. B. Saltman, "Preventive Medicine for Hospital Costs," *Harvard Business Review*, January–February 1983.

discussed, not in its usual sense, but in terms of a variety of "misfits" that can exist between the budgetary system and an organization's various other management systems.

FULL COST ACCOUNTING AND MANAGEMENT CONTROL

The relationship between full cost accounting and management control systems rests in large part on the concept of resources. Whereas full cost accounting was concerned with the resources expended for a particular endeavor, management control is concerned with the question of who controls the use of those resources. The answer to this question can be translated into the concept of *responsibility* and, ultimately, into the establishment of a series of *responsibility centers*.

While it would be useful if the structure for accumulating full costs were also the responsibility structure (i.e., the structure for management control), this, unfortunately, is rarely the case. Consider, for example, the cost of a day of inpatient care. From a full cost accounting perspective, we would wish to add together the various resources which went into that day: room, board, nursing care, medications, and so on. From a management control perspective, we are concerned with the individuals who have control over those resources. For example, physicians who order medications, who decide on the level of nursing care, order tests and procedures, and who determine a discharge date carry a major *responsibility* for the use of resources. A nursing director or supervisor who determines the efficiency and staffing patterns of nurses carries some additional responsibility. The director of housekeeping who is responsible for the efficiency and quality of the cleaning effort also bears some responsibility. And so on.

Conceptually, we can think of management control in terms of a series of *cost-influencing* factors or variables, coupled with the individual or individuals who control them. These factors were discussed briefly in Chapter 4 in the context of full cost accounting, but they now can be given a management control focus. To do so, we must concern ourselves with the issue of *controllability*.

Table 4-2 in Chapter 4 distinguished among five cost-influencing variables: case mix, volume, resources per case, efficiency, and price. Table 6-1 assesses each of these variables in terms of the individual or individuals who exercise control over it. In each instance the controllability is indicated in terms of "much," "some," "little," or "none." As this table indicates, the first variable, case mix, is particularly complex, since it is influenced by a

TABLE 6–1 _____

Controlling Forces over Cost-Influencing Variables

Cost-influencing variable	Controlling force			
	Environment	Physicians	Administrators	Third-party payors
1. Case mix	Much	Some	Little	Little
2. Number of cases	Much	Some	Some	Little
3. Resources per case (mode of treatment)	None	Much	Little	Little
4. Input unit price	Some	None	Some	Little
5. Input efficiency	Little	Little	Much	Little

Source: D. W. Young and R. B. Saltman, "Preventive Medicine for Hospital Costs," *Harvard Business Review*, January–February 1983.

wide variety of demographic, epidemiological, and institutional factors. Physicians, of course, exercise some short-range influence over elective admissions through their patterns of patient referral—an impact which is particularly evident in the mix of cases found in tertiary care institutions, and, to a lesser degree, in the different hospitals in a multi-hospital locale. Physicians also exert a substantial degree of long-term or "lagged" influence over the scope and nature of the services available at any given institution. Despite this degree of physician influence, however, it seems reasonable to conclude that, at least in the short run, case mix is determined primarily by epidemiological and demographic factors, which are external to the hospital, and, therefore, that no one inside the hospital ought to be held financially responsible for that mix. This removal of liability for case mix from a hospital's reimbursement schedule is, of course, a primary goal of case-mix-based reimbursement systems, such as the Diagnostic Related Group (DRG) System in New Jersey.

Second, the number of cases will also affect total costs. As Table 6–1 indicates, this variable is one which, at present, has shared responsibility. The sharing exists because third-party reimbursement systems do not distinguish between a hospital's variable costs, which are volume dependent, and its fixed costs, which are not. The result is that a hospital's per-diem rate includes both fixed and variable-cost components, thereby requiring the hospital to maintain its patient days at or above budgeted levels to fully recover its costs. Under a system that reimbursed fixed costs on a period basis, for example, or which utilized some other means that did not penalize an institution for volume reductions, this variable, like case mix, would be a result primarily of factors external to the hospital.

The third variable, inputs per case or modes of treatment, refers to the mix of hospital resources used to treat different cases, control of which rests almost exclusively within the province of the attending physician. The nature and number of laboratory tests, radiological procedures, and other ancillary services ordered for a patient with a particular admitting diagnosis, for example, is a matter of physician choice, as is the treatment mode selected for that diagnosis: medication therapy, surgery, level of nursing care, and so on. Additionally, a patient's length of stay is also determined, in most instances, by the attending physician. Therefore, since control over this third cost-influencing variable rests with the physician, an effective management control system would be one that assigned management control responsibility in this area to the physician.

Finally, input unit prices and efficiencies are categories comprised of costs generated by the actual production of ancillary and support services within the hospital. These costs include both the cost of labor, materials, and support services purchased from outside suppliers, as well as the efficiency with which these resources are utilized within the hospital. While it seems clear that efficiency is under the control of hospital administrators, input unit prices can be seen as a shared responsibility. In some instances, the administrator will have a fair amount of control (such as with salaries, savings from shared purchasing, and so on). In others, his or her control will be severly limited (such as with per-unit energy costs).

Although readers may not fully agree with this assessment, they should not lose sight of its fundamental conceptual thrust: the alignment of responsibility with controllability. Indeed, if the management control process is to be effective, managers must engage in an analysis of this sort and come to a controllability/responsibility alignment pattern that is reflective of their own organization's characteristics.

MANAGEMENT CONTROL AND THE ATTENDING PHYSICIAN

The above analysis of the relationship between full cost accounting and management control suggests that successful management control systems in both hospital and other health delivery settings are ones which incorporate attending physicians into the management control process. Of the five cost-influencing variables described in Table 6–1, two are not controllable at the hospital level; one has long been controlled by the administrator; and one is shared, between the administrator and forces outside the hospital. Indeed, there is some evidence to indicate that hospital administrators historically have tended to concentrate their cost-containment efforts on input prices, rather than upon the efficiency of input delivery, a situation due in part to a lack of widely accepted standards with which to measure delivery efficiency.[2]

As the above analysis of cost-influencing variables indicates, however, a key component of hospital costs, which *is* controllable at the hospital level but which, at present, is not subject to the direct managerial authority of the hospital administrator, is inputs per case. This variable remains the exclusive responsibility of the attending physician; and yet, in most hospitals, the medical staff makes only minimal contributions to cost-containment efforts. Thus, for hospital administrators designing management control systems, a key consideration is the role played by their attending physicians.

A primary difficulty in incorporating physicians into the management control system is finding a balance between the system's financial effectiveness and its acceptability to the physicians. If the system is so cost containment-oriented that it directly intervenes in the physician's patient-related decisions, many physicians quite likely will attempt to subvert the system as an affront to their medical autonomy. Alternatively, if the system is entirely voluntary at the individual physician level, it is likely to show little cost savings for the hospital.

The problem of physician acceptance is compounded by two additional (and interrelated) limitations on the hospital administrator's maneuverability. The first is the fee-for-service system of physician payment, which confers financial autonomy on attending physicians. The result is a substantial reduction in physician incentives to consider the cost implications of their patient-related decisions, as well as severe constraints on an administrator's ability to incorporate physicians into the hospital's management control system. The second limitation arises from the hospital's "power equilibrium,"[3] which historically has been controlled by

---

[2] See F. Allison, "Administrative Responses to Prospective Reimbursement," *Topics in Health Care Financing*, Winter 1976, pp. 97–111; and R. Vraciu and J. Griffith, "Cost Control Challenge for Hospitals," *Health Care Management Review*, Spring 1979, pp. 63–70.

[3] R. B. Saltman and D. W. Young, "The Hospital Power Equilibrium: An Alternative View of the Cost Containment Dilemma," *Journal of Health Politics, Policy and Law*, Fall 1981, pp. 391–418.

the hospital's medical staff, and seriously impedes an administrator's flexibility by forcing him or her to adopt a collegial, rather than a hierarchical, supervisory arrangement.

One potential response to the above dilemma is the development of a semiautonomous management control module for physicians, in which the emphasis is upon physician self-regulation as a collectively responsible group. Such a module could be built around inputs per case, which is the cost-influencing variable directly under physician control. To provide the management control system context in which this type of activity might take place, we must consider some of the characteristics of such systems. This can best be accomplished by using a dual perspective: structure and process.

THE MANAGEMENT CONTROL STRUCTURE

Structurally, a management control system can be thought of in terms of a network of responsibility centers, or clusters of individuals working together toward some common end, which presumably is consistent with the overall goals of the organization. Since responsibility centers of some sort exist in almost all organizations, the central question is not whether there *are* responsibility centers but rather whether they are structured in such a way that they facilitate the organization's ability to achieve its goals in an effective and efficient fashion. Examples abound of organizations in which responsibility centers have overlapping goals and objectives that frequently come into conflict, or in which some of the important goals and objectives of the organization have not been assigned to any particular responsibility center, or in which managers of particular responsibility centers are not given appropriate incentives to achieve the center's objectives.

In a for-profit context, responsibility centers generally are thought of in terms of four alternative financial choices:

Responsibility center	Responsible for:
Revenue center	Revenue from a particular type of activity
Expense center	Expense associated with a particular type of activity
Profit center	Revenues and expenses associated with a particular activity
Investment center	Revenues and expenses associated with particular activity, computed as a percentage of the assets used by the responsibility center

Since, in a for-profit context, questions of quality and service can be translated almost directly into revenue or expense, there is little need to move beyond the pure financial measure to assess the success of the responsibility centers. In this context, then, the key question becomes, "who controls what financial resources?" The choice of a responsibility center structure ultimately rests on top management's assessment of what resources can and should be controlled by individual managers.

The responsibility/controllability assessment is by no means an intuitively obvious exercise, and the resulting choices can produce a number of unintended consequences. A somewhat classic example of an unintended consequence is the profit center manager who suspends machine maintenance to increase his or her annual profit, thereby trading off the long-term success of the organization for short-term profits.

In a nonprofit context, responsibility center design questions become even more complex. Not only must we worry about the question of which financial resources a manager controls but we must also concern ourselves with managerial control over *programmatic* outcomes. Indeed, in most if not all nonprofit organizations, financial objectives are not objectives at all; rather, they are constraints on a manager's ability to achieve a desired set of programmatic outcomes. In essence, then, programmatic outcomes must be measured in some other way, and attained if possible in the context of the limited financial resources available.

While the above argument would appear to call for a responsibility center structure in which the organization's programs were defined as responsibility centers, this is not always the case. Frequently, a given center will have responsibility for several programs, and, by contrast, some responsibility centers may overlap several programs. For example, in many health care organizations, medical records is a responsibility center that serves all the organization's programs; but it generally is not thought of as a "program." Similarly, nursing is an example of an activity which might either stand alone as a responsibility center serving a variety of programs or departments in a hospital, or be viewed as an activity which can be divided among the organization's programs in such a way that each program manager's responsibility extends to the supervision and management of several nurses.

As the above discussion indicates, there is no one "right" answer to the problem of responsibility center design. Each organization is unique in terms of its strategy, its management philosophy, its programs, and a wide variety of other characteristics. The guiding principle is that of aligning controllability and responsibility, but no clear-cut prescriptions can be given.

THE MANAGEMENT CONTROL PROCESS

In almost all organizations the management control system includes a process, which is a series of events that are followed in an almost rhythmical fashion. Anthony and Welsch[4] have identified four steps in the process: programming, budgeting, measurement, and reporting. Although each step is an important ingredient in the overall process, for logistical purposes the four steps will not be discussed in the order given above. In part this is because some of these steps already have been discussed. Chapters 1 and 2, for example, looked at measurement and reporting from the perspective of financial accounting systems. Chapters 4 and 5 also addressed measurement issues, but from cost accounting and decision-making perspectives. Programming is a somewhat broader issue than just management control, and is thus reserved for Chapter 9, in which the management control system is put into an organizational perspective.

We are thus left with budgeting and reporting, two steps which logically follow one another, but which are too broad to be discussed in a single chapter. Consequently, the focus of the remainder of this chapter will be on budgeting. Chapter 7 looks principally at the questions of reporting, although it also examines measurement in a management control context, as contrasted with the financial and cost accounting contexts discussed previously.

BUDGETING

Although administrators in many health care organizations are coming to rely increasingly on the budget as a management tool, the budgetary process in many of these organizations has not kept pace. Health care managers whose organizations experience financial difficulties frequently find that the budgetary process has failed to play the role it might in assisting both them and the organization's health care professionals to attain important programmatic objectives while living within the organization's financial means. The explanation that the absence of a profit motive makes budgeting difficult is increasingly being seen as a poor excuse, and gradually attempts are being undertaken to make the budgetary process a more meaningful managerial tool.

---

[4]R. N. Anthony and G. A. Welsch, *Fundamentals of Management Accounting* (Homewood, Ill.: Richard D. Irwin, 1981).

One of the most basic problems in budgeting concerns the issue of what, in fact, the budget measures. Indeed, while the budget in health care organizations may be the *only* concerete measure of performance, it usually assesses only one side of a two-sided equation. The other side of the equation—the achievement of programmatic objectives—generally is not measured by the budget, and, in fact, some would argue, is not measurable at all.[5] It is at least partially a result of these difficulties that the budgetary process frequently is accorded a mechanical, rather than a managerial, role in many health and human service organizations.

The budget need not be a purely mechanical process, however. But to see it in its managerial context, it must be viewed in a more global light than generally has been the case. Further, many aspects of the budgetary process as it has been developed in profit-seeking organizations are directly applicable to health and human service organizations as well. The absence of a profit motive is a complicating factor, to be sure, but it need not be a major deterrent to effective use of the budget.

THE BUDGETARY PROCESS

Although clearly very complex, the process of budgeting can be analyzed from a perspective that allows us to view its various elements separately and to demonstrate ways in which many of these elements have been neglected or given insufficient consideration in health care organizations. The process, shown schematically in Figure 6–1, consists of two phases: budget formulation and budget monitoring. Both phases have a behavioral and mechanical aspect. The activities which comprise these two aspects are quite different in each of the two phases, however. Further, the whole process rests on a base which gives it a contingent nature, thereby explaining the development of different budgetary systems in different organizations. The base consists of five components: cost structure, critical success factors, the formal authority system, programmatic goals and objectives, and motivation systems. These components rest, in turn, on a foundation which consists of the organization's environment, its strategy formulation system, and its value system.

Viewed in this way, the budgetary process becomes not only an integral part of an organization—of any organization—but an es-

---

[5]Obviously, utilization review, tissue committees, and other similar performance measurement systems exist for hospitals, but most say little about whether the organization is achieving its *programmatic* objectives.

FIGURE 6-1

The Budgetary Process

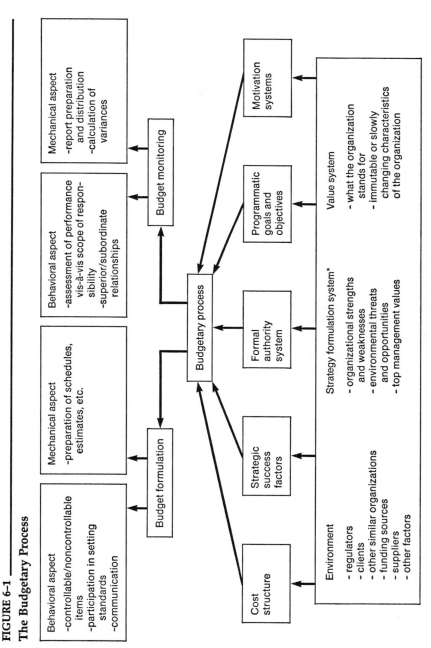

*See K. Andrews, *The Concept of Corporate Strategy* (Homewood, Ill.: Dow Jones-Irwin, 1971).

sential ingredient in the organization's success. The role of budgeting, thus, depends to a large extent on its fit with a variety of other organizational elements. By the same token, the failure of the budget to play a useful role in some organizations might be assessed in terms of its misfits with these other elements. Indeed, it is by means of these misfits that it is possible to address many of the reasons for the failure of budgeting in health and human service organizations.

BUDGETING MISFITS

Misfit #1.   Between the Cost Structure and the Budget Formulation Phase

In the formulation phase, a budget frequently is not built around the cost structure faced by the organization. As indicated in Chapters 4 and 5, many hospital reimbursement systems utilize a per-diem rate as the basis by which third-party payors reimburse hospitals for the care provided. However, the per-diem rate, which is designed to cover three types of costs (i.e., fixed, semi-fixed, and variable), accrues to the hospital on the basis of volume only (i.e., by means of the patient day). Since fixed costs and a portion of semi-fixed costs are time-based (i.e., dependent on the passage of time, not on the number of patient days treated), there is a misfit between the cost structure and the budget. As mentioned above, the resolution of this dilemma consists, in part, of holding managers responsible only for those costs over which they exercise some significant control. The result is a need to distinguish between controllable and noncontrollable costs. While some fixed costs are controllable in a typical budget period (one year), many others are not; they exist because the organization has committed itself to be "ready to serve," and will continue to exist even if no patients are admitted. By contrast, most variable costs and many semi-fixed costs are controllable, but only on a per-unit basis. *Total* variable costs and some semi-fixed costs will increase as volume increases, so that to the extent that volume is beyond a manager's control, so are total variable costs.

Misfit #2:   Between the Cost Structure and the Budget Monitoring Phase

In the budget monitoring phase, a misfit can exist in the form of a reporting system that does not adequately specify the reasons underlying a variance between budgeted and actual figures. Returning to Table 6–1, we can see that a variance betwen budgeted and actual costs may be the result of (1) a change in case mix, (2) a change in volume, (3) a change in input mix per case, (4) a change in the efficiency of input usage, and/or (5) a change in unit price of inputs. Although an accounting technique—variance analysis—has been developed to distinguish among these different elements, it is rarely utilized in the nonprofit sector. As a result, managers in health and human service organizations generally find it extremely difficult to determine the reasons underlying a deviation between budgeted and actual performance. These issues are discussed in greater detail in Chapter 7.

Misfit #3: Between Critical Success Factors and the Budgetary Process

Most organizations are able to identify one or two factors on which their ongoing success is based. In the airline industry, for example, success is highly related to the route structure and the load factor on flights. In health care, as the above examples suggest, one of the most important factors for a hospital is occupancy rate[6] For a home health agency, the critical success factor is visits per day per nurse. In an HMO it is hospital days per thousand enrollees. Serious misfits can occur when strategic success factors are excluded from the budgetary process. A hospital which is reimbursed on a per-diem basis and which does not build occupancy levels into both the budget formulation and monitoring phases for its routine care departments (e.g., medical/surgical, obstetrics, and so on) will almost certainly face serious difficulties.[7] A home health agency, on the other hand, which does not build nursing visits per day into its budget can also be expected to face serious problems, since revenue can fluctuate greatly with only a small change in the average number of daily visits. By contrast, many HMOs have encountered serious financial difficulties when their hospitalization rates per 1,000 enrollees exceeded budgeted levels.

---

[6]This is true, of course, only as long as the reimbursement system requires a hospital to cover a portion of its fixed costs *via* the per-diem rate.

[7]Note that in this instance the budget being discussed is for a hospital functioning *within* a reimbursement system that utilizes a per-diem system of payment. Although the occupancy level would not necessarily be a strategic success factor in *any* hospital, once regulatory agencies have established a per-diem system, the payment mechanism must be taken as a given by individual hospitals in developing their own budgetary processes. The result is that occupancy level becomes a strategic success factor.

Example: The Pleasant Street Home Health Agency charges $30 per visit and has a staff of 50 nurses. Nurses make an average of six visits a day. How much will revenue be affected by a change to 6.1 in the average number of visits per day per nurse over the course of a year?

Analysis: Revenue changes by $36,000, a substantial sum for many of these agencies. Calculations are as follows:

Change in average visit per day	6.1 − 6.0 =	0.1
Number of work days in a year	=	240
Number of nurses	=	50
Revenue per visit	=	$30
0.1 × 240 × 50 × $30 = $36,000		

Misfit #4.   Between the Formal Authority System and the Budgetary Process

Many health care and other nonprofit organizations are organized into programs, and many departments within a hospital are organized into subdepartments. Frequently, however, the budgetary process is not designed to fit this authority system. As a result, managers who make decisions that can affect the budget frequently do not have appropriate budgetary responsibility. Situations of this sort can exist between, say, the service departments in a hospital (e.g., housekeeping, laundry, and the like) and the "production" departments (e.g., medical/surgical, outpatient clinics), where a production department manager is responsible for a portion of the service department cost, but where service department managers are not reponsible budgetarily for the costs in their departments.

Misfits also can occur when budgetary units either overlap or fall between organizational units, such as can occur when the budget for a department has been disaggregated according to some sections within the department but not others, or where budgetary categories are established that do not correspond to organizational sections.

Example: The Department of Medicine at Arlmont Hospital is comprised of several sections: internal medicine, pediatrics, gastroenterology, and cardiology. Each section is managed by a chief of the specialty, and the department itself is under the direction of the chief of medicine. The budget report, which contains both budget and actual cost data, is prepared monthly and contains direct cost information classified into salaries, supplies, and depreciation. The information is broken down by ward, including two adult medicine wards and a pediatrics ward. Each specialty chief is asked to prepare a budget and to assist the hospital in its cost-containment effort.

Analysis: Until the cost data are classified by specialty, rather than ward, only the chief of pediatrics will have the requisite information to prepare and monitor a budget. Additionally, the budget categories may have to be further disaggregated to distinguish among types of personnel and supplies to facilitate greater control.

Misfit #5: Between Programmatic Goals and Objectives and the Budgetary Process

Since many health and human service organizations frequently fail to make programmatic goals and objectives explicit, this misfit may appear to be less pronounced than is, in fact, the case. In organizations that engage in program budgeting, the lack of congruence between programmatic objectives and financial constraints can be made explicit and be addressed directly during the budget formulation phase. Alternatively, issues concerning financial/programmatic congruence may be resolved by default, as can be the case when budget cuts are necessary but managers do not have sufficient information to determine which programs or programmatic efforts are most successful in meeting the organization's objectives.

Misfits of this sort can be corrected by revising the budgetary process to include a component in which department managers are asked to specify programmatic goals and objectives and to commit themselves to the attainment of these in the same way as they committed themselves to the financial objectives of the budget. Generally, the problem is not a particularly easy one to solve, however, and managers often are forced to consider the budget as a financial constraint, rather than as a pool of resources designed to assist in the attainment of some programmatic ends. This issue is discussed more fully in Chapter 7.

Misfit #6: Between Motivation Systems and the Budgetary Process

While managers and other professionals in health care—and, indeed, in most nonprofit organizations—appear to derive much of their motivation from nonfinancial sources, the budget, nevertheless, can play a role in influencing the motivation of these individuals to work toward the organization's objectives. To the extent that managers are committed to programmatic objectives that are not financially feasible, or are encouraged to develop new program ideas that are then thwarted by the budgetary process, there is a misfit between the organization's motivation systems and its budgetary process. In fact, in many instances, the budget is seen rather as a hurdle to overcome than an integral part of the planning process.

In some hospitals, for example, the entire budgetary process in some departments is one of generating statistics in an attempt to convince the fiscal affairs division that the department will provide at least as much revenue for the hospital as during the prior year. In many home health agencies and visiting nurse associations, the budget is a mechanism for obtaining funds from the local United Way. In these instances, the budget is not looked upon as a useful management tool by either managers or professionals in the organization. Indeed, under such circumstances as these the budgetary process is at best divorced from other motivation systems in the organization, and at worst is inconsistent or incompatible with them.

While no simple solution exists to attaining a good fit between motivation systems and the budgetary process, hospitals and other health care organizations can attempt to interest physicians in budgeting and cost containment by an attractive structuring of financial incentives. A hospital may find it very effective, for instance, to pay physicians substantial year-end bonuses that are tied to their overall ability to meet certain budgetary targets. As an example, Massachusetts General Hospital found that, by transforming all of its outpatient clinics into physician-operated group practices, it was able to reduce the rate of growth of its costs quite dramatically.[8] Additionally, there have been several proposals to structure medical services as profit centers and to relate physician remuneration to the financial performance of their particular service.[9] All of these incentive systems effectively incorporate the hospital's physicians into the budgetary process without establishing an external control mechanism which would significantly interfere with their medical autonomy.

There are undoubtedly a variety of other mechanisms which could be used to improve the fit between motivation systems and the budgetary process. The central point to stress, however, is the importance of incorporating attending physicians (and conceivably other health professionals) into an organization's budgetary system. If, for example, a hospital administrator can successfully structure a budgetary system that includes physicans and

[8]Regina Herzlinger, "Can We Control Health Care Costs?", *Harvard Business Review,* March–April 1978, pp. 102–10.

[9]J. E. Harris, "Regulation and Internal Control in Hospitals," *Bulletin of the New York Academy of Medicine,* January 1979, pp. 88–103.

enhances their motivation to balance clinical and financial issues in their decision making, he or she will have taken a major step in bridging the gap between the hospital's budgeting and cost-containment requirements and its physicians' needs for high-quality and accessible care.

Misfit #7: Between the Budget Formulation and Budget Monitoring Phases

In addition to the six misfits discussed above, which are between the components forming the base of the budgetary process and the process itself, there is the possibility of misfits *within* the budgetary process. The area where this problem appears to occur most frequently is between the budget formulation and monitoring phases. Even if managers have made programmatic and financial commitments, and are prepared to take them seriously, the entire process is weakened, and perhaps incapacitated, if the organization's reporting systems do not provide information which is complete (i.e., allows managers to assess the extent to which they are meeting or not meeting their commitments), accurate, and timely. Yet, the reporting systems in many health care organizations operate with such long time-lags that the information is of little managerial use when it arrives, and, as mentioned above, even those systems which are timely generally do not provide sufficient detail on the reasons underlying a budget variance to allow a manager to assess the action that should be taken to correct the situation. Again, Chapter 7 explores some of these issues in greater depth.

TOWARD MORE EFFECTIVE BUDGETING

Although the above discussion drew examples from the health care field, it did not, it should be noted, imply that the budgetary process in health care differed in any fundamental way from budgetary processes in other organizations, profit-seeking or not. Indeed, most of the literature on budgeting that has been drawn from the profit-seeking sector refers to one or more of the areas of fit discussed above. Additionally, since many profit-seeking organizations frequently build nonfinancial objectives (e.g., training and educational programs) into their total planning and budgetary processes, the divergence between the profit and nonprofit sectors is narrowed even further. In short, the rationale that the absence of a profit motive makes budgeting difficult is a weak excuse. The budgetary process could be improved in most health care and other nonprofit organizations if managers were willing to devote the necessary time and effort to eliminating misfits to make the process a more useful management tool.

Looked at somewhat more broadly, if the five cost-influencing variables described in Table 6-1 are to be monitored effectively, hospitals and other health care organizations will require more sophisticated management control systems than those currently in place. These new control systems will need to address three factors:

A budget *formulation* process that incorporates all five cost influencing variables: case mix, volume, resources per case, price, and efficiency.

A budget *monitoring* process that reports on the variances between budgeted and actual expenditures in each area so reporting can be tied to performance.

Accounting techniques that relate the above two activities to the third-party reimbursement system in place, thereby giving a hospital the ability to explain both to itself and to regulators the precise reasons for deviations between budgeted and actual performance.

In the budget formulation area, a revised management control system must incorporate case mix estimates into the projection process, so estimates of the volume of cases of each type or category become the driving force in formulating the budget. Once these estimates are available, they can be converted, via the application of standard (physician-determined) resource inputs per case, to estimates of total resource requirements. Finally, by applying standard efficiency factors and projected unit prices, resource requirements can be converted into dollar amounts.

The above process—albeit in a less sophisticated form—underlies the diagnostic-related group (DRG) rate-setting system currently being tested in New Jersey,[10] and is similar to a procedure-base system in use at the Massachusetts Eye and Ear Infirmary in Boston.[11] Although somewhat costly and time consuming to develop initially, a budget formulation process such as this can ultimately have important benefits for a hospital's management control system, and can be relatively inexpensive to operate on an ongoing basis. By comparing actual results to budgeted ones, and

---

[10]New Jersey Department of Health, *A Prospective Reimbursement System on Patient Case-Mix for New Jersey Hospitals, 1976–1978,* Seventh Quarter Report, 1978.

[11]Charles T. Wood, "Relate Hospital Charges to Use of Services," *Harvard Business Review,* March–April 1982.

doing so by area of control, as depicted in Table 6–1, this budget *monitoring* process becomes an essential complement to the above-described budget formulation process. The value of such a system is that it allows an administrator to relate performance to responsibility, and to hold managers—including physicians—responsible only for those cost-influencing variables over which they exercise a reasonable amount of control. This budget monitoring function is discussed more fully in the next chapter.

MANAGERIAL CHECKLIST

1. What are the responsibility centers in our institution? Are they designed in such a way that managers are held responsible only for those factors—costs and programmatic outcomes—that they can reasonably control?

2. Are physicians incorporated into the management control system in such a way that they are held responsible for variances in inputs per case by case type? If not, what barriers exist to implementing such a system?

3. What misfits exist in our organization's budgeting system? What can be done to eliminate them?

4. Have we developed a variance analysis which can distinguish among case mix, volume, inputs per case, efficiency, and unit prices? If not, what barriers exist to doing so?

5. What drives our budget formulation process? Can case mix estimates be developed in such a way that they become the driving force? If not, why not?

6. Does our budget reporting system include programmatic outcomes as well as financial outcomes? If not, what barriers exist to incorporating programmatic outcomes?

Bibliography

Althaus, J. N. et al. "Decentralized Budgeting: Holding the Purse Strings, Part 2." *Journal of Nursing Administration,* June 1982.

Anthony, R. N., and J. Dearden. *Management Control Systems.* Homewood, Ill. Richard D. Irwin, 1980.

Anthony, R. N., and G. A. Welsch. *Fundamentals of Management Accounting.* Homewood, Ill.: Richard D. Irwin, 1981.

Anthony, R. N., and D. W. Young. *Management Control in Nonprofit Organizations.* Homewood, Ill.: Richard D. Irwin, 1984.

Bisbee, G. E., and M. M. McCarthy. "Planning, Budgeting and Cost Control in HMOs." *Inquiry*, Spring 1979.

Block, J. A., et al. "Rochester Area Hospitals Launch Major Cost Containment Program." *Health Services Manager*, February 1981.

Burroughs, S. "Managing Financial Crisis in the Laboratory." *Pathologist*, January 1981.

Cammann, C., and D. A. Nadler. "Fit Control Systems to Your Managerial Style." *Harvard Business Review*, January/February 1976.

Covaleski, M. A., and M. W. Dirsmith. "Budgeting in the Nursing Services Area: Management Control, Political and Witchcraft Uses." *Healthcare Management Review*, Summer 1981.

Dillon, R. D. "Zero Based Budgeting: An Introduction." *Hospital Financial Management*, November 1977.

Gilman, D. "Cost Control at the Unit Level: Decentralization Cultivates Economy at Johns Hopkins Hospital." *Cost Containment*, February 9, 1982.

Golden, D. W., et al. "A Tool for Predicting the Future: Good Forecasting Builds Good Budgets." *Hospital Financial Management*, August 1981.

Harris, J. E. "Regulation and Internal Control in Hospitals." *Bulletin of the New York Academy of Medicine*, January 1979.

Herzlinger, R. "Can We Control Health Care Costs?" *Harvard Business Review*, March–April 1978.

Hofstede, F. "Management Control of Public and Not for Profit Activities." *Accounting, Organizations and Society*, 1981, pp. 193–211.

Janke, T. A., and A. Liberman. "Budgetinig and the Management Power Equation." *Journal of Mental Health Administration*, Fall 1980.

Joskow, P. L. *Controlling Hospital Costs: The Role of Government Regulation.* Cambridge, Mass.: MIT Press, 1981.

Lusk, E. J., and J. G. Lusk. *Financial and Managerial Control: A Healthcare Perspective.* Germantown, Md.: Aspen Systems Corporation, 1979.

Lutton, R. L. "The Four Quarter Approach—Establishing a Rolling Budgeting Process." *Hospital Financial Management*, May 1981.

Ouchi, W. "A Conceptual Framework for the Design of Organizational Control Mechanisms." *Management Science*, 1979, pp. 833–48.

Pyhrr, P. A. *Zero Based Budgeting.* New York: John Wiley & Sons, 1973.

Saltman, R. B., and D. W. Young. "The Hospital Power Equilibrium: An Alternative View of the Cost Containment Dilemma." *Journal of Health Politics, Policy and Law.* Fall 1981.

Thompson, G. B., and P. A. Pyhrr. "Zero Based Budgeting: A New Skill for the Financial Manager. *Hospital Financial Management*, March 1979.

Vraciu, R. A. "Programming, Budgeting and Control in Health Care Organizations: The State of the Art." *Managing the Finances of Health Care Organizations*, G. F. Bisbee and R. A. Vraciu. Ann Arbor, Mich.: Health Administration Press, 1980.

Vraciu, R., and J. Griffith. "Cost Control Challenge for Hospitals." *Health Care Management Review*, Spring 1979.

Wildavsky, A. *The Politics of the Budgetary Process.* Boston: Little, Brown, 1974.

Young, D. W., and R. B. Saltman. "Medical Practice, Case Mix, and Cost Containment: A New Role for the Attending Physician." *Journal of the American Medical Association*, February 12, 1982.

_____. "Preventive Medicine for Hospital Costs." *Harvard Business Review*, January–February 1983.

7

Measurement and Reporting Processes

As Chapter 6 indicated, management control systems have both structure and process. Of particular importance in the latter area is the rhythmic flow of activities, consisting of four separate but closely related steps: programming, budgeting, measurement, and reporting.[1] Budgeting was discussed at some length in Chapter 6, and, as was indicated in that chapter, programming is reserved for Chapter 9, where it can be put into a broader context. The purpose of this chapter is to complete the discussion of the measurement process begun in Chapters 4 and 5 and to discuss the reporting process in some depth. The discussion on reporting addresses two important techniques: flexible budgeting and variance analysis. Additionally, this chapter takes up an important question for non-profit organizations, that of measuring and reporting *programmatic performance*. Finally, the chapter contains a summary of the criteria for a good management control system. The appendix at the end of the chapter illustrates some of the concepts discussed by means of a sample flexible budgeting system.

---

[1] R. N. Anthony and G. A. Welsch, *Fundamentals of Management Accounting* (Homewood, Ill.: Richard D. Irwin, 1981).

THE MEASUREMENT PROCESS

Fundamental to an understanding of the measurement process is the notion repeated previously that *different costs are used for different purposes*. The reader will recall the discussion in Chapter 5 of the importance of using differential costs for add/drop, contract-out, and other alternative-choice decisions. Full costs, discussed in Chapter 4, were shown to be inappropriate for these types of decisions. In the same vein, a still separate set of cost information is appropriate for the management control system. Specifically, for management control purposes, one is concerned with the distinction between controllable and noncontrollable costs.

In general, we can say that all costs in an organization are controllable by someone. As a consequence, the appropriate and challenging task for management is in designing the management control system so that different managers are responsible for controlling different costs, or more specifically, so that each manager is held responsible only for those costs over which he or she exercises reasonable control. As Chapter 6 indicated, this responsibility/controllability alignment is by no means an easy task. Once determined, however, the organization's costs must then be measured in such a way as to report relevant cost information back to managers in both a useful and timely fashion. This may mean augmenting the full cost-collection process in some way, or it may simply mean that data already being collected for full cost or other purposes must be restructured for use by the management control system.

THE REPORTING PROCESS

Once appropriate information is being collected, a key task for the management control system is the provision of information to managers. This reporting process must meet several criteria if it is to be effective.

First, the information must arrive on a timely basis. Timely, in this context, does not necessarily mean quickly, but rather appropriately, with respect to the managerial action that may be necessary. In some instances, monthly reports that arrive within a few days of the end of each month may be necessary; in others, it may be feasible for the monthly reports to arrive within a week or two. Similarly, daily, weekly, quarterly, or annual reports may be necessary, and each will have an appropriate time-lag between the effective date of the report and the date it must be received by the manager.

A second criterion for an effective reporting process is a hierarchy of information; that is, information which is available in various levels of detail, from highly summarized to highly detailed. Generally, not all managers at all levels in the organization will find it necessary to have the same level of detail in the information supplied to them. A hospital director, for example, most likely will not want detailed efficiency information for each technician in the laboratory. He or she, however, will probably wish to know whether the laboratory is functioning efficiently, and may wish to have information about the efficiency of different sections within the laboratory. Generally, the information on sections in the laboratory would appear at a second level in the hierarchy so it does not impair the reading of the more summarized information. Thus, one might expect to find three or four levels of detail in a good reporting system:

A highly summarized level used by top management only, generally on a department or responsibility center basis.

A breakdown of sections or subdepartments within a responsibility center (such as a department) that is available to top management for reference purposes as needed, but which is used primarily by responsibility center managers.

A breakdown of personnel within sections or subdepartments, which is available to responsibility center managers for reference purposes as needed, but used primarily by section or subdepartment managers.

A detailed transaction-by-transaction listing for both personnel and supplies, which generally is not used unless in-depth reference is needed. This last level effectively constitutes the building blocks for the more summarized information described above, as well as for both the financial accounting and full cost accounting systems.

Obviously, the levels of detail must be tailored to each individual organization and its needs. For smaller organizations, where management is intimately aware of programs and activities, a highly summarized level and a transaction level may be all that is necessary. As potential problems are identified, they can be discussed with the individuals involved—using transaction information, as necessary, to answer questions. For larger organizations, a second level of summary may be necessary. And for very large organizations, all four (or even more) summaries may be needed.

Several factors are central to a decision concerning the appropriate number of summary levels: the managerial time associated with the reports, the kinds of actions that can be taken using the reports, the amount of responsibility given to individuals at different levels in the organization, and the cost of preparing the reports. A careful weighing of these factors is an essential ingredient in designing an effective and usable reporting system.

A third criterion for an effective reporting process is the presence of relevant and accurate data on the reports. Although accuracy needs no elaboration, the term *relevant* does. In many instances, one finds reporting systems with a great deal of information that is of marginal or no use to managers receiving the reports, while certain crucial information is missing entirely. A good example is that of year-to-date information, which, while generally of some use to a manager, often is not included on the management reports. Conversely, if the organization has a highly seasonal pattern of operations, year-to-date information, unless adjusted for seasonality, will be of little use. Unit cost information is another example of information which may or may not be of use. If a manager has no control over volume, then total unit cost information is of little value, and, indeed, may be quite misleading. Instead, the relevant information would be either controllable or variable costs per unit, which, presumably, are not affected by volume and, therefore, are costs that can be controlled by the manager. Clearly, what is relevant for one organization may not be relevant for another.

A final criterion for an effective reporting system is a behavioral one, namely, that the system must be taken seriously. It is not sufficient to simply prepare and distribute reports. Unless top management communicates to managers at various levels in the organization that the reporting system must result in appropriate management intervention, the system will have little value. Clearly, however, for this last criterion to be met the system must be timely, contain relevant and accurate data, and report those data in a hierarchical fashion.

In the context of the above criteria, two reporting techniques stand out as particularly relevant and important: flexible budgeting and variance analysis. Both techniques have been used extensively in for-profit organizations and are potentially quite useful in health care as well. For the most part, however, health care organizations have made only limited use of them.

FLEXIBLE BUDGETING

The key concept that underlies flexible budgeting is the distinction between controllable and noncontrollable costs. In many organizations, individual department managers appear to exert a great deal of control over both their department's fixed costs and the variable costs per unit of service, but exert no control over total *units* of service. As a result, they exercise little control over *total* variable costs. The management control solution to this problem is the *flexible budget* (i.e., a budget adjusted for volume changes prior to measuring a manager's performance).

Example: The manager of the dental clinic of the Tanglewood Community Health Center estimated that 2,000 patients would need exams and cleanings. She estimated that each exam and cleaning would take approximately a half hour of a dental hygienist's time, at an hourly rate of $10. Other costs associated with an exam and cleaning were supplies, electricity, and water, which totalled about $1 per procedure. The fixed costs associated with the exam and cleaning activity were $4,000. The result was the following budget:

Number of procedures		2,000
Hygienist cost (½ hour at $10/hr.)	$5	
Other variable costs	1	
Total variable costs per procedure	$6	
Variable-cost budget		$12,000
Fixed costs		4,000
Total costs		$16,000

During the reporting period, a total of 2,500 patients had an exam and cleaning, and the total costs of the department were $20,000.

Analysis: A flexible budget (sometimes called a performance budget) for the department would look as follows:

Number of procedures	2,500
Variable costs per procedure	$ 6
Variable-cost budget	15,000
Fixed-cost budget	4,000
Total budget	19,000
Less actual expenditures	20,000
Spending variance	$ (1,000)

Note that, although it would appear initially there was a budget overrun of $4,000, in fact only $1,000 was a "spending" overrun, since the remaining $3,000 can be attributed to the volume change over which the manager had no control.

Although the flexible budget is a partial answer to the problem of aligning responsibility and controllability, it does not answer all the important questions. Returning to the above example, we might still have some questions about the $1,000 spending overrun. Among the possible explanations are (1) a higher hygienist wage rate, (2) a higher per-unit supply costs, (3) more hygienist time per procedure, (4) more supply usage per procedure, (5) different supply usage, and (6) higher fixed costs. Indeed, were the answer contained in some of the reasons above, we might wish to explore the issue even further. If, for example, more hygienist time than budgeted were used, we might wish to know why. Were there new hygienists on the job who required training, and thus were slower than anticipated in exams and cleanings? Or were there some patients for whom exams and cleanings were more complex than others, resulting in more time needed to complete the procedures? Or perhaps patients arrived late, and scheduling was disrupted, slowing the hygienists down? And so on. While accounting techniques cannot answer all the above questions, the technique of variance analysis permits us to look into the six listed possibilities.

VARIANCE ANALYSIS

Variance analysis is an accounting technique that permits a close examination of the difference between budgeted and actual (or standard and actual) information. The technique allows us to break the difference into categories that are meaningful for managerial action. As the reader will recall, Table 6–1 (in Chapter 6) demonstrated that the difference between a hospital's budgeted and actual costs could be divided into five categories: case mix, volume, inputs per case, efficiency of input delivery, and price per unit of inputs. Variance analysis is the technique that allows us to distinguish among these five factors.

The concept of variance analysis can perhaps best be illustrated graphically. Consider the example of labor costs in a given organization. Total labor costs for a given employee or category of employees can be calculated, using the number of hours worked and the wage rate per hour. Assume that our labor budget is $400, resulting from an estimate of 100 hours work at $4/hour. Graphically, this can be represented by a rectangle, with the verticle axis indicating the wage rate and the horizontal axis the number of hours, as shown on the next page.

Assume now that our actual labor costs for the period in question were $600. A typical budget report might indicate the variance as follows:

Item	Budget	Actual	Variance
Labor cost	$400	$600	$(200)

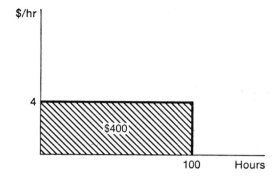

In this instance, the "$(200)" indicates a negative variance (i.e., actual expenses greater than budget). While this information may be somewhat useful to managers, it does not indicate *why* the variance occurred, or, more specifically in this instance, whether it was the result of a higher wage rate than anticipated, more hours than anticipated, or some combination of the two.

If the variance were solely the result of a higher wage rate, it could be viewed graphically as follows:

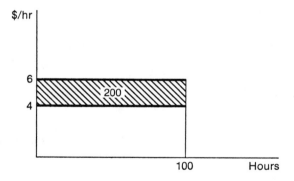

If, on the other hand, it were a result solely of more hours than budgeted, it could be viewed as shown on the next page.

Finally, if it were a result of a combination of both a higher wage rate and more hours, it could be depicted by a variety of wage/hour combinations; one example is shown on the next page.

Note that, in this last instance, we have a problem because the small rectangle shown on the upper right portion of the graph is the result of a combination of both the wage variance *and* the hour (or volume) variance. This combination variance typically is referred to as the "grey area," in that it cannot reasonably be as-

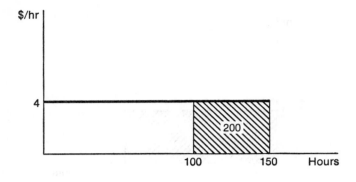

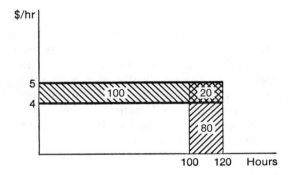

signed to either the higher price or the higher volume, but rather to the *combined effect* of the two. In this instance, then $100 of the total variance can be attributed to the higher wage rate, $80 to the higher number of hours (volume), and $20 to the combination effect.

If we had this kind of information, the budget report could be made much more managerially useful; it might look something like the following:

Item	Budget	Actual	Variance
Labor costs	$400	$600	$(200)
Wage variance			(100)
Volume variance			(80)
Combined variance			(20)

The increased managerial utility of this report comes directly from the fact that, in most organizations, different managers are responsible for different elements of a total variance, and that, in line with the responsibility/controllability concept discussed in Chapter 6, it is important to designate the precise amount of the variance attributable to each individual manager. It then becomes possible to discuss the reasons for the variance with the managers who are involved, and to take whatever actions are deemed appropriate. It is important to note in this context, however, that the variance is not designed to be used as a "club"; rather, it is to be used as a means for diagnosing the reasons *why* costs diverged from budget, and for exploring them with the appropriate managers so that, if possible, actions can be taken to bring costs back in line.

The accounting technique used to calculate a variance follows three relatively simple rules:

---

1. For any kind of cost variance, subtract the *actual* figure from the *budgeted* figure and multiply the result by all other items at their budgeted levels.
2. For any kind of revenue variance, subtract the *budgeted* figure from the *actual* figure and multiply by all other figures at budgeted levels.
3. The combination effect is the difference between the total variance being explained and the sum of all individually calculated variances.[2]

Let us return to the example illustrated above and perform the calculations according to the three rules. Since there is no revenue variance, we need not concern ourselves with it; the cost variances could then be explained as follows:

$$\text{Wage variance} = \left(\begin{array}{c}\text{Budgeted}\\\text{wage rate}\end{array} - \begin{array}{c}\text{Actual}\\\text{wage rate}\end{array}\right) \times \begin{array}{c}\text{Budgeted}\\\text{hours}\end{array} = \text{Variance}$$

$$\$4.00 - \$5.00 \times 100 = (\$100)$$

$$\text{Volume variance} = \left(\begin{array}{c}\text{Budgeted}\\\text{hours}\end{array} - \begin{array}{c}\text{Actual}\\\text{hours}\end{array}\right) \times \begin{array}{c}\text{Budgeted}\\\text{wage rate}\end{array} = \text{Variance}$$

$$100 - 120 \times \$4.00 = (80)$$

$$\text{Combination} = (\text{Total variance}) - \left(\begin{array}{c}\text{Sum of}\\\text{individual}\\\text{variances}\end{array}\right) = \text{Variance}$$

$$-200 - -180 = -20 = (20)$$

---

[2]Most accounting texts arbitrarily assign the combination effect to one of the individual variances. Obviously, this unfairly assigns this variance to a manager who has only partial control over it. The problem can be solved by keeping the combination effect as a separate item.

Note that, although this technique was performed in a situation where there were only two items involved, it could be performed equally well where several items could have a variance. The only difference is that the multiplication would involve several items at budgeted levels, rather than just one, as shown above.

Example:　The Conejo Family Planning Clinic has budgeted return visits as follows:

	Number of visits	Time per visit	Nurse practitioner wage	Total cost
Budget	7,000	10 minutes	$12/hour ($.20/minute)	$14,000
Actual	6,000	12 minutes	$15/hour ($.25/minute)	$18,000

The administrator is interested in obtaining a better understanding of the reasons behind the budget overrun.

Analysis:

Variance	Budget	−	Actual	×	Other items at budget	=	Total variance
Volume	7,000	−	6,000	×	10 × .20	=	2,000
Wage	.20	−	.25	×	7,000 × 10	=	(3,500)
Efficiency	10	−	12	×	7,000 × .20	=	(2,800)

	Total variance	−	Sum of individual variances		
Combination	−4,000	−	(2,000 − 2,800 − 3,500)	=	300
Total					(4,000)

An alternative calculation would be to first develop a performance budget, as follows:

	Number of visits	Time per visit	Nurse practitioner wage	Total cost
Budget	6,000	10 minutes	$12/hour ($.20/minute)	$12,000
Actual	6,000	12 minutes	$15/hour ($.25/minute)	$18,000

Now the efficiency and wage variances can be calculated, as shown on the next page.

The advantage of this alternative is that it eliminates volume as a factor influencing the other two variances, and thus allows us to examine the wage and efficiency variances in a somewhat cleaner context. If volume is truly beyond the control of the managers of the organization, an approach such as this would be preferable.

Variance	Budget	–	Actual	×	Other items at budget	=	Total variance
Wage	.20	–	.25	×	6,000 × 10	=	(3,000)
Efficiency	10	–	12	×	6,000 × .20	=	(2,400)
	Total variance	–	Sum of individual variances				
Combination	(6,000)	–	(5,400)			=	(600)
Total							(6,000)

In sum, variance analysis can be an important tool for understanding the reasons why costs have deviated from budget. It is important to bear in mind, however, that while variance analysis can highlight the reasons for such a deviation in terms of price, efficiency, mix, and so forth, it cannot explain why a particular unit in an organization was, say, more or less efficient than budgeted. Thus, variance analysis can be used to assist managers in asking the right questions and in identifying the lower-level managers to whom those questions should be asked. As with many other accounting techniques, however, variance analysis should be considered as a tool to assist managers in learning more about the activities of their organizations. Used properly, it can be both a powerful and valuable tool.

PROGRAMMATIC MEASUREMENT AND REPORTING

In addition to reporting on cost data, an effective management control system in a health care or other nonprofit context must consider the measurement and reporting of *programmatic* data. Indeed, in most nonprofit organizations, the financial reporting system indicates at best how well the organization is performing within its financial constraints, but says nothing about how effective it is in achieving its programmatic objectives. Since the objectives of health and human service organizations go well beyond the satisfaction of financial constraints, the measurement and reporting processes must do so also.

Most readers in the field of community health are familiar with the reporting requirement designed by the Bureau of Community Health of the Department of Health and Human Services (DHHS). These reporting requirements, generally referred to as the BCRR (Bureau of Community Reporting Requirements), address a wide range of programmatic concerns, such as number and type of encounters, program objectives, quality, unmet needs, and others. A minimal attempt is made to relate programmatic output to costs, and thus to address the issue of congruence between financial and programmatic concerns. Unfortunately, as most users of this information know, it is of little use managerially. Therefore, for community health centers and other health organizations, the issue of designing adequate programmatic measurement and reporting systems still remains.

Central to the measurement and reporting of programmatic results, is the question of quantifiability of information. Anthony and Young[3] have identified a "continuum of output measures," which range from relatively unmeasurable but highly meaningful indicators of performance to easily measurable but not terribly meaningful ones. Their three categories—social indicators, results measures, and process measures—indicate the nature of the dilemma. Almost all health and human service organizations would agree that their principal objective is to have an impact on the health status of the communities they serve. But the measurement of health status is inherently difficult, and, even if it were measurable, the establishment of a linkage between the activities of a particular organization in a community and the community's health status would be all but impossible.

Just as social indicators are difficult to determine and measure, process measures are rather easy. Patient days, outpatient encounters, surgical procedures, laboratory tests, x-ray procedures, home visits, and the like are all easy to measure and report. Unfortunately, they say little about whether an organization is achieving its programmatic objectives, or the impact it is having on the health status of its community.

It is thus in the category of results measures that the focus of performance measurement must take place.[4] Here the challenge to managers at all levels in the organization is to develop a set of objectively measurable indicators of performance, so programmatic objectives can be negotiated between top and middle management during the budget formulation process, and then be measured and reported at regular intervals during the budget year.

As a consequence of developing and negotiating results measures, managers need to receive two types of reports: financial and programmatic. To the extent feasible, these reports should be integrated, so that managers can determine the resources being con-

---

[3]Robert N. Anthony and D. W. Young, *Management Control in Nonprofit Organizations: Text and Cases* (Homewood, Ill.: Richard D. Irwin, 1984).

[4]It is also important to distinguish between performance and performance measurement. See David W. Young, *The Managerial Process in Human Service Agencies* (New York: Praeger Publishers, 1979), chap. 1.

sumed in the attainment of various results. As with financial reporting systems, programmatic reporting must provide accurate, timely, and useful information to the appropriate managers.

In attempting to develop results measures, readers may find it useful to consider several criteria. First, programmatic reporting should attempt to distinguish between inputs and outputs. While it may be useful to measure patient days in a hospital setting, for example, and, in fact, it may be *necessary* to do so for purposes of third-party reimbursement, an organization concerned with measuring its performance will need to relate these inputs to some kind of desired output. The measurement of average length of stay is one such effort, relating patient days to discharge (an output). But for the information to be managerially useful, it must also be related to the ability of individual managers to *control* outcomes; therefore, *average* length of stay generally is not sufficiently specific. A much more meaningful measure might be average length of stay by diagnosis, or, in a department of surgery, average length of stay by procedure. An even more meaningful measure might be total resources consumed (days of care, nursing utilization, ancillary procedures, operative procedures, and the like) by diagnosis.

A second criterion concerns the relationship between inputs and outputs. Once one begins to measure both, questions arise concerning desired ratios between the two. Although the tendency may be to attempt to provide a given level of output with as few inputs as possible, such an approach may have negative consequences for an organization's programmatic performance over the longer run. This problem is particularly apparent in an HMO (health maintenance organization) setting, for example, where the organization receives a fixed-dollar amount per enrollee each year and must, on the average, spend less than that to survive financially. The tendency to focus managerial attention on resources consumed per patient, and to minimize that ratio, could lead to decisions to eliminate activities of a preventive nature, such as primary care visits or diagnostic tests. Thus, once an organization begins to measure ratios of outputs and inputs, it must also begin to establish standards or norms for those ratios.

Third, organizations that begin to develop performance measures and programmatic reporting procedures must be careful not to allow the needs of external users of information to fully govern the choice of results measures. Here, however, many organizations will find themselves facing a dilemma in which *their* programmatic objectives are inconsistent or incompatible with the payment mechanisms of their funding agencies. In many states, for example, inpatient care in a hospital is fully reimbursable, while outpatient care is not. An organization which, for programmatic reasons, emphasizes a shift from, say, inpatient to outpatient surgery may find that the financial consequences of such a shift are prohibitive. Nevertheless, in some areas of an organization's activities, it may be possible to develop results measures which more adequately indicate programmatic performance and which do not involve a potential compromise in financial viability. In an ambulatory care setting, for example, although most third-party payors reimburse on the basis of encounters, a more appropriate measure of programmatic performance would appear to be total resources consumed per episode of illness, classified by diagnosis. A performance measurement system could be developed to report on this important indicator, while the organization continued to bill third parties on a per-encounter basis.

Fourth, organizations which begin to develop results measures must be certain that the content of their programs is not influenced by the kinds of measures which are most easily developed for the reporting system. Instead, energy must be devoted to developing output measures that reflect as clearly as possible each program's objectives. Chapter 9 discusses the important relationship among an organization's values, its strategies, and its programs. Not only must this relationship be preserved, but it must serve to influence programmatic objectives, which then become translated into output indicators for reporting purposes.

Fifth, and related to the above, it is important to recognize that some programmatic objectives will be difficult or simply impossible to measure. This is an unfortunate fact of life in health and human service organizations. In some instances, it may be necessary to develop surrogate measures of output, such as social work visits or psychiatric encounters, rather than attempt to develop objective measures for social or mental well-being. Indeed, in some instances, the attempt to attach a quantifiable measure of results to an inherently unquantifiable activity may be highly misleading.[5]

Finally, as with financial reporting systems, an attempt must be made to relate responsibility to controllability, and to develop hierarchically summarized levels of reporting which are appropriate to various levels of management. While a patient-by-patient summary of resources consumed by diagnosis might be appropriate for, say, a department of medicine, a diagnosis-by-diagnosis

---

[5]The Davidson Community Health Center case (found in Anthony and Young, *Management Control*) is a good example of an organization which made such an attempt.

summary would most likely be more appropriate for top management of the hospital.

From a more general perspective, it is important to recognize that the criteria for a good management control system discussed in the next section are equally appropriate for either financial or programmatic reporting systems. The reader should consider both types of reporting systems in reviewing this section.

CRITERIA FOR A GOOD MANAGEMENT CONTROL SYSTEM

The discussion in this chapter and in Chapter 6 can be summarized by setting forth a number of criteria which characterize a good management control system. These criteria can be grouped into three categories: structure, process, and behavioral aspects.

Structure

Perhaps the most important structural aspect of a management control system is that its responsibility centers are well-defined, and that they fit well with the authority structure of the organization. Well-defined means that the controllability/responsibility relationship has been assessed, and that managers are held responsible for those factors which are under their control. In this respect, it is most important that a good decision by a manager be reflected by a good result on the reports that that manager receives (i.e., if the decision affects his or her responsibility center in a positive way, the reporting system should so indicate).[6]

Process

The process which the management control system follows should be a rhythmical one characterized by four phases: programming, budgeting, measurement, and reporting.

The *programming* process should clearly identify the organization's programs, the programs should fit with the organization's overall strategic focus, and the objectives for each program should be clearly delineated.

The *budgeting* process should identify not only the relationship

---

[6]See R. N. Vancil, "What Kind of Management Control Do You Need?", *Harvard Business Review*, March–April 1973. Vancil calls this effect the "fairness criterion."

between programs and responsibility centers but the financial and programmatic expectations for each program. Specifically, managers should be held accountable not only for the dollar amounts associated with their programs but for programmatic objectives as well.

The *measurement* system should collect data relating to both costs and programmatic objectives as identified in the budgetary process. It is important to stress that it may be necessary to collect different kinds of cost data for the budgetary activities of the organization than are collected for cost accounting purposes.

The *reporting* system which presents this information to managers should be characterized by reports that are timely, accurate, and relevant to the responsibility center, which separate controllable from noncontrollable costs, which show the relationships between programmatic output and the costs incurred in achieving that output, and which contain information of varying levels of detail appropriate to the managers who will be using the reports.

Behavioral Aspects

Perhaps the most important behavioral aspect of a control system is that it be taken seriously by top and middle management. Top management's active participation in the control system in both the budget formulation and budget reporting processes is necessary if middle and lower-level managers are to take the system seriously, and are thus to feel obligated to achieve the expectations outlined during the programming and budgeting processes. Additionally, to the extent feasible, the control system should be characterized by what Vancil[7] has called "goal congruence," namely, that the programmatic and financial goals of individual managers, as determined by the responsibility center structure, programming and budgeting processes, and the like, should be consistent with the overall goals of the organization.

Finally, to the extent that managers participate in the programming and budgeting phases of the control process, their participation should be an integral part of that process. As such, the managerial commitment to the programming and budgeting processes can be appropriate to the organization's needs.

As the reader no doubt has realized, the level of effort necessary to accumulate and structure cost and programmatic information for both full cost and management control purposes can be

[7]Ibid.

extensive and time-consuming. For this reason and others, many organizations have come to rely on computerized management information systems to assist them in their activities. The next chapter examines the topic of management information systems, and discusses the many issues which can arise in their development and implementation.

MANAGERIAL CHECKLIST

1. Is our accounting system set up in such a way that cost data which are used for full cost reporting can be restructured for management control purposes? If not, what level of effort would be necessary to restructure it?

2. What reports are produced from our management control system? Who receives them? Do they arrive in a timely enough fashion to facilitate management action? If not, what must be done to assure that they do?

3. What is the hierarchy of our reporting system? Is top management burdened with too much detail? Do middle managers and supervisors have sufficient detail to allow them to take whatever action is necessary to correct deviations from planned activities?

4. Do managers frequently complain that they are unable to determine what action to take because the reports they receive do not contain "relevant" information? If so, what different or additional information would be necessary, and what would be the cost of collecting it and including it on the reports?

5. Is the reporting system used in a serious way? Are reports discussed among managers? Does top management use the reports as a basis for requesting action plans from middle managers when actual activities deviate from planned ones?

6. Is volume beyond the control of some managers? If so, do we have a flexible budgeting system which adjusts for volume changes? If not, what kind of effort would be necessary to develop such a system?

7. What factors in our organization, other than volume, might cause variances from budget? Case mix, inputs per case, efficiency, unit prices, wage rates, and so on? Are we calculating these variances as part of the reporting system? If not, what effort would be required to do so? Would the results better depict the responsibility/controllability alignment and, thereby, facilitate more effective managerial action?

8. What performance measures does our organization use? Do they adequately distinguish between result measures and process measures? Are the linkages between process activities and results as clearly defined as possible?

9. Does our reporting system present programmatic as well as financial information? If not, what programmatic information might be included, and what level of effort would be necessary to do so? Can it be tied to individual managers within the organization and included as part of the budgetary process? Can a hierarchical reporting system be developed?

10. Does our reporting system link programmatic and financial information so we can determine the cost of attaining our programmatic objectives? If not, can such a linkage be made? At what cost? Can standards be developed for the ratios of outputs and inputs?

11. To what extent are our programmatic objectives consistent with those of our funding agencies? If inconsistencies exist, how are they being managed such that we meet the needs of both our funders and patients/clients as effectively and efficiently as possible?

Bibliography

Anthony, R. N., and G. A. Welsch. *Fundamentals of Management Accounting.* Homewood, Ill.: Richard D. Irwin, 1981.

Anthony, R. N., and D. W. Young. *Management Control in Nonprofit Organizations.* Homewood, Ill.: Richard D. Irwin, 1984.

Dirksen, C. J. "Determining How and Why Your Costs are Changing." *Hospital Financial Management,* December 1978.

Finkler, S. A. "Flexible Budgets: The Next Step in Health Care Financial Control." *Health Services Manager,* May 1981.

Hays, T. I., Jr. "Variable Budgeting in the Pharmacy." *Hospitals,* January 16, 1979.

Horngren, C. T. *Introduction to Management Accounting.* Englewood Cliffs, N. J.: Prentice-Hall, 1978.

Layman, R. "Flexible Budgeting for Small Hospitals." *Hospital Financial Management,* October 1980.

Scott, T. J. "Variable Budgeting: To Accurately Monitor a Hospital's Performance." *Hospital Financial Management,* May 1980.

Sorenson, E. L. "Flexible Budgeting—Easier Than You Think." *Hospital Financial Management,* April 1979.

Vancil, R. N. "What Kind of Management Control Do You Need?" *Harvard Business Review,* March–April 1973.

Young, D. W. *The Managerial Process in Human Service Agencies.* New York: Praeger Publishers, 1979.

APPENDIX: A Sample Flexible Budgeting System

INTRODUCTION

The principal objective of a good budgeting and control system (BCS) is to place responsibility for budget determination and cost control in the hands of the managers most able to control the resources needed to deliver a set of health care services. By so doing, top management can expect that an institution's resources will be used as effectively and efficiently as possible in meeting the needs of its patients.

The BCS described in this appendix is a flexible budgeting system, one which could quite easily be developed from an existing cost accounting system. The purpose of the appendix is to both illustrate the concept of flexible budgeting and to indicate its relationship to a full cost accounting system. The system is described in the context of a hospital, but, as the reader will see, it could be adapted quite easily to many other types of health and human service organizations. As indicated in Chapter 6, there are two aspects to a BCS: budget formulation and budget monitoring. Each will be described separately below.

BUDGET FORMULATION PROCESS

The process of formulating the budget typically is initiated several months prior to the beginning of the budget year. At that time, department managers should have available to them patient statistics, cost, and budget information for the prior fiscal year as well as for the first several months of the current fiscal year.

Using this information, coupled with their knowledge of programmatic changes being undertaken in their organization, managers can formulate two types of budgets: operating and capital. Although the two types are distinct, they are also highly interrelated, since they must rely on a common set of assumptions concerning the amount, quality, and level of care to be provided by each department. Nevertheless, each will be discussed separately.

Operating Budget

The operating budget consists of two general categories of costs: controllable and uncontrollable. Controllable costs are those that are *reasonably* (not necessarily *totally*) under the control of a department manager. Uncontrollable costs are those costs associated with a department, but over which the manager exercises very little if any control. These distinctions will become clearer in the paragraphs that follow.

To illustrate, let us assume a situation in which two items comprise the controllable category of the operating budget: salaries and supplies. The remaining two categories of costs (i.e., contract services and depreciation) will be considered uncontrollable. Contract service costs are uncontrollable at the department level because fixed-price contracts are let by the hospital; depreciation, although controllable through the capital budget process, is not controllable by a department manager once the capital purchase decisions have been made. Both contract service and depreciation amounts will appear on a department's operating budget for information purposes, however.

For purposes of budgeting, we will use the term *responsibility center*, rather than "department" or "cost center," because some department managers will find that their departments consist of several responsibility centers. A list of responsibility centers and their costs for Spy Pond Hospital for January–June 19XX is contained in Exhibit 7A–1. We will assume that this information is available in August 19XX, when the budget preparation process begins for the next calendar year, 19YY.

Using the cost information in Exhibit 7A–1, it is possible to derive a unit cost figure for each responsibility center's controllable costs. In most instances, the unit will be a "patient-day"; but in some responsibility centers, another unit will be more useful. For example, in the clinic the appropriate unit is a visit; in radiology it is a film; in the laboratories, a test; and so on. Exhibit 7A–2 contains the same cost information as Exhibit 7A–1, but the information is now structured in terms of units and controllable costs per unit (obtained by dividing each controllable cost figure for the six-month period by the appropriate number of units). For example, the maternity costs are calculated as shown on the next page.

The value of this approach is that it permits an operating budget to be prepared by estimating various items independently and then checking them for consistency. The total process for preparing the operating budget consists of six steps, described here for the 19YY budget year:

Item	Source	Amount
1. Total costs	Exhibit 7A–1	$128,400
2. Days care	Hospital records	1,368
3. Salaries cost	Exhibit 7A–1	$70,600
4. Salaries/unit	Salaries cost/days care	$51.60
5. Supplies cost	Exhibit 7A–1	$40,500
6. Supplies cost/unit	Supplies cost/days care	$29.60
7. Uncontrollable cost	Services + depreciation (10,400 + 6,900)	$17,300

Step 1: Project the total number of units for the responsibility center, bearing in mind that the totals in Exhibit 7A–2 (example: days care) are for six months only.

Step 2: Estimate personnel needs and associated salary levels, using the form shown in Exhibit 7A–3. Note that the columns permit a manager to distinguish between additional salary needs for existing positions (column 4) and growth needs represented by new positions (column 5). If the projections contained in column 4 are for other than cost-of-living needs (example: merit increases) they should be explained in the form contained in Exhibit 7A–4.

Step 3: Verify the validity of the projections as follows: (1) divide the total in column 4 by the estimated number of units for the current fiscal year; (2) divide the total in column 5 by the expected *increase* in units for the new fiscal year; (3) the two per-unit numbers should be approximately the same. Any increases of more than 10 percent in the per-unit cost should be explained.

Step 4: Estimate supply needs similar to personnel needs, using Exhibit 7A–5 and specifying: (1) the inflationary increase for existing supplies; (2) changes in supplies needed for existing patient levels (use change); and (3) the changes in supplies needed for new patient levels (volume changes). The exhibit can include either increases or decreases, with decreases shown in parentheses: ( ).

Step 5: Prepare a justification of the use increases or decreases, using Exhibit 7A–6. These may be based on changes in either efficiency, quality, or care protocols.

Step 6: Verify the validity of the volume increases on Exhibit 7A–5 as follows:

---

1. Add the total with the inflation increase to the use increase.
2. Divide this total by the total units for the prior fiscal year.
3. Divide the total in column 5 by the expected increase in patient days for the new fiscal year.

EXHIBIT 7A–1

SPY POND HOSPITAL
Cost Breakdown by Category and Responsibility Center
January–June 19XX
($000)

Responsibility center	Salaries	Supplies	Contract services	Depreciation	Total
Inpatient:					
Maternity	70.6	40.5	10.4	6.9	128.4
Gynecology	66.8	50.4	6.3	5.9	129.4
Pediatric	57.6	58.9	11.3	9.0	136.8
Premature	17.0	7.7	4.1	2.9	31.7
General surgery	93.6	91.0	12.1	11.9	208.6
Medicine	75.5	94.2	10.8	11.9	192.4
Orthopedic	46.8	22.1	4.4	3.2	76.5
Anesthesiology	31.5	1.3	5.8	44.9	83.5
Intensive care	16.3	20.2	1.5	11.9	49.9
Total	475.7	386.3	66.7	108.5	1,037.2
Ancillary and clinical support:					
Nursing	605.4	—	—	31.9	637.3
X-ray	46.8	17.3	1.0	10.2	75.3
Laboratory	94.6	14.8	—	23.5	132.9
Physical therapy	59.6	—	—	3.2	62.8
Pharmacy	9.7	20.3	0.2	1.3	31.5
Central sterile	8.5	10.5	1.3	5.1	25.4
Social service	30.1	3.6	0.8	0.5	35.0
Total	854.7	66.5	3.3	75.7	1,000.2

Outpatient clinics:					
Medicine	14.5	53.3	0.1	0.8	68.7
ENT	7.0	2.4	0.1	1.2	10.7
Dermatology	7.0	19.4	0.1	0.8	27.3
Ophthalmology	10.5	0.7	0.1	4.2	15.5
General surgery	22.1	7.0	0.1	0.8	30.0
Walk-in	34.6	6.0	0.1	1.4	42.1
Gynecology	15.8	3.6	0.1	0.8	20.3
Pediatrics	15.0	6.2	0.1	0.9	22.2
Dentistry	5.7	—	0.1	0.4	6.2
Emergency	32.3	14.7	3.1	3.6	53.7
Total	164.5	113.3	4.0	14.9	296.7
Miscellaneous services:					
Hotel	190.3	25.0	26.4	15.1	256.8
General	180.4	1.7	100.4	52.0	334.5
Engineering	100.6	5.3	382.3	30.0	517.6
Administrative and financial	150.8	3.1	234.7	20.9	409.5
Total	621.5	35.1	743.8	118.0	1,518.4
Hospital totals	2,116.4	601.2	817.8	317.1	3,852.5

SPY POND HOSPITAL
Cost Breakdown for Budget
January–June 19XX

Responsibility center	No. beds	No. units Days care	No. units No. visits	No. units Other	Total cost (a)	Controllable costs Salaries/unit (b)	Controllable costs Supplies/unit (c)	Uncontrollable costs (d)
Inpatient:								
Maternity	11	1,368	—	—	128.4	51.60	29.60	17.3
Gynecology	14	2,108	—	—	129.4	31.68	23.92	12.2
Pediatric	28	3,216	—	—	136.8	17.92	18.32	20.3
Premature	8	1,172	—	—	31.7	14.52	6.56	7.0
General surgery	29	4,012	—	—	208.6	23.32	22.68	24.0
Medicine	29	3,225	—	—	192.4	23.40	29.20	22.7
Orthopedic	7	944	—	—	76.5	49.56	23.40	7.6
Anesthesiology	—	—	—	1,241(e)	83.5	25.36	1.04	50.7
Intensive care	2	186	—	—	49.9	87.64	108.76	13.4
Total	128	16,231	—	—	1,037.2			175.2
Ancillary and clinical support:								
Nursing	128	16,231	—	—	637.3	37.32	—	31.9
X-ray	—	—	—	14,054(f)	75.3	3.33	1.23	11.2
Laboratories	—	—	—	62,649(g)	132.9	1.51	.24	23.5
Physical therapy	—	—	—	6,051(h)	62.8	9.85	—	3.2
Pharmacy	—	—	—	5,808(i)	31.5	1.67	3.50	1.5
Central sterile	—	—	—	1,241(e)	25.4	6.85	8.46	6.4
Social service	—	—	—	1,672(j)	35.0	18.00	2.15	1.3
Total	128	16,231	—	—	1,000.2			79.0

Clinical (outpatient):						
Medicine	—	1,575	68.7	9.20	33.84	0.9
ENT	—	441	10.6	15.87	5.49	1.3
Dermatology	—	1,062	27.3	6.59	18.26	0.9
Opthalmology	—	357	15.5	29.41	1.96	4.3
General surgery	—	1,626	30.1	13.59	4.30	0.9
Walk-in	—	1,452	42.0	23.82	4.13	1.5
Gynecology	—	916	20.2	17.24	3.93	0.9
Pediatrics	—	744	22.1	20.16	8.33	1.0
Dentistry	—	403	6.2	14.14	—	0.5
Emergency	—	11,537	53.8	2.80	1.28	6.7
Total		20,113	296.7			18.9
Miscellaneous services:						
Hotel	—	—	256.8			
General	—	—	334.5			
Engineering	—	—	517.6			
Administrative and financial	—	—	409.5			
Total			1,518.4			
Hospital totals			3,852.5			

a. From Exhibit 7A-1. In thousands of dollars.
b. Salaries from Exhibit 7A-1 ÷ Number of units.
c. Supplies from Exhibit 7A-1 ÷ Number of units.
d. Services + depreciation. In thousands of dollars.
e. Number of operations.
f. Number of films.
g. Number of tests.
h. Number of procedures.
i. Number of prescriptions filled.
j. Number of patient visits.

EXHIBIT 7A–3 _____

SPY POND HOSPITAL
Personnel Budget

Responsibility center _____   Fiscal year _____

Position description	Name of incumbent	Salary			
		Current	With increases	New	Total
(1)	(2)	(3)	(4)	(5)	(6)
Total salary dollars					

Column:
   3. Salary for current fiscal year, for incumbents only.
   4. Expected salary with increase for next fiscal year, for incumbents only.
   5. Expected salary for next fiscal year, for new positions only.
   6. Sum of columns 4 and 5.

EXHIBIT 7A–4 _____

SPY POND HOSPITAL
Personnel Budget Justification

Responsibility center _____   Fiscal year _____

Position description	Name of incumbent	Justification of increases other than cost of living

EXHIBIT 7A–5

SPY POND HOSPITAL
Supply Budget

Responsibility center _____   Fiscal year _____

Description of supply	Current	With inflation increase	Use change	Volume change	Projected total
(1)	(2)	(3)	(4)	(5)	(6)
Total dollars					

Column:
3. Prior year total plus increases due only to higher prices.
4. Change in prior year total due to use of different supplies or more or less of same supplies by existing patient load.
5. Change in prior year's total due to changes in patient volume.
6. Sum of columns 3, 4, and 5.
Note: Any item can show a decrease as well as an increase. Indicate decreases with parentheses.

4. The two per-unit numbers should be approximately the same. Any increase of more than 10 percent in the per-unit cost should be explained.

An example of the six-step process follows: From Exhibits 7A–1 and 2, we can determine that the Maternity Department at Spy Pond Hospital will spend an estimated $141,200 (70,600 × 2) on salaries and $81,000 (40,500 × 2) on supplies during the 19XX fiscal year. It expects to deliver 2,736 days of care during that period (1,368 × 2) for a cost per day of $51.60 for salaries and $29.60 for supplies.

Step 1: The department expects an increase in utilization, based on a recent increase in its occupancy rate to 75 percent, a rate which it expects will persist for the next 12 months. Therefore, its projected patient days for 19YY are 11 beds × 365 days × .75 = 3,011.

Step 2: The totals on Exhibit 7A–3 would look as follows, assuming a 10 percent inflation rate:

EXHIBIT 7A–6 _____

SPY POND HOSPITAL
Supply Budget Justification

Responsibility center _____   Fiscal year_____

Description of supply	Type of increase	Amount of increase	Justification for non-inflation increase
	(1)	(2)	

Column:
   1. Specify use (U) or volume (V).
   2. Should correspond to total increase shown in Exhibit 7A–5.

_____

Current	With increase	New	Total
141,200	155,320 (*a*)	15,612 (*b*)	170,932

   a. 141.200 increased by 10 percent for cost of living. No other wage increases were included.
   b. 275 (3,011 − 2,736) additional patient days at $56.77 per day (155,320 ÷ 2,736).

Step 3:   Since the rate used for new days is the same as the inflated rate at the existing level of patient days, no justification is necessary. Therefore, $170,932 is the salary budget for 19YY. The per-diem salary budget is $56.77 (170,932 ÷ 3,011).

Step 4:   The totals on Exhibit 7A–5 might look as follows, assuming a 10 percent inflation rate:

Current	With inflation increase	Use changes	Volume changes	Projected total
81,000	89,100 (*a*)	(1,368) (*b*)	8,819 (*c*)	96,551

   a. 81,000 increased by 10 percent.
   b. A reduction of $0.50 per-patient day due to use of equally effective but less-costly supplies. All other supply usage projected to remain the same. $0.50 × 2,736 = 1,368.
   c. 275 additional patient days at 32.07 per day [(89,100 − 1,368) ÷ 2,736].

Step 5: See explanation in footnote *b* above. Note that the estimation was on a per-diem basis, and multiplied by the *current* volume. This effect is incorporated into the volume *change* by means of the revised rate, which included the $1,368 reduction.

Step 6:
  1. $89,100 - 1,368 = 87,732$
  2. $87,732 \div 2,736 = 32.07$
  3. $8,819 \div 275 = 32.07$
No increase in per-unit cost.

Totals for Contract Services and Depreciation, which are noncontrollable, will be calculated by the Central Administration. Contract service needs will be based on the projected number of patient days (or other units), and depreciation will be a combination of last year's figure plus the depreciation associated with the capital budget request described below.

Capital Budget

All requests for capital equipment are included on Exhibit 7A–7. They should be listed in priority order, with the most essential equipment first. On Exhibit 7A–8, each responsibility center manager should (1) describe the sorts of problems (if any) which are taking place with existing capital equipment, (2) provide an estimate of the one-time cost of repair, and (3) project the ongoing preventive maintenance (PM) needs to assure the continued

EXHIBIT 7A–7 _____

SPY POND HOSPITAL
Capital Budget Requests

Responsibility center _____   Fiscal year _____

Description of items	Quantity needed	Estimated cost	Reasons for need

EXHIBIT 7A–8

SPY POND HOSPITAL
Capital Equipment Maintenance Needs—
Existing and Requested Equipment

Responsibility center _____   Fiscal year _____

Description of item and nature of problem	Estimated one-time repair cost	Description of preventive maintenance needs	Estimated annual cost of PM

smooth operation of the equipment. An estimate of the preventive maintenance needs of the equipment requested in Exhibit 7A–7 also should be included.

BUDGET MONITORING PROCESS

An integral part of any budgetary system is the process of monitoring the budget to assure that performance against it is as good as possible. In using a flexible budgeting system, a central report is the "performance budget." This report is prepared for each responsibility center, generally on a monthly basis, and is based on the center's per-unit rates established during the budget formulation process. These rates are used to calculate the performance budget for the salary and supply categories. The performance budget assumes that volume (usually days of care, but other units are used for some responsibility centers) is not under the control of the responsibility center manager. The performance budget thus represents what the budget *would have been* if the exact volume had been known at the time of preparation. A sample budget report for the Maternity Department is contained in Exhibit 7A–9. An explanation of this report follows:

---

1. Maternity has a budgeted rate per day for salaries of $56.77 (see example in the section on budget formulation) and projected 3,011 days of care. Thus, its original salary budget for March was based on 251 days of care (3,011 ÷ 12). The salary amount budgeted for March, thus, was $14,249 (251 × $56.77). The salary budget for the first three months of the fiscal year (January–March) was $42,748 (753 × $56.77).
2. For the month of March, the department actually delivered 300 days of care, bringing its total for the year to date to 1,000. Thus, its performance budget for salaries for March was $17,031 (300 × $56.77). For the year to date, its performance budget was $56,770 (1,000 × $56.77).
3. Its actual salary expenditures for March were $20,000. For the year to date, they were $55,000. Thus, it overspent its performance budget for March, but is slightly below budget for the year to date. This effect is shown in the variance columns.

EXHIBIT 7A-9

SPY POND HOSPITAL
Responsibility Center Budget Report—All Cost Categories

Responsibility center: _Maternity_   Fiscal year _19YY_   For month _March_

Cost category	Budgeted rate/day	This month Original budget	This month Performance budget	This month Actual expenditures	This month Variance	Year-to-date Original budget	Year-to-date Performance budget	Year-to-date Actual expenditures	Year-to-date Variance
Salaries:									
Days		251	300			753	1,000		
Amount	56.77	14,249	17,031	20,000	(2,969)	42,748	56,770	55,000	1,770
Supplies:									
Days		251	300			753	1,000		
Amount	32.07	8,050	9,621	9,000	621	24,149	32,070	31,500	570
Total controllable		22,299	26,652	29,000	(2,348)	66,897	88,840	86,500	2,340
Services		953		900	53	2,859		2,600	259
Depreciation		674		674	—	2,022		2,022	—
Total uncontrollable		1,627		1,574	53	4,881		4,622	259
Total - all categories		23,926		30,574	(6,648)	71,778		91,122	(19,344)
Explanation of variances									
Volume variance		22,299	26,652		(4,353)	66,897	88,840		(21,943)
Spending variances									
Controllable					(2,348)				2,340
Uncontrollable					53				259
Total variance					(6,648)				(19,344)

The same principle can be applied to the supply category; and adding salaries and supplies together gives us the total original budget, performance budget, actual expenditures, and variance, which are under the control of the responsibility center manager. These amounts are reported on the Total Controllable line.

For purposes of completing the responsibility center report, services and depreciation figures are entered in the Original Budget and Actual Expenditures columns only, and a variance is calculated. The totals for these two categories are entered on the Total Uncontrollable line, indicating that they cannot be controlled in any reasonable way by the manager of the responsibility center.

Finally, the total costs for the responsibility center are calculated and variances are summarized. Here the difference between the original budget and the performance budget indicates the impact that volume of care alone had on the budget. Consequently, the difference between the performance budget and actual expenditures (i.e., the controllable variance) reflects a combination of greater or lesser (1) case mix, (2) intensity of services, (3) efficiency, and (4) unit price and wage levels.

A second-level report in the BCS can give managers additional detail on the elements which lie behind the salary and supply totals. Exhibit 7A–10 is for supplies, and separates the total into three parts: physician-ordered, nursing-determined, and other. Such a report can assist a responsibility center manager in assessing the reasons underlying a variance in the supply category. Similarly, Exhibit 7A–11 subdivides salaries for purposes of further analysis.

SUMMARY

While the BCS shown here may not be the exact tool that a hospital manager wishes to use, it nevertheless provides a framework which integrates budget formulation and monitoring. Additionally, it can help move a hospital toward a budgeting system that holds managers responsible only for those costs they can control. The sample BCS, thus, may play a useful role in assisting managers to develop systems which are the most appropriate for their own institutions.

SPY POND HOSPITAL
Responsibility Center Budget Report—
Cost Category Detail: Supplies

Responsibility center _____   Fiscal year _____   For month _____

Supplies	Budget rate/ day	This month				Year-to-date			
		Original budget	Performance budget	Actual expenditures	Variance	Original budget	Performance budget	Actual expenditures	Variance
Physician-ordered Days Amount									
Nursing-determined Days Amount									
Other: Days Amount									
Total: Days Amount									

Comments:

SPY POND HOSPITAL
Responsibility Center Budget Report—
Cost Category Detail: Salaries

Responsibility center _____   Fiscal year _____   For month _____

| Salaries | Budget rate/ day | This month | | | Year-to-date | | |
		Original budget	Performance budget	Actual expenditures	Variance	Original budget	Performance budget	Actual expenditures	Variance
Rate and days care									
Physicians									
Nurses									
Technicians									
Administrative									
Other									
Total									

Comments:

8

Management Information Systems

Previous chapters have emphasized the notion that different costs are used for different purposes. Indeed, as was discussed in Chapter 7, one of the most difficult aspects of managing a health or human service organization is obtaining cost and other data structured in a way that is useful for ongoing decision making and control. In many organizations a great deal of data are available in raw form, but the time and effort necessary to organize and structure them in several different formats for particular decision-making purposes is so time-consuming and costly that the effort frequently is not made. In an attempt to resolve this dilemma, managers increasingly are turning to the use of computerized management information systems (MIS).

Unfortunately, what may seem as a panacea all too often turns out to be a costly, time-consuming effort with minimal if any satisfactory results. In part the problems are technical, but in many instances they are behavioral and managerial as well. Although much has been written concerning the technical aspects of management information systems, relatively little attention has been devoted to the behavior and managerial issues associated specifically with designing and implementing a MIS[1] This chapter attempts to shed some light on these latter issues.

---

[1]A notable exception is R. E. Herzlinger, "Why Data Systems Fail in Non-Profit Organizations," *Harvard Business Review*, January–February 1977.

The chapter begins with a discussion of the difference between management information systems and management control systems, and develops a framework which puts management information systems in the context of planning and control systems in general. Next, the chapter examines the reasons for utilizing a MIS, and the barriers which exist to the development of one. Finally, the general question of implementation is discussed, including both the wide variety of issues that can arise during the implementation of a MIS, and the notion of alternative implementation strategies.

FRAMEWORK FOR MIS

The relationship between management control systems and management information systems perhaps can be viewed most easily if we think in terms of the framework developed by Robert Anthony, which distinguishes among the activities of strategic planning, management control, and operational control.[2] He defines strategic planning as

> the process of deciding on objectives of the organization, on changes in these objectives, on the resources used to attain these objectives, and on the policies that are to govern the acquisition, use, and disposition of these resources. (P. 16.)

Management control, by contrast

> is the process by which managers assure that resources are obtained and used effectively and efficiently in the accomplishment of the organization's objectives. (P. 17.)

And, finally, operational control

> is the process of assuring that specific tasks are carried out effectively and efficiently. (P. 18.)

Although the three elements of the framework overlap somewhat at the margins, they nevertheless identify three distinct kinds of managerial activities and concerns. In this context, one must recognize that strategic planning is an inherently subjective activity, frequently utilizing ad hoc or "soft" data and managerial intuition. Operational control, by contrast, is inherently objective, frequently carried out through the use of decision rules that are relatively well-established and easily quantified. A good example

---

[2]R. N. Anthony, *Planning and Control Systems: A Framework for Analysis* (Boston: Harvard Business School Division of Research, 1965).

is the reordering of inventory or the preparation of billing statements.

Management control shares some features of both strategic planning and operational control. It has a subjective element in that it frequently requires judgment and decisions which are by no means clear-cut. On the other hand, as Chapters 6 and 7 indicated, it can and must be characterized by a flow of information at regular intervals to provide managers with feedback on the effects of their decisions. It is in this latter respect that the relationship between the management control system and the management information system is so important.

Table 8–1 indicates not only the relationship between management control systems and management information systems but the nature of the relationship between MIS and both strategic

TABLE 8–1

Relationship between Planning and Control Activities and Management Information Systems

Planning and control activities	Data collection	Processing/ presentation	Management use
Strategic planning	Information needs constantly changing; data frequently not available; close approximations acceptable; derived from external sources.	Processing rules changing; presentation needs constantly changing; detail less important than aggregate trends.	Relatively subjective; somewhat infrequent; focus is on future.
Management control	Some subjective decisions concerning what data to collect, from whom and from where; needs change, but not as frequently as in strategic planning; precision is important, although approximizations will do on occasion; data mainly internal, although some external data frequently is important (e.g., competitor's charges).	Some difficulties in assessing needs and determining processing rules, but once in place, change is slow. Linkages among systems are important; summaries (with supporting detail) are important.	Some subjective decisions require a regular flow of data; some uses frequent, some infrequent; focus is on present but with implications for future.
Operational control	Relatively easy to determine needs; data collection frequently is time-consuming; precision is important; data come from internal sources.	Relatively easy; well-defined and slow to change; detail is important.	Relatively easy; use is the same for many organizations; high frequency or on an "as needed" basis (e.g., inventory reorder); focus is on present.

planning and operational control. The table looks at three important aspects of a MIS: data collection, data processing and presentation, and management use. As can be seen from an examination of the table, a MIS is of limited use in the strategic planning effort, given that (1) the relevant data needs are constantly changing and frequently not available from within the organization; (2) the way in which the data must be processed and presented depends on the kinds of analyses being performed, and thus will be changing constantly; and (3) the managerial effort is a relatively subjective one and, therefore, does not lend itself readily to the kinds of data available through a MIS.

By contrast, a MIS can be quite useful in operational control activities. Data collection is relatively easy, processing and presentation follow a standardized set of rules, and managerial use is rather straightforward. Although data collection can be time-consuming, the processing effort would be much more time-consuming and much more error-prone were the information not computerized. Perhaps the best example is payroll, where the effort necessary to calculate an employee's withholding tax and other deductions, while relatively simple at each step, is both time-consuming (given the large number of steps involved) and highly likely to contain errors when a similar set of calculations is performed manually for several hundred or thousand employees.

It is, therefore, at the intersection of the management control row and of each of the three MIS columns that many of the interesting and challenging MIS issues arise in organizations. It is here that difficult decisions need to be made on (1) what data to collect, where to obtain them, and from whom they are to come; (2) how the data are to be analyzed and flow within the MIS, including among subsystems of the MIS; (3) how users' needs are to be assessed; and (4) what impediments exist to utilizing the information in a managerial way. In this context, a central question to be answered in terms of the relationship between MCS and MIS is whether an organization needs a computerized or manual MIS. This is the subject of the next section.

WHY A (COMPUTERIZED) MIS?

Many health and human service organizations, recognizing the need for more effective ways to maintain and process information, are moving in the direction of computerized management information systems. Although computer-based information systems have been used rather extensively in the for-profit world for some time, they have not been as thoroughly tested and evaluated in the health and human services. Thus, a manager facing the problem of information becoming increasingly difficult to process and control, must ask essentially two questions: "Could a computerized management information system help me manage my organization better?" and, "If so, how do I decide what kind of system to utilize?"

The answer to the first question clearly is a highly situational one; it will depend on the particular needs of the organization, the divisions or programs of the organization that might have a need for a computer-based system, the skills and attitudes of the staff members involved, and so on. There are, however, two broad issues which generally must be taken into consideration regardless of the organization or program making the decision.

The first and most fundamental issue concerns the nature of the organization's data needs. Generally a computer is most beneficial when an organization's or program's data needs possess at least one of the following characteristics:

The data are voluminous, must be presented in managerially useful forms, but are not managerially useful in their "raw state" (e.g., encounter information in a clinic).

There are several managers who use the same set of data, but each needs the data presented in a different format (e.g., cost data for cost reports as well as for budget reports).

Different individuals in the organization who are widely separated geographically need relatively constant access to the same set of data (e.g., regional offices of a home health agency or hospitals in a multi-hospital system).

There are complex processing formulas (e.g., full cost accounting reports, patient scheduling).

Large quantities of data must be processed for managerial use in a short amount of time (e.g., budget reports).

Clearly, the more of these characteristics that are present at any given time, the greater the organization's need for a computer.

The second issue for consideration in making the computer-based decision is the organizational one. Included in this category of concerns are questions of: how professionals in the organization will react to the introduction of a computer; the extent to which the computer-based system will give managers greater potential for control over their programs and budgets, and how they will use that potential; the issue of confidentiality of patient or client data; and the cost of the system as compared to that of other activities in which the organization might engage.

WHAT KIND OF MIS?[3]

Given the need to explore the possibility of utilizing a computerized MIS, a manager typically will encounter a variety of systems available, at a variety of costs.

The task of choosing the "right" one can be quite difficult, particularly if the manager has had little previous contact with information system technology. Thus, it may be useful to outline a framework which can be used for evaluating and comparing different types of information systems. The framework can be divided into five different areas of analysis: performance objectives, flexibility needs, timing considerations, risk element, and costs.

Performance Objectives

In the area of performance objectives, a manager must be concerned with two questions: (1) Will the MIS be client- or patient-oriented, program-oriented, personnel-oriented, or some combination of all three? (2) Will reports produced by the system be used for clerical time-saving, for management, for research, for reporting to third parties, or for some combination of these uses?

The answers to these questions form the nucleus of almost any information system in health and human services organizations. Further, the two issues may be combined to produce a rather extensive list of specific questions that the manager should address. That list might look as follows:

A Client-Oriented or Patient-Oriented System:

Basic questions—for regular third-party reporting, some internal management, community sharing, and some research:

1. Who are my clients/patients?
2. What are their characteristics?
3. What costs are involved in their care/treatment?

Advanced questions—for more sophisticated internal management, community planning, and research:

1. How well am I meeting my clients'/patients' needs?
2. Are my services and effectiveness in meeting those needs improving or worsening? How? Why?

---

[3]Many of the ideas expressed in this section originally appeared in D. W. Young, "Computerized Management Information Systems in Child Care: Techniques for Comparison," *Child Welfare*, July 1974.

3. Are the kinds of services needed by my clients/patients changing?
4. How do client characteristics influence care/treatment costs?

A Program-Oriented System:
Basic questions:

1. What are my programs?
2. How long do clients/patients remain in programs?
3. What are my program costs? Per encounter? Per client/patient day? Per episode of care?

Advanced questions:

1. What are my criteria for evaluating the relative advantages and disadvantages of ongoing programs?
2. Using these criteria, which of my programs are the best?
3. If my budget for next year were less than my present budget, which programs would I eliminate or cut back? Which services would be curtailed?

A Personnel-Oriented System:
Basic questions:

1. What was the total professional workload for last month? Average per professional? Range?
2. How are my professionals geographically organized?
3. What percent of my professionals' time is being spent in clerical activities? Is it increasing or decreasing? By how much?

Advanced questions:

1. Are my professionals specializing (e.g., with aged people, with family budget assistance, with children, with particular problems, such as alcoholism, smoking)? Should they?
2. What are my professionals' areas of greatest expertise? Are those areas being used to their full potential?
3. Are my professionals operating as individuals or as part of a team? Which type of operation is better?
4. What kinds of results are my professionals achieving? At what costs?

The interrelationships among these three areas of system orientation is illustrated schematically in Figure 8–1. As indicated, a variety of additional questions may arise from an examination of areas A, B, C, and D of the figure.

Once decisions have been made concerning the kinds of questions the MIS will be answering, a manager is ready to begin looking at some of the more tangible areas of analysis in assessing alternative information systems.

FIGURE 8–1

Informational Interrelationships among Clients, Programs, and Personnel

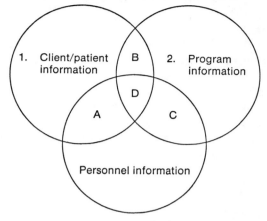

Area	Basic question(s)
1. Client/patient	Who are clients/patients? What are their characteristics? Costs?
2. Program	What are programs? What are program costs?
3. Personnel	Who are personnel? What are their abilities?
A. (Personnel—Client/Patient)	Which personnel work with which clients/patients and how well?
B. (Program—Client/Patient)	Which clients/patients are in which programs? Are their needs met?
C. (Personnel—Program)	Which personnel work with which programs and how well?
D. (Personnel—Client/Patient—Program	Which personnel deal with which clients/patients and in which programs and how well?

Flexibility Needs

The principal decision on flexibility is whether to contract with an outside vendor for a standardized set of reports or to develop an inhouse MIS. Although standardized reports generally are considered the most convenient from an operational point of view, the information needs of an organization frequently exceed what is available from outside vendors. Whether vendors will be able to satisfy these supplemental or emerging reporting requirements, and at what cost, are important questions to attempt to answer prior to contracting out. On the other hand, if a system is developed internally, report formats and content can be determined on an as-needed basis, and reports generally can be designed and prepared by the organization's own personnel. With this option, however, the organization loses the expertise and economies of scale of the vendor, and incurs some fixed costs to maintain its computer capability.

In addition to looking at report preparation questions, managers should consider such issues as the ability of a system to interact with other information systems, programs, or departments, as well as with other organizations for purposes of central planning and reporting. An organization that is growing or diversifying, for example, should assess the extent to which various MIS options have the ability to keep pace with its strategic changes. Frequently, the answer becomes some combination of internal capability and outside vendor support.

Timing Considerations

In the area of timing, the key question is, "How much time will pass until the system is designed and operational?" Depending on the system being used or considered, this time period can be rather lengthy.

Some of the more important activities to be carried out during system design and implementation are the following:

Determination of data base elements.

Design and preparation of data collection forms.

Design of report formats.

Preparation and testing of computer programs.

Training of professional, clerical, and managerial staff in the process of form completion and updating.

Training of staff in techniques for effective utilization of reports.

Original data collection and verification.

Original report distribution, review, and correction where necessary.

If an information system is being designed specifically for an organization, a good deal of time can be spent in system design, computer programming, and system testing. Obviously, these activities are not necessary if a standardized system is being purchased from an outside vendor. Remember, however, vendors also must design, program, and test their systems, and an organization purchasing a standardized system should be certain that the system is indeed functioning as claimed. Assuming this is the case, the system generally will not become operational immediately. Training and data collection activities will be necessary, for example; and the system may have to be adapted to the organization's particular needs, so installation activities may take some time. In general, though, total elapsed time will be much less with a standardized system than with one designed specifically for an organization.

Clearly, it is not possible to provide precise guidelines for the amount of time to be spent in system design or implementation activities, or both, since several unknown variables are involved. Indeed, the time necessary to move a system from the stage of conceptualization to operation is influenced by a wide variety of factors: the type of computer system being used, the kind and amount of information being collected, the availability of administrative and professional personnel for participation in training and other meetings, the adaptability of clerical staff to new procedures, and, if necessary, the speed with which computer programming and related system design activities are carried out. In this context, it is most important that managers considering alternative information systems obtain estimates of both the time needed for each of these activities and the amount and type of effort required from the organization's clerical, managerial, and professional personnel.

Risk Element

The implementation of any new system—either a standardized one or one designed specifically for an organization—involves a risk. A manager considering an information system should ask two questions concerning risk: "What are the chances the system won't perform as claimed?" and "What are the consequences if it does not?"

Answers to these questions are not easily forthcoming. However, several methods can be used to limit the agency's risk. First is utilization of a standardized system or a modified version of a standardized system that is already operating satisfactorily. Second is an independent review of alternatives by some competent third party, such as the organization's accounting firm. Finally, a manager may wish to consider some sort of legal document that spells out the obligations of both parties, sets performance and timing objectives, specifies costs, and provides for compensation should the system not perform as represented.

Obviously, this latter activity is not possible if the organization's internal MIS department is designing the system. In this case, careful monitoring by the managers desiring the system (or a MIS committee, if one exists) generally is necessary to assure that the system is designed properly and implemented in a timely way. This is not an activity that can be delegated and ignored, and examples abound of systems which either fail to meet managerial needs or are implemented well behind schedule, or both. Regular review and follow-up by key managers are as important in MIS design as they are in any of the organization's more programmatic activities.

Cost

Obviously, the question of cost is one of the most serious to be considered. Information system costs fall into two general categories: one-time setup costs, and ongoing operational costs. Costs in each category can vary widely, depending on a number of factors.

Considerations in the setup category include the following:

---

1. Whether the system is being designed specifically for the organization or a standardized system is being purchased.
2. Type of computer system being used, and related equipment and storage needs.
3. Number and complexity of reports desired when the system becomes operational.
4. Extent of participation of agency personnel in the design of the system and in training meetings.
5. Amount of time needed to complete original data submission forms and to verify results.

Considerations in the operational cost category include:

---

1. Computer operating charges (or vendor charges).
2. Data processing personnel salaries and fringe benefits.
3. Professional, clerical, and managerial time necessary to submit pertinent information on an ongoing basis and to review reports.

Both cost categories are discussed below.

One-time Setup Costs. *Specific versus standardized system.* Generally, a system designed specifically for an organization costs more than a standardized one. Computer programming and testing costs, which can be high, account for the majority of the differential. Such factors as systems analysis, design modifications, and general time-lapses (creating a need for relearning and retraining) account for the remaining differential between the two approaches.

Equipment and storage costs. These one-time costs consist of such items as storage files, computer purchase and installation charges (if an organization is purchasing or leasing its own computer), and peripheral equipment, such as tape and disk drives, and other related office equipment.

Number and complexity of reports. If a system is designed specifically for the agency, the cost of computer programming varies to a large extent with the number and complexity of reports desired. Usually, the one-time cost associated with a standardized system does not depend on the kind and quantity of reports desired, but the ongoing costs will.

Participating by agency personnel in meetings. Adequate grass-roots support for an information system in a health and human service organization is difficult to obtain unless the organization's personnel participate in both system design and training meetings. The importance of this should not be overlooked, but neither should the cost. Time spent in design and training meetings is time that cannot be spent with clients or patients. At best, this is a "hidden" cost that can be absorbed by the organization. At worst, the cost may be a direct outlay for short-term staff to cover professional and clerical responsibilities, while regular staff participate in meetings.

Initial form completion and verification. This cost is similar to the participation cost, although generally it can be absorbed into the day-to-day routine and, thus, remains a "hidden" cost, rather than a direct outlay. In some instances, however, it may be necessary for an organization to incur some sizable temporary help costs if initial form completion and verification encompasses a large number of items (and must be done quickly).

Operational Costs. *Computer operating charges.* Computer operating charges are a function of several factors. For organizations with their own systems, the most important consideration is whether the computer is leased, purchased, or contracted out (i.e., computer time is rented from another organization, such as a service bureau). If the organization is leasing or purchasing its computer, the cost is a fixed monthly item (either a direct outlay or a depreciation expense). Alternatively, use of a service bureau means that the cost will vary in almost direct proportion to usage. The difference, then, is one of fixed versus variable costs in which, at a certain volume of activity (hours of computer usage), lower unit costs will result if the organization uses its own computer. As indicated above, organizations that use standardized systems will incur operating charges based essentially on the number, frequency, and complexity of the reports they receive.

The other important factor to consider in assessing computer operating charges is technology. Generally, more sophisticated technology is more expensive, although the introduction of mini and micro-computers in recent years has made the whole task of technology assessment much more complicated than previously. In fact, the hardware-related portion of total MIS costs has fallen dramatically over the past 10 years, being replaced by personnel-related costs.[4]

Data processing personnel. Organizations utilizing a computerized management information system will find it necessary to have data processing support personnel, including data entry clerks, operations staff, programmers, and system analysts. The number and type of support personnel needed will depend not only on the standardized-versus-internal decision but on the nature, scope, and complexity of the MIS itself.

Professional staff time. Professional staff frequently need to participate to some degree in regular data submission and updating, and the amount of time required will depend on the kind of system in use. If, for example, the system is designed to report on professional activity, it may be necessary to complete daily, weekly, or monthly information forms. If, however, the system maintains information on client or patient characteristics, data submission and updating may be required less frequently, and it may be possible for clerical, rather than professional, staff to perform data submission activities. In addition, professional staff frequently are required to review and work with the system's output reports. While this activity generally should improve their effectiveness, it nevertheless requires time on their part. Unless this time substitutes for time which previously was spent reviewing manual output, it will require additional effort.

As previously discussed, the time that a professional spends on information forms and reports is time that cannot be spent with clients or patients, and thus involves "hidden" costs. A manager considering the use of alternative information systems should assess the amount of professional time required by each system, since the effective cost of this time quite easily can exceed the cost of many of the other computer-related activities.

Managerial time. Managerial time requirements are as important as professional ones. Reports must be read, and generally action of some sort is necessary. If the information system is well

---

[4]See B. Allen "An Unmanaged Computer System Can Stop You Dead," *Harvard Business Review,* November–December 1982.

designed, however, useful and meaningful reports should emerge and the managerial time, thus, should be well spent. Nevertheless, this time, too, has a cost that must be assessed as part of the MIS decision.

This section on costs has received considerable emphasis, since costs undoubtedly will play a major role in a manager's final decision. Despite this emphasis, though, a manager should not lose sight of the other criteria of performance objectives, flexibility needs, timing considerations, and the risk element, because these criteria also will help him or her to determine which of several alternative information systems will be most useful to the organization.

IMPLEMENTATION ISSUES

Although implementation issues were mentioned in the last section, the emphasis was placed on the relevant cost and other considerations, rather than on the managerial activities needed to ensure a successful implementation effort. Nevertheless, many managers are painfully aware of MIS endeavors that have failed, been marginally successful, or been much more costly than planned because of difficulties in implementation. Thus, this topic, too, deserves some discussion.

Although there is no standardized solution to implementation problems, several issues frequently arise. The first is the question of the *scope* of the MIS. Although an organization may feel it needs an extensive and complex MIS, many MIS efforts have been less than successful because of attempts to design and implement *the* complete and integrated system, instead of following a "stages" approach. In many instances, a small but successful implementation effort not only can get the MIS off to a good start but will give many people in the organization confidence in the ability of management to implement the system. Thus, while it may not always be feasible, a stages approach is a central implementation issue worthy of management's consideration.

A second issue is the organizational location of the MIS department. In some organizations, the MIS becomes the responsibility of the planning department; in others, the MIS director reports to the organization's executive director; in still others, he or she reports to the controller or to the assistant director. While there is no prescribed "best" reporting relationship, there are two important considerations: (1) the MIS skills of the general manager to whom the MIS manager reports, and (2) the general manager's power within the organization. The skills are necessary if the MIS department is to be managed and controlled effectively. Additionally, the extent to which people in the organization take the MIS effort seriously will depend to a great extent on the importance they feel top management gives to the effort. Top management can signal its support quite noticeably by where in the organization it places line responsibility for the MIS.

A third issue is the role of the professional staff in the implementation effort. Since an organization's professionals frequently will not be particularly supportive of the MIS effort, and since their support frequently is important to the success of the implementation process, managers need to give serious consideration to securing their support. Involvement in the design phase (or the system decision phase, if a standardized system is being purchased), development of reports that are meaningful to the professional staff, minimizing their role in data input, and communicating the importance of the system to them are all ways in which management can work to secure the support of the organization's professionals.

Finally, with internally designed systems, there is the issue of the role of the system designer. In the first place, a manager must consider whether the designer is to be an employee of the organization or a consultant. There are advantages to each, and, once again, there is no right answer. On the one hand, as an employee of the organization, the system designer may be able to devote more time to the system. On the other hand, the consultant, by not being as available as an employee to various members of the organization, may be able to give top management an incentive to become involved and to play a central role in the system's success. Additionally, a consultant may bring a broader base of expertise, and thus be better able to assist the organization in avoiding pitfalls in the implementation process.

Apart from the choice between an employee and a consultant, there remains the question of the designer's role in the organization. Is he or she to be an advisor to other managers or top management, or to have full responsibility for implementation? How is he or she to be managed, particularly if top management has only a limited understanding of the kinds of problems that can arise during implementation and of their associated cost and timing implications? Finally, should the designer or top management have responsibility for maintaining appropriate communications with others in the organization about progress with the MIS effort, requirements for staff, and so on?

In summary, a wide variety of managerial issues are associated with a successful MIS effort, issues which go well beyond the purely technical ones of software and hardware choices. In particular, managerial action is required in (1) the decision to use a computerized MIS; (2) choices about the kind of system to be used, its focus, and its cost to the organization; and (3) the implementation process. The intent of this chapter has been to provide managers with a framework for considering the nature of their actions and choices in these areas.

MANAGERIAL CHECKLIST

1. What characteristics does my organization possess that indicate the need for a computerized MIS, such as voluminous data, multiple users of the data base, geographically dispersed users, complex processing formulas, short turnaround times for reports? If some of the characteristics exist and we do not have a computer-based system, what are the financial and organizational impediments to developing one? How might they be overcome?

2. What kinds of questions might a MIS answer for our organization? Are these questions patient-related, program-related, personnel-related, or some combination of the three? How specific have I been in identifying these questions? Can I be even more specific? How might these questions change as we move in new strategic directions?

3. How much flexibility do we need (have) with our MIS? Will a system purchased from an outside vendor satisfy all our needs, both current and anticipated? If not, should we develop our own system or move toward an internal system supplemented by some combination of standardized systems purchased from outside vendors? What will our fixed costs be under various options? Our variable costs?

4. If we are considering alternative information systems, do we have estimates of the amount of time necessary for system design and implementation? What amount and type of effort will be required from our own personnel during these activities? Is this feasible? If not, what options exist?

5. What risks are involved in our MIS strategy? Have we adequately dealt with these either in a contract with the vendor or in working relationships between our internal MIS department and the relevant program managers?

6. Have we analyzed the potential MIS costs for both one-time setup and ongoing operational activities? If the costs in either category are excessive, how might they be influenced by changing various decisions about either the questions we wish the MIS to answer or the flexibility we wish it to have? What other trade-offs might be made? What "hidden" (i.e., personnel-related) costs exist?

7. What is our implementation strategy, either for a new MIS or for modifications to an existing one? Can we follow a stages approach?

8. Where in the organization do we wish to locate responsibility for the MIS? Will this location adequately signal top management's support for the MIS effort?

9. What steps are planned to involve professional staff in the MIS decision and, if relevant, the design phase of the effort? What additional efforts might be taken to secure their support?

10. Who will take responsibility for the system design—an internal employee or an outside consultant? Does the designer have the requisite knowledge of the organizational activities being implemented on the MIS? Will he or she have top management's support? What role will he or she play in the implementation process? How is he or she to be managed?

Bibliography

Allen, B. "An Unmanaged Computer System Can Stop You Dead." *Harvard Business Review,* November–December 1982.

Anthony, R. N. *Planning and Control Systems: A Framework for Analysis.* Boston: Harvard Business School Division of Research, 1965.

Austin, C. J. *Information Systems for Hospital Administrators.* Ann Arbor, Mich: Health Administration Press, 1979.

Ball, M. J., and T. N. Boyle, Jr. "Hospital Information Systems: Past, Present and Future." *Hospital Financial Management,* February 1980.

Brooks, F. P., Jr. "The Mythical Man Month." *Datamation,* December 1974.

Buss, M. D. J. "Penny Wise Approach to Data Processing." *Harvard Business Review,* July–August 1981.

Coffey, R. M. *How a Medical Information System Affects Hospital Costs: The El Camino Hospital Experience.* MCHHR Research Summary Series, Washington, D.C.: U.S. Department of Health, Education and Welfare, Publication Number (PHS) 80-3265, March 1980.

Drazen, E., and J. Metzger. *Methods for Evaluating Costs of Automated Hospital Information Systems.* MCHHR Research Summary Series. Washington, D.C.: U.S. Department of Health and Human Services, Publication Number (PHS) 81-3283, July 1981.

Goldstein, R. C., and R. L. Nolan. "Personal Privacy vs. the Corporate Computer." *Harvard Business Review,* March–April 1975.

Herzlinger, R. "Management Non-Information Systems in Health Care Organizations." *Health Care Management Review,* Spring 1976.

_____. "Why Data Systems Fail in Non Profit Organizations." *Harvard Business Review,* January/February 1977.

Hodge, M. H. *Health Planning Review of Medical Information Systems.* MCHHR Research Report Series. Washington, D. C.: U.S. Department of Health and Human Services, Publication Number (PHS) 81-3303, May 1981.

Kuntz, E. F. "Hospital Information Systems: Hospitals Plug in to Micros Despite Limited Software." *Modern Health Care,* April 1982.

Malvey, M. "Single Systems, Complex Environments: Hospital Financial Information Systems." *Managing Information Series*, vol. 2. Beverly Hills, Calif.: Sage Publications, 1981.

Nolan, R. L. "Managing the Crises in Data Processing." *Harvard Business Review*, March–April 1979.

Pillow, C. I. "Providing the Right Data to the Right Person at the Right Time." *Hospital Financial Management*, June 1981.

Potgio, F. L. "Shared Data Processing—A New Approach." *Hospital Financial Mangement*, June 1981.

Schoech, D. *Computer Use in Human Services*. New York: Human Sciences Press, 1982.

Srinipasan, C. A., and P. E. Dascher. "A Method to Improve Software Management." *Hospital Financial Management*, June 1981.

U.S. Department of Health, Education and Welfare. *The Design of Management Information Systems for Mental Health Organizations*. NIMH Series C, No. 13, 1976, Washington, D.C.

————. *Demonstration and Evaluation of a Total Hospital Information System*. MCHSR Research Summary Series, DHEW Publication Number (HRA) 77-3188, July 1977, Washington, D. C

Young, D. W. "Computerized Management Information Systems in Child Care: Techniques for Comparison." *Child Welfare*, July 1974.

9

The Administrative Systems Perspective[1]

As the reader no doubt has noticed, the focus of the preceding eight chapters has shifted from rather specific topics, such as financial and cost accounting, to ones which require much more in the way of managerial judgement. The result is that the last few chapters have been somewhat more conceptual than the first few, providing what might best be called a language system, rather than information on specific techniques or processes. The purpose of this final chapter is to become even more conceptual, and to put some of the ideas set forth in the last few chapters into an overarching—or an "administrative systems"—framework.

ADMINISTRATIVE SYSTEMS DEFINED

Although the classical view of an organization is one represented by the boxes on an organizational chart, all managers know that

---

[1]This chapter summarizes many of the ideas and concepts previously discussed in D. W. Young, *The Managerial Process in Human Service Organizations* (New York: Praeger Publishers, 1979).

an organizational chart provides, at best, only a preliminary overview of what actually goes on within an organization. Indeed, there are many processes and managerial activities that take place which are not depicted on the organizational chart. This is true in all types of organizations, including those involved in health and human services.

One of the most widely cited definitions of an organization—in fact, the one John Kenneth Galbraith has referred to as the classic definition—is that given by Chester Barnard in 1938 when he wrote *The Functions of the Executive.*[2] Barnard defined an organization as "a system of consciously coordinated activities or forces of two or more persons." The concept of administrative systems discussed in this chapter has its roots in two aspects of this definition: *system* and *conscious coordination.* From an administrative systems perspective, then, an organization can be viewed as a series of systems, of which some operate independently and some interact with others. The key concept in terms of the conscious coordination of activities that Barnard referred to is the maintenance of a "fit" among these systems. This concept was discussed in Chapter 6 in terms of misfits between the budgetary system and other organizational systems. In that chapter as well as this one, "fit" means that the systems, if they are to be successful, and, in turn, if the organization is to be successful, must reinforce rather than contradict one another.

There are three broad categories of administrative systems: organization, reporting, and planning. These categories and the specific systems in each are shown in Figure 9–1. Managers of health and human service institutions generally interact in some way with all three classes of systems, and, therefore, must frequently concern themselves with the ways in which these systems reinforce or contradict one another. Thus, although this chapter is divided into three parts, each representing one cate-

FIGURE 9–1 _____

Administrative Systems Overview

Organization systems	Reporting systems	Planning systems
Formal authority	Financial	Strategy formulation
Patient processing	Program	Program Adaptation
Conflict resolution		Budget formulation
Value maintenance		
Motivation		

---

[2]C. I. Barnard, *The Functions of the Executive* (Cambridge, Mass.: Harvard University Press, 1938).

gory, the importance of focusing on the whole set of systems cannot be overemphasized. Indeed, the concept of *fit* should constantly be kept in mind; that the specific system in operation within an organization is not only important in and of itself but must also be considered in terms of its fit with the other administrative systems.

ORGANIZATION SYSTEMS

As Figure 9–1 indicates, five organization systems are important in health and human services management: (1) the formal authority system, (2) the patient (or client) processing system, (3) conflict resolution systems, (4) value maintenance systems, and (5) motivation systems.

The Formal Authority System

A variety of formal authority systems can exist in organizations. At one end of the spectrum is the hierarchical or authoritarian system. This is very much a top-down system—orders are given by an individual who is clearly in charge, and those orders are fanned out through the rest of the organization. There is little questioning of the orders; they are simply obeyed. A good example of an authoritarian system can be found in a military organization, such as the U.S. Army.

At the other end of the spectrum is the collegial system. Here the authority process is a much more interactive one, and there is a great deal of participation by many members of the organization in the decision-making process. Decisions frequently are made by individual organizational units or members in those units, and the information flow is both from the top down and from the bottom up. A good example is a university.

While most professionals in health and human service organizations may have a preference for a collegial authority system, they should recognize that such a system can be quite costly. A great deal of time and energy is required in the decision-making process, since, rather than simply accepting orders and carrying them out, members of the organization actually participate in the formulation of decisions.[3]

Lying somewhere between these two extremes is the somewhat unusual authority system of the modern hospital, in which

---

[3]For additional details on this contrast, see W. G. Ouchi, *Theory Z: How American Business Can Meet the Japanese Challenge* (Reading, Mass.: Addison-Wesley Publishing, 1981).

a rather continual power struggle exists among physicians, administators, and other occupational groups. The result is what might best be called a hospital power equilibrium, in which each of these groups attempts to better its position vis-à-vis the others.[4] Although the nature of the interactions are not shown, the two lines of authority are quite clearly indicated in the fairly typical hospital organizational chart contained in Figure 9–2.

The Patient Processing System

There is a process that exists within all health or human service organizations whereby patients or clients are identified and "processed." For example, in a hopital, inpatients typically are identified through either the admitting office, the emergency room, or the outpatient department. From the point of identification, various steps are taken to deliver services, and ultimately patients are discharged. By contrast, in a community health center or other ambulatory facility, many patients are identified when they "walk in" or call for an appointment. The patient processing system, thus, will be very different, requiring follow-up notices, phone calls on occasion, and so on. A patient also is not "discharged" as definitively as in a hospital.

Clearly, a thorough understanding of the patient processing system is essential for effective management of an organization. Since the system involves a number of decisions, made by a variety of individuals within the organization, frequently including the patient, assurances must be made that it works well. If necessary, modifications must be made to insure that patients' or clients' needs are met, and such modifications are quite difficult unless the system itself is accurately defined and well understood.

Conflict Resolution Systems

Although the word *conflict* can have a somewhat pejorative connotation for many individuals, it frequently can be quite beneficial to an organization's clients. One of the advantages of organizational conflict is that it allows important managerial and professional concerns to surface and be resolved.

> *Example:* Consider two community health centers. At Center A, a nurse practitioner (NP) and a social worker (SW) spend a great deal of time with a patient during his or her initial visit, formulating a

---

[4]For additional details, see R. S. Saltman and D. W. Young, "The Hospital Power Equilibrium: An Alternative View of the Cost Containment Dilemma," *Journal of Health Politics, Policy, and Law,* Fall 1981.

FIGURE 9-2
Hospital Organization Chart

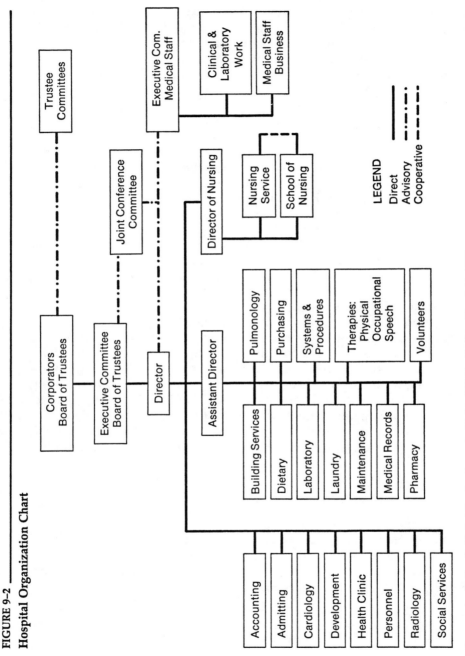

Source: Application for Project Construction, submitted to HEW by Faulkner Hospital in 1971.

care plan when necessary. A physician spends only minimal time with the patient. The NP and SW then discuss the care plan with the physician to reach a final decision. At Center B, the physician spends a great deal of time with the patient, while the NP and SW are only minimally involved. The physician determines the care plan and informs the NP and SW of what will be expected of them under it.

Given these two types of "patient processing systems," it is possible to identify several areas where conflict can take place among the three individuals responsible for the patient, with the first center rather clearly having a greater potential for conflict than the second. Indeed, one also could speculate that patients themselves could also become involved in a conflictive way more in Center A than in Center B. A logical question, then, is, "Why would Center A have a system of processing patients that produces so many potential conflicts when it could just as easily have a system like Center B's, which produces minimal conflicts?"

Analysis: It would appear that the patient processing system in Center A, with all the conflicts it generates, is in the end result much better for the patient, since a variety of people, presumably with different perspectives that bear on the patient's health, participate in the decision-making process. The ultimate result is that patients do not become victims of a processing system based more on clinical assessments than on their needs within the larger social system.

Conflict can be detrimental to an organization, however, if not managed properly and resolved. Among other difficulties, unresolved conflict can result in different members of the organization carrying out different activities, with respect to a given patient, which are quite possible mutually contradictory and potentially damaging. One example of this dilemma can be found in those hospital settings where nurses and physicians have not resolved the conflict over how much information should be communicated to patients about their health status. The result, frequently, is that patients and their families receive conflicting or incomplete information and become understandably upset.

In short, conflict must be resolved. The amount of resolution that is necessary clearly depends on the amount of conflict that is generated. In the above example concerning community health centers, for instance, one would find Center B having much less of a need for conflict resolution than Center A. Of perhaps greater importance, we would expect to find Center A devoting many more resources (i.e., time) to conflict resolution, and that its "productivity" is lower than Center B. Thus, the choice to use a more interactive patient processing system has implications not only for the conflict resolution system but for the organization's reporting and motivation systems as well.

Apart from the *amount* of conflict resolution, there is also a question about the *nature* of conflict resolution. Conflict can be resolved by one of several different modes, and again it may be useful to look at two ends of a spectrum. At one end is what might be termed *forcing*, a mode characterized by a highly structured, top-down approach, where the conflict is appealed to an authoritarian party and that person simply makes a decison. At the other end is what might be referred to as *direct confrontation*, here the individuals involved in the conflict work out their differences together, without the intervention of authority figures, third parties, and the like. As Figure 9-3 indicates, the time impli-

FIGURE 9-3

Modes of Conflict Resolution and Time Implications

	Direct confrontation	Forcing
Management time	Low	High
Professional time	High	Low

cations differ considerably in the two modes. With direct confrontation, the organization's professionals spend considerably more time working out their differences than with a forcing mode in which "management" (which might be a supervising professional) spends more time.

In this context, it is important to recognize that there are conflict resolution systems in almost all organizations. The patterns of behavior—or processes—may or may not be formally stated, but, in fact, they exist and are used for conflict resolution. What is important is that these conflict resolution processes fit well with both the patient processing system and the formal authority system.

Value Maintenance System

The need for value maintenance systems is based on the premise that an organization can indeed have values. That is, an organization can have a set of behavior-inducing beliefs—a culture—which give it its distinctive character.[5] Returning to the two centers mentioned previously, let us assume that one has an extremely clear set of organization values, which can be characterized as the following: (1) the best interests of the patient, (2) the spirit of change, and (3) preventive care. Everything that exists in that organization—every departmental unit, every program, every service that is delivered—can be characterized as fitting into one or more of these organization values.

Assume further that there is a much less clear value system at the other center. One group of professionals feels that the organization should be concerned with the delivery of curative health services. Other groups believe that community involvement, health education, and research are important. While all of these may be noble values, they frequently may be mutually incompatible, with the consequence that programs could be developed that fit one of the values but not others. The result may be a less than harmonious climate within the organization.

The principal reason organizational values are important is that they constitute one of two ways of assuring that people in an organization will do what is necessary for the viability of that organization. Specifically, if people in an organization believe in and subscribe to the organization's values, they are much more capable of making decisions that are consistent with and supportive of the overall direction of the organization without the need for intervention by supervisors or others in the decision-making process.

Thus, given a well-defined and consistent set of organization values—which is clearly a prerequisite for effective value maintenance systems—three specific value maintenance systems can be identified: hiring/firing, training, and communication. These systems can assist a manager to instill in the organization's members a sense of what the organization is all about, as well as what is important organizationally. This, in turn, can significantly influence how members of the organization go about making decisions. It also can influence the nature of the conflict resolution process, in that conflicts can be resolved more easily if everyone

---

[5]One of the earliest statements of the importance of organizational values can be found in P. Selznick, *Leadership in Administration* (New York: Harper & Row, 1957). More recent and specific examples can be found in Ouchi, *Theory Z.*

involved has the same general understanding of what is important for the organization and the people it serves.

However, when there are differences in values among members of the organization, conflict resolution can be and frequently is an extremely difficult process. A good example is found in the differences that frequently occur within a hospital between fiscal personnel and physicians, or between fiscal personnel and the outpatient department, or between physicians and nurses. These differences in values—not just different cognitive and emotional orientations, but fundamental differences in the perception of what the organization is all about—can make conflict resolution very difficult indeed. As a consequence, one way of smoothing the conflict resolution process may be to retrace one's steps and pay some attention to values and value maintenance systems.

Motivation Systems

Although a great volume of literature in the management field is addressed to the topic of motivation, Chester Barnard[6] was one of the first to point out that the concept of motivation extends well beyond monetary rewards. Lorsch and Morse[7] provide what is, perhaps, one of the best descriptions of how the motivation process works, stressing that there is an important three-way fit to be attained among (1) personality predispositions of an organization's members, (2) the "internal environment" and, (3) the "external environment." The important result of this three-way fit is that an individual achieves a strong sense of competence. For example, where the external environment (i.e., the world that exists outside the organization) is relatively certain, and when members of the organization prefer dependent authority relationships and have a relatively low tolerance for ambiguity, a high level of organizational control is appropriate (i.e., highly structured ways of organizing people's behavior). By contrast, in an uncertain environment, where members prefer more autonomy and have a higher tolerance for ambiguity, a low level of organizational control seems appropriate (i.e., few controls and an unstructured organization of behavior). The same control structure that is used for workers on an assembly line, for example, will most likely be totally inappropriate for scientists engaged in exploratory research.

Drawing on these concepts, we might conclude that health and

---

[6]Barnard, *The Functions of the Executive.*

[7]Jay W. Lorsch and John J. Morse, *Organizations and Their Members: A Contingency Approach* (New York: Harper & Row, 1974).

human service professionals typically operate in relatively uncertain environments, and that they both desire autonomy and tolerate ambiguity well. Additionally, given the fact that many health and human service agencies are highly constrained in terms of salary scales and promotional possibilities for their professional staff, some thinking about the implications of the Lorsch and Morse findings would appear to be extremely useful.

The dilemma that health and human service managers face, with respect to motivation, arises from what appears to be a lack of congruence between the low level of control being called for by the internal environment, on the one hand, and the demand for accountability being forced upon them by their external environments, on the other. That is, an uncertain environment in conjunction with professionals' (particularly physicians') desire for autonomy and tolerance for ambiguity implies the need for a low level of control. But the external environment—public sector agencies, third-party payors, and the like—frequently is seeking means to increase the level of control, and part of the burden can fall on the organization's professional staff. Hospital administrators who have attempted to interest their medical staffs in assuming some cost-containment responsibility are no doubt acutely aware of this dichotomy.

In short, much of the conflict existing between professionals and administrators in health and human services organizations can be seen much more clearly if looked at through the lenses of Lorsch and Morse. A serious misfit exists between the internal and external environment; a misfit which begins with motivation but which can be traced through all administrative systems described thus far (and many of those to be discussed in the rest of this chapter).

As a consequence, in seeking adequate motivation processes, health and human service managers have two general areas of concern. First, trade-offs that must be made between professionals' need for a low level of control within the organization, and the organization's own need for suitable programmatic and financial controls. Second, ways to bridge the gap between the low level of control needed by professionals, and the increasing demand for accountability by the external environment. Furthermore, not only does there appear to be a desire for autonomy and a high tolerance for ambiguity, on the part of health and human service professionals, but there also appears to be a great deal of "process-orientation." That is, professionals generally expect a concern on the part of the organization not only for the end results of a particular effort but for the means of getting to those results. Additionally, they wish to be a part of the planning process, particularly when the plans being formulated will affect their day-to-day activities. Organizations that have collegial-type authority systems may find it fairly easy to satisfy this process orientation, but it clearly is a much more difficult task in a hierarchical authority system.

What, then, can health and human service managers do about the motivation process, given that it is one of only five organization systems with which they must interact, and given that there are two other categories of administrative systems—reporting and planning—that are also involved in the management process? The answer, in part, lies with an organization's middle managers, who can and must play a vital linking-pin function. Specifically, they must somehow bridge the gap between the requirements of the organization and the external environment, on the one hand, and the needs and predispositions of their staff, on the other. This is no small role, yet it has become an increasingly important one. Lawrence and Lorsch[8] have termed such a person an *integrator*, and have stipulated that the integrative function can be carried out either by such a person or by various other means (i.e., teams, cross-functional committees, the hierarchy, paper-flow systems, and the like).

In short, requests that health and human service organizations make of their professionals frequently do not result from decisions that managers themselves have made; rather, they result from decisions that have been imposed upon them by their external environments. But the need remains to both communicate these decisions to professionals and others and to motivate them to perform well in carrying out the implications of the decisions.

Apart from the integrative function, what can be done in terms of motivation? First, it is important to consider utilizing "value maintenance systems"—to infuse the organization's professionals with a sense of what the organization is all about. In many organizations, given the nature of professional education, it would appear that some of the organization's values will be quite compatible with those of its professionals, and, hence, this process should be easier than in many profit-seeking organizations.

Second, managers concerned with motivating their professional staff can focus on motivation techniques and processes—an internal environment—which reinforce a professional's internally derived motivations and values. To some extent, the team approach used by one of the community health centers described earlier does this, in that it allows health care professionals to

---

[8]P. R. Lawrence and J. W. Lorsch, *Organization and Environment* (Boston: Division of Research, Harvard Business School, 1967).

share experiences with each other in discussions and decision-making efforts. Similarly, training meetings, which allow professionals to raise issues of concern to them, also work toward this end.

Third, it would appear that managers also can provide more "feedback." This term in its broadest sense includes an effective communication system, going beyond the reporting activities described in Chapters 6 and 7 to various other means of sharing information: committees, professional seminars, newsletters, and so on. Further, it includes active participation by professionals in those decision-making processes which have not been totally circumscribed by higher levels in the organization or by the external environment. Not only would feedback of this sort appear to reinforce professionals' predispositions but it would help to make them more aware of the organization's external constraints.

Finally, managers at all levels play a rather key integrating role in translating an organization's procedures and requirements into terms that are compatible with the predispositions of its professional staff. To the extent that managers recognize this role as an important one—regardless of whether the organization defines it as such—they can begin to structure the integrative mechanisms that help to bridge the administrative/professional gap.

Figure 9–4 summarizes the organization systems category. As might be expected, the more specific one becomes in describing these systems, the more the lines between them begin to blur.

FIGURE 9–4

Organization Systems Summarized

Formal authority	Patient processing	Conflict resolution	Value maintenance	Motivation
Hierarchical versus collegial	Contingent on type of organization	Amount versus nature of resolution	Hiring/firing Training Communication	Internal versus external environment
Two lines of authority	Authoritative versus collegial	Forcing versus direct confrontation modes		Certainty of environment
				Preferred authority relationships
				Tolerance for ambiguity
				Process orientation
				Integrative function
				Feedback

The implication, of course, is that a manager's focus must constantly remain on the big picture—the totality of the organization—regardless of the specific system with which he or she is interacting. Moreover, as the discussion in this section has indicated, managers must also be concerned with the highly interdependent nature of their activities within an organization, and thus must be cognizant of the importance of attaining some consistency among those activities (i.e., a *fit* among the various administrative systems).

REPORTING SYSTEMS

As was discussed in Chapters 6 and 7, a wide range of reports and reporting systems exists in most organizations, including those in health and human services. Nevertheless, as discussed in Chapter 7, these systems generally can be classified into one of two kinds: program reporting and financial reporting. Because these systems were discussed separately in Chapter 7, it is not necessary to do so here. Instead, they will be briefly defined and put into their administrative systems context.

Program reporting systems, the reader will recall from Chapter 7, are those which provide managers with information on the organization's programs: number of clients or patients served, nature of the services delivered, results of the services, and the like. Financial reporting systems are those that provide managers with information on costs, revenues, expenses against budgets, and so on—data of a financial nature. Chapters 4 and 5 looked at some basic cost-measurement and reporting questions. Chapter 6 expanded that discussion to responsiblity reporting, and discussed some potential misfits between an organization's budgetary system and some of its other administrative systems. But there are potential misfits of a somewhat broader nature as well.

One such area is that of "financial programmatic congruence," a concept discussed in Chapter 6. In its broader context, this concept might be thought of in terms of a three-way relationship among resources, patients, and programs. For example, in some hospitals, an inpatient admission generates resources automatically in terms of a per-diem payment, although, depending on the nature of the patient and his or her clinical characteristics, the per-diem amount may not always fully cover the direct or even the incremental costs which the hospital incurs as a result of the new admission. This is particularly true when the payment is an all-inclusive per-diem, such as some states have under Medicaid. In a community health center or outpatient department, a visit typically is the link among programs, clients, and resources. In an HMO, Veterans Administration hospital, or other fixed-budget organization, the linkage is less clear. Subscribers generate resource inflows, but utilization of programs by subscribers leads to resource outflows. Sometimes a given programmatic endeavor (e.g., a preventative program of some sort) means small resource outflows in the short term to avoid larger resource outflows in the long term.

What frequently happens as a result of this intersection among patients, resources, and programs is a process of cross-subsidization, a process which becomes exceedingly complex when, for example, an outpatient department, social service department, nursing program, teaching and research endeavors, or others are included in a hospital's activities. What often can happen under such circumstances as these is a loss of control over the use of financial resources, since managers who are pursuing some programmatic goals of the organization may utilize scarce resources, which affect other departments, programs, or the organization as a whole. This is particularly true when, as is frequently the case, some service center managers (e.g., social service), have no budgetary constraints, but the costs of their programs are distributed via the stepdown to revenue centers that do (see Chapter 4).

In a similar fashion, some managers, in attempting to stay within financial limits, may compromise programs in ways that contradict the overall objectives of the organization. For example, while most hospital managers would agree that hospital beds should not be filled inappropriately, and that patients should not be kept in the hospital after the date when they could be discharged, a per-diem system of payment certainly encourages hospitals to extend the convalescent portion of a patient's stay as much as possible. The result is a financial/programmatic misfit, which, if not carefully managed, may result in a hospital engaging in a variety of programmatic endeavors in the name of good health care (e.g., timely discharges or outpatient surgery), but for which it is financially penalized by its reimbursement system. Unmanaged, this lack of financial/programmatic congruence can lead to serious financial difficulties.

Two fairly concrete examples of misfits may be useful in illustrating the seriousness of this issue:

> *Example 1:* In one hospital, clinical department managers receive reports which contain large allocated amounts for service departments, such as medical records. The clinical managers are held re-

sponsible for those amounts, yet have no control over them, while managers of the departments who *could* control the amounts receive *no* reports.[9]

Analysis: The result of this reporting system is that managers of the service departments have no budgetary accountability whatsoever. They spend as they choose, and their expenditures are passed on to managers of clinical departments. Obviously, in this instance, there is a very poor fit among the financial reporting system, the authority system (as measured in this instance by the organizational structure), and, possibly, the budget formulation system (discussed later).

Example 2: In a large municipal hospital undergoing programmatic change, an important objective for the radiology department was to reduce patient waiting time. The programmatic reports, which were developed to monitor waiting time, identified and measured the time-gap from arrival in the department until the film results were reported. Unfortunately, however, there were four time-gaps of importance, two of which overlapped: (1) arrival in the department until entry into the procedure room, (2) time in the procedure room, (3) exit from procedure room until return to patient's room, and (4) exit from procedure room until results were reported.[10]

Analysis: Without this more detailed information, it was not possible to identify key organizational units, assign responsibility and standards to each, and measure performance. Again a poor fit— this time between the desired patient processing system and the program reporting system.

This last example raises an important point, namely that a program reporting system that tracks patients through an organization's patient processing system would seem to be essential to measuring performance in health and human service organizations. A reporting system such as this could identify important points in the patient processing system so that management could review the progress of patients through the organization. Exception reports could highlight instances where the patient processing system was not functioning as designed, so appropriate management intervention could take place.

A central point to emphasize in this context is that, without

---

[9]See the King Community Hospital case in R. N. Anthony and R. E. Herzlinger, *Management Control in Nonprofit Organizations: Text and Cases* (Homewood, Ill.: Richard D. Irwin, 1980).

[10]See the Cook County Hospital (B) case in J. B. Silvers and C. K. Prahalad, *Financial Management of Health Institutions* (Flushing, N.Y.: Spectrum Publications, 1974).

adequate reporting systems, managers may not fully understand the kinds of financial/programmatic trade-offs they are making. As a result, these trade-offs may be made by default, rather than by conscious managerial decision. Thus, with reporting systems, as well as with organization systems, the concept of fit is an important one. Moreover, the nature of financial/programmatic congruence depends in many respects on the kinds of decisions an organization is making as a result of its organization and its planning systems. As such, the reporting systems must fit with all of the other administrative systems.

PLANNING SYSTEMS

The final area where misfits can develop is between organization or reporting systems, or both, and the planning systems, the third category of administrative systems. There are essentially three types of planning systems: strategy formulation, program adaptation, and budget formulation. All of these relate to the way in which an organization is defining itself, its programs, and its planned use of resources.

The Strategy Formulation System

In considering an organization's strategy formulation system, it is important to distinguish among three important factors: values, strategies, and programs. In even the smallest organization, there is a strategy formulation process going on. It may be quite rigorous and systematic or, alternatively, it may be one which operates very informally and intuitively. Regardless of this distinction, the strategy formulation process is how top management first examines the environment in which the organization is functioning and assesses the kinds of signals being sent by that environment—financial and programmatic. It next compares this environmental information with the organization's strengths and weaknesses, as well as with both the organization's values and its managers' own personal values. Ultimately, it decides on some directions in which the organization should be heading. Indeed, the environment (i.e., the entire range of social, cultural, political, and economic forces within which the organization operates) can both be a source of opportunity and provide threats to the organization's survival. Occasionally, it can simply exert constraining influences.

This strategic process is a complex one and cannot be fully covered in this chapter.[11] It is important to recognize, however, that one of the most difficult aspects of the process is assessing the nature of the environmental signals. How, for example, does top management go about learning what efforts are being called for by public and private organizations? How does it gain a better understanding of patient or community needs? How does it ascertain what kinds of resources are available to support its efforts? How does it determine what other similar organizations are doing? And so on. Keeping in touch with the executive and legislative branches of government at all levels is certainly one means of doing this for some health and human service organizations, as is a continuing dialogue with community leaders, consumer/patient groups, and local industry. And, as antitrust suits begin to emerge in the health care industry in some states, the court system provides still another source of environmental information. But the question still remains: "How does top management obtain this kind of information, particularly in a complex and rapidly changing environment."

One means that many organizations use for acquiring environmental information is to solicit it from middle managers and professionals. Thus, if top management in an institution supports them, middle managers and professionals can be a rather unique source of information about the environment in which the organization is operating, particularly in large, multi-institutional settings. Middle managers and professionals frequently know about community acceptance of their programs, community needs, industry needs (such as employee assistance programs), and the like. These individuals also can be valuable in "processing" this information and deciding what is important. As a result, many organizations increasingly are beginning to involve middle management in the strategy formulation process.

The Program Adaptation System

It is important to distinguish strategy from programs. In a very real sense, programs are the operational definition of an organization's strategy; and, in well-managed organizations, we would expect to see an "umbrella effect" among values, strategy, and programs. In such a situation, strategy is consistent with values, and programs are consistent with strategy or strategic directions. This umbrella effect is shown schematically in Figure 9–5.

---

[11]For additional details see Kenneth R. Andrews, *The Concept of Corporate Strategy* (Homewood, Ill.: Dow Jones-Irwin, 1971).

FIGURE 9–5 _____

The Adaptive Umbrella

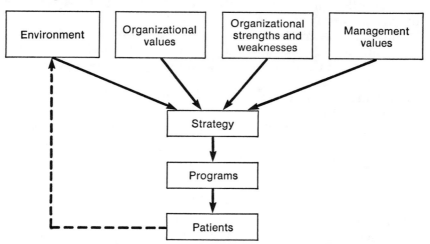

Source: David W. Young, *The Managerial Process in Human Service Agencies* (New York: Praeger Publishers, 1979).

Example: In one of the health centers previously mentioned, the organizational values are (1) the best interest of the patient, (2) the spirit of change, and (3) preventive care. These values have led to a strategy that emphasizes home care and health education (which support the values of the best interest of the patient and prevention). Given these strategies, the organization can engage in program efforts that reinforce the strategic directions.

If managers are to develop new programs or to change the content of existing programs, however, they must have a clearly articulated organizational strategy, as well as a good understanding of how their programs or program changes fit into that strategy. This, then, is the essence of the program adaptation system.

Underlying an organization's program adaptation systems are various processes that must be carefully managed: the flow of program information from professionals to middle managers, and ultimately to top management; the latitude given middle managers to engage in their own program development; the process of program review for financial viability; and so on. Unless both professionals and middle managers, as well as top management, have a clear understanding of how this overall process works, an organization can have a very difficult time successfully adapting its programs to meet changing needs. In addition, middle managers in particular must be able to identify the linkage between the strategy formulation system and the program adaptation system, and they must have a good understanding of the role that they play in the entire process.

Figure 9–6 indicates some of the elements of the adaptive process, using a four-stage approach. As the exhibit indicates, the environment frequently provides different input to different groups in the organization. That input must then be gathered formally (and sometimes informally) and distilled, and then analyzed in terms of its fit with the organization's strategy and capabilities (both financial and otherwise). If feasible, changes are then implemented in terms of either new strategic directions, new programs, or changes in the content of existing programs.

The Budget Formulation System

Obviously, one constraint that operates in almost all organizational settings is the financial one, which leads to the last planning system: the budget formulation system. Given that there are programmatic and strategic objectives an organization wishes to achieve, the annual budget process (which may be more frequent than annually) *can be* one that establishes *both* financial and programmatic commitments for the year ahead. Although Chapter 6 discussed budgeting in some detail, and Chapter 7 addressed the question of budget-related reporting, it is worth emphasizing some key points in the context of an administrative systems perspective.

First, it is possible to budget not only for financial objectives but for programmatic goals and objectives. Further, if the process is carried out properly, it should be possible to obtain some commitment from managers to attain programmatic goals and objectives, and to do so within the financial limitations of the budget. Unfortunately, the budgetary formulation process frequently consists of a great deal of number-generation, with very little commitment to those numbers; it is driven by a third-party reimbursement process for many organizations; and it often includes no discussion of goals or objectives for particular departments or responsibility centers.

Second, it is important to maintain a good fit between the budgetary process and the organization's other administrative systems. For example, it is very difficult to have a participative budgeting process in a very hierarchical, authoritarian organization. Additionally, the budget must rely on a clear understanding of the patient processing system, and must fit well with the or-

FIGURE 9-6

Stages of the Adaptive Process

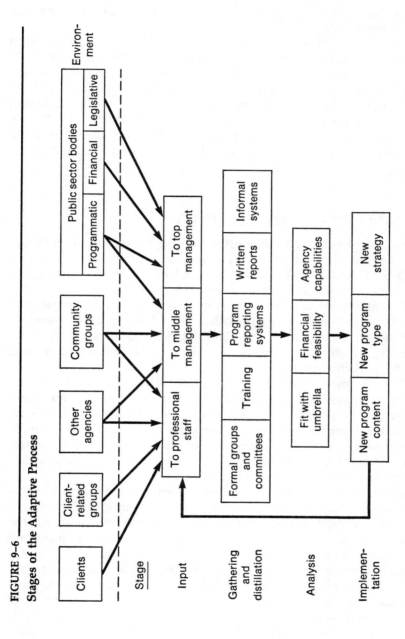

Source: David W. Young, *The Managerial Process in Human Service Agencies* (New York: Praeger Publishers, 1979).

ganization's programs. In fact, if possible, each program should be budgeted separately in terms of both financial and programmatic commitments.

Finally, it is extremely important that the budget formulation process and the budget reporting system fit together well. Otherwise, it is quite difficult to determine if managers are performing as planned or not. Moreover, without a good fit between these two systems, managers may make both programmatic and financial commitments, which they wish to achieve, but will have no idea whatsoever if they are meeting their objectives, because the information either is unavailable to them or arrives with such a long time-lag that it is virtually useless.

SUMMARY OF THE CHAPTER

Three categories of administrative systems have been identified in this chapter: organization, reporting, and planning (see Figure 9–1). In the first category, there are a formal authority system, a patient processing system, conflict resolution systems, value maintenance systems, and motivation systems. In the category of reporting systems, there are both financial and programmatic reporting systems. And, in the planning systems category, there are a strategy formulation system, a program adaptation system, and a budget formulation system.

These systems allow us to put much of the material in the first eight chapters of this book into a broader context than might otherwise be possible. Indeed, while accounting and control are certainly important activities, they should not be seen as ends in themselves—or even as activities that stand alone in an organization. Rather, they are part of a much larger set of organizational processes, or administrative systems.

What makes the administrative system perspective a particularly useful way to view an organization is that it deals not only with the content of each system but with the ways in which the systems interact. This interaction or "fit" is extremely important to the success of an organization. While many managers may feel highly constrained in terms of modifying the administrative systems within their own organizations, they also may have far more latitude than is readily apparent. This chapter has attempted to show where some of that latitude may exist. By exercising this latitude, and by attempting to improve both the content of their administrative systems and the fit among these systems, managers have the ability to have a significant impact on the performance of their organizations.

MANAGERIAL CHECKLIST

1. Is our patient (or client) processing system clearly identified? Would it be helpful to monitor patients' progress through the system and identify points where the system is not functioning as designed? What level of effort would be required to do so?

2. Where does conflict arise in our organization? Is this a useful conflict, because it leads to better decisions? What modes of conflict resolution do we use? Do they fit well with our formal authority system? With the patient processing system? If not, what might be done to correct the misfits?

3. What are our organization's values? What is it that gives our organization its distinctive character? Do members of the organization subscribe to these values? If not, what changes might be made in our hiring/firing, training, and communication systems to reinforce these values?

4. What are some of the key factors which motivate professionals in our organization? What role does middle management play in developing and implementing motivation systems? Do these systems reinforce the professionals' internally derived motivations and values? If not, how might the system be changed?

5. What sorts of financial/programmatic trade-offs are we making, and at what cost? Can we quantify this precisely enough to allow us to determine which programs should be curtailed or eliminated if budgetary shortfalls occurred? If not, what effort would be necessary to develop more quantitative information?

6. To what extent are middle managers involved in the strategy formulation process? What efforts are being made to incorporate their knowledge of the organization's environment into our strategic thinking?

7. How does the process of program adaptation work in our organization? What specific steps must a new program, or a modification to an existing program, pass through to be implemented? What informal processes influence the decison? Can these processes be better managed to lead to more effective and viable programs?

8. Do we budget for both financial and programmatic commitments? If not, what effort would be necessary to do so?

Bibliography

Andrews, K. R. *The Concept of Corporate Strategy.* Homewood, Ill.: Dow Jones-Irwin, 1971.

Anthony, R. N. *Planning and Control Systems: A Framework for Analysis.* Boston: Harvard Business School, 1965.

Anthony, R. N., and R. E. Herzlinger. *Management Control in Nonprofit Organizations: Text and Cases.* Homewood, Ill.: Richard D. Irwin, 1980.

Barnard, C. I. *The Functions of the Executive.* Cambridge, Mass.: Harvard University Press, 1938.

Flexner, W.A., et al., eds. *Strategic Planning in Health Care Management.* Rockville, Md.: Aspen Systems Corporation, 1981.

Kovner, A. R., and D. Neuhauser, eds. *Health Services Management: Readings and Commentary.* Ann Arbor, Mich.: Health Administration Press, 1978.

Lawrence, P. R., and J. W. Lorsch. *Organization and Environment.* Boston: Division of Research, Harvard Business School, 1967.

Levey, S., and T. McCarthy, eds. *Health Management for Tomorrow.* Philadelphia: J. B. Lippincott, 1980.

Lorsch, J. W., and J. J. Morse. *Organizations and Their Members: A Contingency Approach.* New York: Harper & Row, 1974.

Ouichi, W. G. *Theory Z: How American Business Can Meet the Japanese Challenge.* Reading, Mass.: Addison-Wesley Publishing, 1981.

Selznick, P. *Leadership in Administration.* New York: Harper & Row, 1957.

Silvers, J. B., and C. K. Prahalad. *Financial Management of Health Institutions.* Flushing, N.Y.: Spectrum Publications, 1974.

Saltman, R. S., and D. W. Young. "The Hospital Power Equilibrium: An Alternative View of the Cost Containment Dilemma." *Journal of Health Politics, Policy and Law,* Fall 1981.

Young, D. W. "Administrative Theory and Administrative Systems: A Synthesis Among Diverging Fields of Inquiry." *Accounting, Organizations and Society,* 1979, pp. 235–44.

————. *The Managerial Process in Human Service Organizations.* New York: Praeger Publishers, 1979.

Index

Focusing on managers, administrators and physicians -- not accountants and financial specialists -- *Financial Control in Health Care* emphasizes finance and control as important elements in managerial decision making. Due to the competitive nature of health care today, these people need to have a thorough working knowledge of accounting, finance and management control principles.

In this timely, sensible -- and useful -- book, health care administrators learn how these principles can be applied effectively in a health care setting. *Financial Control in Health Care* offers insights for approaching and solving organizational problems. Discussions include financial accounting, financial analysis and management, full and differential cost accounting, management control systems, and management information systems. A final chapter places these topics into a broad management context.

Financial Control in Health Care is an optimistic blueprint for the future of the U.S. health care system, pointing the way for responsible decision making and successful management control.